THEORY AND INTERPRETATION OF NARRATIVE
JAMES PHELAN, PETER J. RABINOWITZ, AND ROBYN WARHOL, SERIES EDITORS

FOR VANESSA, MAX, AND MILLY

THE RETURN OF THE OMNISCIENT NARRATOR

Authorship and Authority in Twenty-First Century Fiction

PAUL DAWSON

THE OHIO STATE UNIVERSITY PRESS
COLUMBUS

Copyright © 2013 by The Ohio State University.
All rights reserved.

Library of Congress Cataloging-in-Publication Data
Dawson, Paul, 1972–
The return of the omniscient narrator authorship and authority in twenty-first century fiction / Paul Dawson.
pages cm—(Theory and interpretation of narrative)
Includes bibliographical references and index. ISBN-13: 978-0-8142-1233-2 (cloth : alk. paper) ISBN-10: 0-8142-1233-6 (cloth : alk. paper)
1. Fiction—Technique. 2. Omniscience (Theory of knowledge) in literature. 3. Narration (Rhetoric) I. Title. II. Series: Theory and interpretation of narrative series.
PN3355.D246 2013 808.3–dc23
2013031509

Cover design by AuthorSupport.com
Text design by Juliet Williams
Type set in Adobe Sabon

∞ The paper used in this publication meets the minimum requirements of the American National Standard for Information Sciences—Permanence of Paper for Printed Library Materials. ANSI Z39.48–1992.

9 8 7 6 5 4 3 2 1

CONTENTS

Acknowledgments		vii
INTRODUCTION	The Return of Omniscience in Contemporary Fiction	1
CHAPTER 1	Omniscience and Narrative Authority	25
CHAPTER 2	The Direct Address and the Ironic Moralist	62
CHAPTER 3	Prolepsis and the Literary Historian	88
CHAPTER 4	Style and the Pyrotechnic Storyteller	111
CHAPTER 5	Polymathic Knowledge, the Immersion Journalist, and the Social Commentator	136
CHAPTER 6	Voice and Free Indirect Discourse in Contemporary Omniscient Narration	166
CHAPTER 7	Paralepsis and Omniscient Character Narration	195
CHAPTER 8	Real Authors and Real Readers: A Discursive Approach to the Narrative Communication Model	222
CONCLUSION		247
Notes		251
Works Cited		255
Index		267

ACKNOWLEDGMENTS

THIS BOOK would not have been written without the support of my wife, Vanessa Dawson. From her unwavering encouragement and belief in my capacity to tackle a new field, to expert grant-writing advice, to patient sighs and glazed eyes at the mention of words such as paralepsis, she has sustained me.

My research has benefited enormously from generous financial support in the form of an Australian Research Council Discovery Project grant, plus an Early Career Researcher Grant and a Faculty Research Grant from the Faculty of Arts and Social Sciences at the University of New South Wales.

Jim Phelan and Peter Rabinowitz have made this a better book with their comprehensive, challenging, and insightful comments. I am grateful for their enthusiasm, and for that of the external reader. I thank Sandy Crooms, too, for her warmth and help with the process of submission and publication.

Much of this book was written during my time as a Visiting Scholar in the Department of English at the University of California, Berkeley. I extend my warmest thanks to Dorothy Hale, who acted as my faculty host during this period. My discussions with Dori about the novel and narrative theory have each and every time been exceptionally rewarding. I have also gained much from talking with Namwali Serpell and Kent Puckett. I must thank Mary Mellin, who facilitated the administrative side of my time at the University of California, Berkeley, and Joanna Picciotto, who generously allowed me to use her office during my stay.

I extend my gratitude to many of my colleagues in the School of the Arts and Media at the University of New South Wales. Julian Murphet and George Kouvaros both provided me with excellent mentorship during this book's early life as a research grant proposal. John Attridge, Chris Danta, Helen Groth, Roslyn Jolly, Stephen Muecke, Sean Pryor, and Louise Ravelli have all helped me clarify my thoughts. Lee Williamson was instrumental in helping me secure a grant to write this book. I must especially thank my two excellent research assistants, Lynda Ng and Grace Hellyer, who did so much grunt work on my behalf and provided sounding boards for ideas.

Many of the claims in this book have been tested at annual conferences for the International Society for the Study of Narrative since 2008. The feedback from delegates at these conferences has been very helpful in shaping my argument. In particular I would like to thank the following Narrative Conference regulars who have discussed ideas or shown interest in my work: Porter Abbot, Frederick Aldama, Sarah Copland, Susan Lanser, Christine McBride, Brian McHale, Henrik Nielsen, Gerald Prince, Brian Richardson, Richard Walsh, and Robyn Warhol. Last, I want to acknowledge my wonderful whiskey-drinking friends in narrative, none of whom actually helped write this book: Matt Bolton, Lizzie Nixon, and, particularly, Emily Anderson, who is always there to help prop up the bar.

Early versions of my argument have appeared in: "Historicizing 'Craft' in the Teaching of Fiction," *New Writing: The International Journal for the Practice and Theory of Creative Writing* 5.3 (2008); and "The Return of Omniscience in Contemporary Fiction," *Narrative* 17.2 (2009). A version of chapter 8 appears as "Real Authors and Real Readers: Omniscient Narration and a Discursive Approach to the Narrative Communication Model," *Journal of Narrative Theory* 42.1 (2012).

INTRODUCTION

The Return of Omniscience in Contemporary Fiction

"What happened to the omniscient author?" Gone interactive.
—Jeanette Winterson, *The Powerbook* 27 (2001)

In the first year of the new millennium Helen published a novel which one reviewer described as "so old-fashioned in form as to be almost experimental." It was written in the third person, past tense, with an omniscient and sometimes intrusive narrator.
—David Lodge, *Thinks* 340 (2002)

THIS QUOTE from the last paragraph of David Lodge's novel *Thinks* captures with ironic pithiness the central premise of this book and the paradox it seeks to investigate. Despite long being considered a relic of the nineteenth-century novel, the ostensibly outmoded figure of the omniscient narrator has become a salient feature of contemporary British and American literary fiction. From the 1990s, and particularly since the turn of the millennium, a number of important and popular novelists have produced books which exhibit all the formal elements we typically associate with literary omniscience: an all-knowing authorial narrator who addresses the reader directly, offers intrusive commentary on the events being narrated, ranges freely across space and time, provides access to the consciousness of characters, and generally asserts a palpable presence within the fictional world.

These authors range from relatively new writers such as Zadie Smith, Adam Thirlwell and Nicola Barker, to established literary figures such as Jonathan Franzen, David Foster Wallace and Rick Moody, to literary icons such as Tom Wolfe, Salman Rushdie, Martin Amis, and Don DeLillo. They include writers who have won or been shortlisted for two of the most significant literary prizes in the Anglo-American world, the Booker and the Pulitzer, such as David Lodge, A. S. Byatt, Gail Jones, and Edward P. Jones. Many of these writers have received sustained scholarly attention for their significance to postmodern and postcolonial fiction, and have generated much debate about the contemporary novel through their nonfiction writing, notably Wolfe, Wallace, and Franzen.

Despite the critical scrutiny these writers have received, their collective contribution to the development of new modes of omniscient narration in contemporary fiction has yet to be recognized. Indeed, criticism today still seems to be in thrall to an historical narrative about the anachronicity of omniscience fostered by modernism. For instance, Timothy Aubry opens a 2008 article on the "politics of interiority" in middlebrow fiction with this claim:

> Although occasionally called upon to perform certain emeritus functions, the omniscient narrator has retired decisively from the scene of contemporary United States fiction. In the place of this appealingly wise but problematic figure emerges an array of speakers no less ignorant, prejudiced, and confused than the reader. . . . A modernist innovation originally, the refusal of omniscience has become a fixed principle, especially within what is frequently referred to as middlebrow fiction. (85)

Aubry's characterization of an omniscient narrator as "appealingly wise" betrays the continued association of this narrative voice with canonical works of nineteenth-century fiction, and hence an unwillingness to consider how formal conventions of omniscience may have been adapted to a different historical context, invoking a different figure of authorship.

One reason for the critical neglect of contemporary omniscience is that surveys of the novel today—unlike, say, Joseph Warren Beach's *The Twentieth Century Novel* (1932)—tend to concern themselves less with formal developments than with interpretative criticism in relation to broader theories of nationalism, history, gender, postmodernism, and postcolonialism. Excursions into literary form are rare, and may be summed up by Brian Finney's claim in his 2006 book, *English Fiction Since 1984: Narrating a Nation,* that what unites British novelists of the last two decades is a belief that "an omniscient narrator is an anachronism" (12). Even avowedly formalist and narratological accounts of contemporary fiction continue to cast omniscience as an outmoded narrative voice which writers have rejected in favor of more radical experiments with form. This, for instance, is Brian Richardson's argument in his 2006 book, *Unnatural Voices*. In an exhaustive survey of twentieth-century fiction, Richardson claims that there "is a general move away from what was thought to be 'omniscient' third-person narration to limited third-person narration to ever more unreliable first-person narrators to new explorations of 'you,' 'we,' and mixed forms" (13). There is much truth to these general claims, of course, but the emergence of new types of omniscient narration complicates their currency and requires a re-evaluation of existing histories of novelistic form.

This book seeks to answer why so many contemporary writers have turned to omniscient narration, given the aesthetic prejudice against this narrative voice which has prevailed for at least a century. The Anglo-American study of novelistic method which emerged early in the twentieth century established conventional critical wisdom regarding omniscient narration. According to this tradition, exemplified by Percy Lubbock's *The Craft of Fiction* (1921), the artistic "progression" of the novel can be understood as a series of innovations to efface the intrusive presence and superior knowledge of the author. The most favored form of narration in this tradition was that of a third-person narrator who does not comment on the action, and tells the story solely from a character's perspective, revealing only what that character could know: in other words, the modernist impersonality championed by Henry James. As a result, the omniscient narrator employed in classic eighteenth- and nineteenth-century novels has been considered both technically obsolete and morally suspect in the twentieth century. "In the age of perspectivism," Eugene Goodheart pointed out in 2004, "in which all claims to authority are suspect, the omniscient narrator is an archaism to be patronized when he is found in the works of the past and to be scorned when he appears in contemporary work. Omniscience is no longer an entitlement of the novelist" (1).

An aesthetic prejudice against omniscient narration, based on a claim for its artistic supersession and historical redundancy, continues to be perpetuated by the industry of creative writing programs, from which the majority of new writers now emerges. Handbook after handbook on fiction writing reiterates the poetics of modernist criticism enshrined in the Anglo-American study of novelistic method by dispensing the "practical" advice that limited third-person narration offers the technical solution to the disadvantages of other "points of view," as well as reminding readers that omniscient narration is too old fashioned to sell books.[1] In a 2007 writing handbook, *How to Write Fiction (and Think About it)*, Robert Graham claims that: "From the earliest literature all the way through to the end of the nineteenth century, the author speaking, the author acting as an omniscient narrator, was standard practice" (47). Graham asserts that omniscient narration has fallen from favor since Chekov, before providing this advice to aspiring writers:

> If you're going to use an omniscient narrator in the twenty-first century, chances are you will not want to wear your omniscience on your sleeve; nobody likes a show-off. . . . Alternatively, you need to use a tone so arch, so dripping in irony, that the reader is bound to realise you know fully well the omniscient narrator went out of fashion in 1899. (56)

How, then, are we to evaluate novels which employ an ostensibly redundant nineteenth-century form in the twenty-first century?[2] Are they conservative and nostalgic by virtue of their form, or are they experimental and contemporary in their use of this form? We are accustomed to an historical trajectory of the novel which holds that modernist and postmodernist fiction throughout the twentieth century can be characterized, in part, as a rejection of the moral and epistemological certainties of omniscient narration. But to claim, along with Goodheart, that "omniscient narration is a lost cause, a sign of successive triumphs of modernism and postmodernism" (2) is to operate with a static understanding of novelistic form. In this book I argue that the contemporary revival of omniscience in fact emerges out an encounter with some of the technical experiments of postmodern fiction.

Movements in contemporary fiction have been described by various new millennium terms such as "hysterical realism," "recherche postmodernism," "neo-realism," and "neo-Victorian fiction." These terms indicate that postmodern fiction, as it has been defined in classic studies of the 1980s by Brian McHale and Linda Hutcheon, continues to undergo new developments. In his 2005 book, *From Modernism to Postmodernism*, Gerhard Hoffmann identifies the last decade of the twentieth century as a period in which the "post-postmodern" novel emerged, characterized by "the return to traditional forms of narrative and storytelling" but without "a return to the belief system of traditional realism" (623). In this book I approach omniscient narration as the exemplary narrative voice of post-postmodern fiction. My contention here is that while the philosophical underpinnings of classical realism were challenged by postmodern fiction, the ironic appropriation of formal elements of omniscience, exemplified by the intrusive narrator of John Fowles's *The French Lieutenant's Woman* (1969), has now been absorbed into mainstream literary fiction, facilitating a general shift away from the modernist ideal of an impersonal narrator and toward an aesthetic of maximalism in which the narrator's voice is always present.

I want to further argue that the reworking of omniscience in contemporary fiction can be understood as one way in which authors have responded to a perceived decline in the cultural authority of the novel over the last two decades. Claims for the death of the novel have been a critical commonplace since the mid-twentieth century, part of the rhetoric of postmodernism, but the latest iteration accompanies significant widespread shifts in the literary-historical conditions which determine the status and function of the novel in the public sphere. These determining conditions over the last decade or so include: increased sales and cultural capital for literary nonfiction such as memoirs, the personal essay and popular history; the commercial orientation of multinational publishing houses, large chain bookstores, and online booksellers such as Amazon; the competing claims of cinema, television, and new media; the broader challenge to traditional print culture presented by technological advances in online publishing, print on demand, ebooks and ebook readers such as the Kindle and the iPad; and the attendant proliferation of demotic opinion in public debate via blogs, customer reviews, and opinion polls made possible by the same technology. All of these conditions contribute to a sense of the fragmentation of the public sphere and a diminishment of the cultural capital of literature and literary fiction.

These conditions feature in current discourses of anxiety about the cultural status of literature, ranging from broader social concerns about literacy in the age of digital media to more specific literary debates about the social function of the novel. Sven Bikerts provides an epochal framework for this anxiety in *The Gutenberg Elegies: The Fate of Reading in an Electronic Age,* originally published in 1994 and reissued in 2006. "The decade of the 1990s," Bikerts claims, "was a classic historical watershed" (xi), marking the irrevocable influence of digital technology on the way people think and relate to each other. For Bikerts, "the societal shift from print-based to electronic communications is as consequential for culture as was the shift instigated by Gutenberg's invention of movable type" (192). The effect, he argues, was to transform our sense of society being composed of isolated individuals who seek solace in the introspective contemplation and subjective immersion in deep time afforded by literature, to one of information seeking citizens interconnected by a digital grid which keeps them perpetually in the present moment. This "network consciousness" (202), Bikerts argues, is at odds with the experience of inwardness cultivated by serious reading, and this explains the waning influence of literature in contemporary culture. A natural consequence is that "the writer's social and cultural status is as low as it has been for centuries. If there is anything consoling to be said, it is that the *need* for the writer is right now probably as great as ever" (208).

The claim that digital technology has had a significant influence on modes of thinking, on interpersonal relations, on the nature of reading, and on the material form of print literature itself, is, I think, uncontroversial. Many scholars, however, eschew Bikerts's nostalgic lament for the supersession of literary fiction. Michael Wutz's 2009 book, *Enduring Words: Literary Narratives in a Changing Media Ecology,* exemplifies a field of scholarship devoted to the study of intermediality, tracing the effects of modern technology, from the gramophone and photography to the internet, on the structure of literary fiction, and on the materiality of books themselves, to demonstrate the enduring power of the printed word to productively engage with new technologies.[3] This field of scholarship nonetheless accepts the premise of a diminished cultural status for literary fiction. As Joseph Donatelli and Geoffrey Winthrop-Young claimed in the introduction to a 1995 special issue of *Mosaic:* "It is not surprising, therefore, that a period which is witnessing the slippage of the authority of the book as a media form, should pay such close attention to the circumstances under which it first gained prominence" (2).

The tenor of Bikerts's lament also resonates throughout public discourse. A palpable sense of escalating crisis is no more overtly expressed than in the 2004 National Endowment for the Arts report, *Reading at Risk: A Survey of Literary Reading in America* and the 2007 follow-up *To Read or Not Read: A Question of National Consequence,* issued with the imprimatur of the federal government and supported by a battalion of statistical data. The executive summary of the 2004 NEA report claims that it "contains solid evidence of the declining importance of literature to our populace. Literature reading is fading as a meaningful activity, especially among younger people" (ix). The key findings suggest that the "percentage of adult Americans reading literature has dropped dramatically over the past 20 years" (ix); the decline in literary reading is accelerating; this decline can be correlated with the competition of "an enormous array of electronic media" (xii); and represents a larger social problem because it "foreshadows an erosion in cultural and civic participation" (xii). The Summary and Conclusion section, in fact, provides methodological qualifications to these "findings," and in opposition to the rhetoric of a crisis of book culture manifested in these reports, Ted Striphas asserts, in *The Late Age of Print* (2009), that "books remain key artifacts through which social actors articulate and struggle over specific interests, values, practices, and worldviews" (3). However, he says, the late age of print means "books exist in a more densely mediated landscape than ever before" (3).

The emergence of contemporary omniscience, I would venture, can be situated within the discourses of anxiety generated by this densely mediated landscape. The concerns about book culture which I have outlined are present in the nonfiction writing of many of the authors under scrutiny in this book, and arguments for a causal link between perceptions of literary decline and the cultural projects of postmodern or late postmodern or post-postmodern novelists have been made respectively by Jeremy Green, Kathleen Fitzpatrick, and Robert McLaughlin.

In *Late Postmodernism* (2005), Green states that his book "addresses the ways in which literature, particularly the American novel, has been described under the rubric of postmodernism and asks how these accounts should be modified in the light of recent literary activity" (3). For Green, this literary activity is the body of work produced in the 1990s by both the first "generation" of postmodern writers such as Pynchon and Barth, and later writers such as DeLillo, Richard Powers, and David Foster Wallace. Green's book, however, as he makes clear, "is less a typology by which new writing might be categorized, than an attempt to comprehend the conditions under which literary novels are now written and understood. These conditions shape the readership, the literary and political ideologies, the self-understanding, and the aesthetic choices available to writers" (3). Green's main goal, then, is to elaborate what he calls the literary field, the institutional conditions of novelistic production and reception which, in the 1990s, featured "widespread dismay over the current conditions and future prospects of the novel" (5). According to Green, the literary field has shaped a sense of crisis of which novelists of late postmodernism are acutely aware and seek to negotiate through their writing:

> The novelist's sense of impending obsolescence is bound up with a perceived loss of cultural authority. Although the backward glance that imagines better times for the novel earlier in the century—with the novelist at the center of a de facto coalition of high, low, and middlebrow

cultural interests—is fanciful and nostalgic, the anxiety over present conditions remains powerful and indicative of genuine change. (7)

In very similar fashion, Kathleen Fitzpatrick's *The Anxiety of Obsolescence* (2006) investigates the sense of cultural crisis engendered specifically by television and new technologies which threaten to undermine the authority of print culture and hence of those who write novels. The question which Fitzpatrick takes up in her book, "is not whether print culture is dying at the hands of the media, but rather what purpose announcements of the death of print culture serve" (3). Her claim is that

> the anxiety of obsolescence, a cultural pose struck by the beleaguered postmodern novelist, has at its root three discourses with which it is mutually constitutive. These discourses—the death of the novel, the threat of new technologies, and the rise of postmodernism—all bespeak obsolescence in the interest of creating a protected space within which a threatened form might continue to flourish. (47)

Through case studies of the work of Thomas Pynchon and Don DeLillo, Fitzpatrick focuses specifically on the gendered and racial implications of this cultural pose, arguing that it operates discursively as an attempt to shore up the high cultural elitist position of largely white male authors, with television figured as the feminized space of mass culture: "This is, at its root level, the function of the anxiety of obsolescence: the release of the white male author from responsibility through an at times histrionic concern for his own imminent demise, a conversion of the forms and gestures of oppressed cultures to his own project of maintaining his cultural (and social) centrality" (233).

Green and Fitzpatrick argue, like Striphas, that, despite protestations of doom, the novel continues to flourish in terms of both aesthetic achievement and cultural importance, albeit under changed and complex conditions. They also point out how anxiety over the fate of the novel and the authority of fiction writers is manifested in the way authors establish a public voice to frame the reception of their fiction. "As writers have become aware of these shifts," Green argues, "they have tried to make sense of the new pressures and difficulties of an altered cultural landscape through their writing, through essays and statements, but above all within novels themselves" (15). Both Green and Fitzpatrick proceed to read their chosen authors' specific concerns—cultural memory, the public sphere, and the political vocation of the novel for Green; and the machine, the spectacle, and the network for Fitzpatrick—as thematized and dramatized largely at the level of story or plot structure.

My focus in this book is specifically on the formalist category of narrative voice, and, rather than providing interpretations of individual works as thematic explorations of cultural crisis, I wish to demonstrate how the narrative voice of contemporary omniscience is symptomatic of the broad anxiety within the literary field over the cultural capital of literary fiction, and hence the public authority of the novelist. I do not mean to assert that each writer under scrutiny here has deliberately chosen omniscient narration out of concern for their relevance to contemporary culture, but that the increasing presence of this narrative voice as a viable option for writers can productively be related to changes in the institutional conditions of literary production and reception. If there is a crisis of cultural authority at play in the literary field, it makes sense that a mode of narration vested by convention with the highest narrative authority would become ripe for renovation. How contemporary writers have adapted the narrative authority of classic omniscience to a more fragmented and relativistic intellectual environment is at the core of this book. "If religion is the opium of the people," comments the narrator of *White Teeth*, "tradition is an even more sinister analgesic, simply because it rarely appears sinister" (193). This aphoristic statement is a typical assertion of narrative authority which nonetheless evinces a modern skepticism toward two discourses of authority which have informed the concept of omniscience.

Evidence for my claim that a turn to omniscience is vitally linked to a sense of the novelist's cultural authority can be found in the statements of authors themselves. In 1993, the Pulitzer Prize–winning novelist Richard Russo delivered a lecture to students which was later published as "In Defense of Omniscience." In this lecture he argued that the capacity to handle "true" or "full" omniscience is a mark of the strongest novelists and at odds with the advice dispensed in writing workshops. Russo describes as advantages the qualities of omniscience which the Anglo-American tradition exemplified by Lubbock criticizes: it is the best way to provide the "necessary information" of the story, and it has a clear and confident authorial voice: "there is always a narrator, a voice that embodies a clearly defined attitude, an authorial pose, a consistent and recognizable way of seeing and understanding" (12). Russo is not just describing narrative technique here, but a figure of authorship embodied in the narrative voice: "Omniscience means, of course, all knowing, and it favors writers who know things and are confident about what they know and generous enough to want to share their knowledge" (15).

His conclusion is instructive for the way he wishes to promote the authority of the mature, professional writer in contemporary culture, showing how such an author can respond to the challenge of omniscience. He does so in the context of explaining why apprentice writers shy away from this mode of writing:

> Omniscience, in the end, is a mature writer's technique. Our being drawn to it has something to do with years, with experience of life, with the gradual accumulation of knowledge and pain and wisdom. Omniscience not only invents a world; it tells us how that world works and how we should feel about the way it works. Few writers at twenty-five or even thirty are ready to assume such a mantle. Omniscience is permission to speak and speak with authority we know we really don't have, about a world that in our century (in any century?) is too complex to know. Ultimately, omniscience forces us to pretend we know more than we do, and we're afraid we'll get caught. (17)

This attempt to claim cultural authority for the novelist is also a pragmatic strategy, for Russo's lecture was a way of preparing the public reception of his 1993 novel *Nobody's Fool*. It is clear that he is inviting readers to see the omniscient narrator of his novels as not only a voice who knows about the fictional world, but the voice of Russo himself imparting his accumulated wisdom about life. This is a traditional understanding of authorial omniscience, shored up by Russo's argument that omniscient narration, the "voice of choice" for the eighteenth century, and the point of view most suited to the Victorian novel, is "the point of view that has never been anything but the mainstay of storytelling in our own century, regardless of the literary movement then in vogue (experimentalism, minimalism, postmodernism, any other 'ism')" (9). My aim in this book is not to offer a quantitative survey of recent fiction across all genres, from popular to highbrow, to determine the extent to which omniscient narration features. In talking about the "return" of omniscience, I mean to address contemporary novels whose use of omniscient narration can be related to the "literary movement" of postmodernism and thus to identify new modes of omniscience which differ from that defended by Russo.

Omniscient narration is not simply one "point of view" for writers to choose from among others, for the presence of this narrative voice in contemporary fiction carries the weight of association with the supposed high point of the novel itself: a period before the competing claims of new media forms, from radio, to cinema to digital age multimedia, in which a public sphere sought guidance in ethical conduct from literature, and novelists could assume, at least in the rhetoric of their narration, a shared set of cultural values with their readers. In his 1968 book, *The Form of Victorian Fiction,* J. Hillis Miller argued that the standard Victorian convention of the omniscient narrator "is so crucial to nineteenth-century English fiction, so inclusive in its implications, that it may be called the determining principle of its form" (63), describing this narrator as the voice of a "general consciousness." Scholes and Kellogg explain in *The Nature of Narrative* why this convention of the omniscient narrator lost authority as a viable point of view in the twentieth century. They argue against the accepted view that it fell out of favor because writers discovered ways of "dramatizing" a story without the need for authorial commentary or exposition, instead claiming that omniscient narration became philosophically untenable as a result of a broader shift in cultural sensibilities:

> The whole movement of mind in Western culture from the Renaissance to the present—the very movement which spawned the novel and elevated it to the position of the dominant literary form—has been a movement away from dogma, certainty, fixity, and all absolutes in metaphysics, in ethics, and in epistemology.... With this broad cultural development in mind, we can see how the authoritarian monism of the fully omniscient mode of narration has become less and less tenable in modern times, while the multifarious relativism of that same mode has seemed increasingly relevant. (276)

In other words, presenting the multiple perspectives of characters remained a feature of twentieth-century fiction, but not their subordination to the single ideology of an author's omniscient narrative voice. "It is not the narrator's narrating that disturbs the modern reader," Scholes and Kellogg claim, "nor his employment of multiple perspectives, it is the resolution of these perspectives into a single truth or reality" (277).

This is a compelling explanation for the "disappearance" and continued untenability of omniscient narration which has retained its currency today, and when examples of omniscient narration in postwar fiction have been discussed, they have generally been described in terms of nostalgic anachronism or "playful" parody. For instance, Morton P. Levitt argues in *The Rhetoric of Modernist Fiction* that the use of omniscience after the war was a deadly conservative reaction to modernist experimentation. He calls this the "New Victorianism" and proceeds to savage more recent novels by Muriel Spark and Margaret Drabble as extensions of this conservatism. "Again and again," Christian Gutleben claims in *Postmodern Nostalgia,* "the prerogatives of the omniscient narrator are usurped in the retro-Victorian novel" (105), arguing that the very use of the form in historical fiction is necessarily parodic.

Neither of these postures characterizes contemporary omniscience for me. But if there has been a "revival" of omniscience, does this mean the whole movement of mind in Western culture changed in the last two decades? Certainly not, so we need to be more supple with our identification of a narrative mode with a philosophical or ideological view. We find today fictional works with an "authoritarian monism" at the level of narrative voice which nonetheless demonstrate an awareness of the relativity of this voice in relation to extraliterary discourse in the public sphere. Which is to say that contemporary omniscient narrators retain the intrusive presence of earlier narrators, but not the assumption that they can address a sympathetic general readership with universal comments about society and human nature. "I know you are not convinced by this," says the omniscient narrator of Adam Thirlwell's *Politics* in a direct address to readers. "You are unpersuaded. Where is the realism? you say. Where is the accuracy of the European novel? Where is the truth to nature of Balzac or Tolstoy?" (131).

Kent Puckett claims, in *Bad Form,* that the nineteenth century "saw both the European novel and an omniscient narration whose voice was the voice of that novel's cultural authority come into their own" (6). If omniscient narration is so closely identified with the form and status of the nineteenth-century novel, I am interested in the specific claims for cultural authority which enable this narrative voice to function in contemporary fiction. By virtue of the fact that the omniscient narrator has traditionally been seen as the "voice" of the author, this mode of narration invokes a particular figure of authorship, and hence relies upon the prevailing status of the novel to authorize its presence in literary culture. With this in mind, we can see that the "universal" moral authority of the classic omniscient narrator is indeed unavailable to contemporary writers, for they can no longer claim the luxury of being spokespersons of authority, asserting accepted truths on behalf of a general consciousness. Writers today must situate the omniscient authority of their narrators in relation to other extraliterary claims to knowledge or expertise in postmodern culture where literature can no longer claim to be a privileged discourse.

I am mindful here that it is easy to both caricature nineteenth-century omniscience and to overstate the cultural authority which novelists enjoyed: to assume that the intrusive commentary characteristic of much Victorian fiction aspires to singular truth rather than simply being an authorial opinion, and that the garrulousness of its omniscient narrators is evidence of a privileged status for their authors. To do so is to subscribe to modernist (and postmodernist) critiques of the authoritarianism of omniscience, and to perpetuate current lamentations for an idealized past in which everyone read literature and novelists wielded greater influence and respect. Equally, however, it would be absurd to claim that literary form is static or that the institutional conditions and cultural status of literature have not changed.

It is interesting to note that, by the mid-twentieth century, when the modernist ideal of effacing the textual presence of the author, of a retreat from overt opinion into the interior lives of characters, became entrenched as an aesthetic principle, it was buttressed by both the "intentional fallacy" of the New Criticism, and the fundamental narratological distinction between an author and narrator. In other words, the meaning and structure of a work could be separated from consideration of authorial intent. Yet at the same time, the presence of the author in the public sphere became increasingly important to the marketing of fiction. This can be evidenced by the advent of the *Paris Review* interviews in the 1950s, establishing the genre of the author interview, and the emergence of writers festivals around the globe. In these forums, alongside a public presence in journalism and books of essays, authors are called upon to explain the genesis and motivations of their work, and to comment on broader social issues which their fiction engages with, as if to supplement what cannot be made overt in the fiction. These opportunities for authors to assert a public presence beyond their fiction may seem to give the lie to the cultural irrelevance of novelists, but the more an author operates within the marketplace of celebrity the less distinct novelists become as privileged cultural figures. Such a tension was on display in the much publicized and critically discussed decision of Jonathan Franzen to refuse an invitation to appear on Oprah Winfrey's Book Club. As Franzen wrote, of the reception of his first novel, *The Twenty-Seventh City*: "I had already realized that the money, the hype, the limo ride to a *Vogue* shoot weren't simply fringe benefits. They were the main prize, the consolation for no longer mattering to the culture" ("Why Bother?" 38).

The figure of authorship associated with the favored narrative voice of modernism, the Flaubertian/Joycean impersonal artist laying bare the psychological interior of characters, today seems a less viable trope than that of the author as an intellectual intervening in contemporary cultural debates. Contemporary omniscient narrators perform this trope most overtly, and one way to understand the difference between classic and contemporary omniscience lies in the different figures of authorship they project, not just as an artist in the literary field, but as an intellectual in the broader public sphere. Two of the best-known assertions of novelistic authority in classic omniscience are Austen's famous defense, in *Northanger Abbey,* of the novelist's capacity to offer "the most thorough knowledge of human nature" (34), which she pits against the value of commonplace books and periodicals, and the "belated historian" of George Eliot's *Middlemarch* who has "so much to do in unraveling certain human lots, and seeing how they were woven and interwoven" (142). We can see how these comments, taken as the voice of the author, lend themselves to the characterization of the nineteenth-century novelist as sage knower of human nature and guide to ethical conduct. Contemporary novelists are more accurately characterized as public intellectuals competing with other nonliterary discourses of "knowledge": journalistic, historical, scientific, critical, etc. As Franzen claimed in an interview: "The poetic, the subjective, and particularly the *narrative* account of what a person is and what a life means—I feel like the novelist's vision is engaged in a turf war with the scientific, biological, medical account" (Antrim).

No other narrative voice or "point of view" is as contested as that of literary omniscience, and this is because the term refers to both the author and the narrator. This slippage between the two, however, encouraged by the analogy with God, is precisely what makes manifestations of literary omniscience a barometer for the figure of authorship which circulates in public discourse. Rather than maintain a strict narratological distinction between author (or creator) and narrator (or knower), I think it is important to understand how the combination of these two concepts produces narrative authority. Most of the authors I have mentioned have produced manifestos, essays, interviews or critical works in which their thoughts on the cultural function of contemporary literature are clear, and which seek to establish the conditions by which their work may be received.[4] It is possible, then, to establish a discursive continuum from narratorial commentary in a work of fiction (by which I mean narrative statements whose ideological provenance cannot be attributed to a character) to critical pronouncements in a work of nonfiction which establish mutually reinforcing claims for an author's cultural capital. Rather than interpreting a novel through an author's paratextual statements I want to situate an author's fictional narrative voice as one element of public discourse alongside their nonfictional "authorial" voice.

This approach is particularly apposite for understanding the function of contemporary omniscience because critics of the novels I have identified typically condemn their narratorial commentary as inartistic authorial intrusion. For instance, in his article "Character in Contemporary Fiction," Brian Phillips claims that the characters in Jonathan Franzen's *The Corrections* often lack life because "Franzen adjourns to analysis and the ease of his own vocabulary" (640) when he is unable to manage the subtleties of free indirect discourse (FID). Phillips's example is this internal analysis of character motivation: "how sweet the optimism of the person carrying a newly scored drug that she believed would change her head; how universal the craving to escape the givens of the self" (324). If we eschew aesthetic prejudice, however, we can see the narrative voice of *The Corrections* precisely as an invocation of Franzen's authorial voice in his famous 1996 *Harper's* essay, which offers a critique of "the retreat into the self" (80) and "the rhetoric of optimism that so pervades our culture" (91).

This essay, which was republished in the wake of the novel's success as "Why Bother?" in his collection, *How to Be Alone,* outlines Franzen's lament for the novel's loss of authority since the nineteenth century and its increasing obsolescence in contemporary society as a result of "the banal ascendancy of television, the electronic fragmentation of public discourse" (36). *The Corrections,* then, is an overt example of a novelist's deployment of omniscient narration as part of a broader project to reassert the authority of the novel in contemporary culture. The fact that *The Corrections* has been simultaneously championed as signaling a return to the social realist novel after the death of postmodernism and a post-postmodern extension of postmodern language games that combines realism with experimentation, is indicative of the paradox of contemporary omniscience.

The discursive continuum between narrative and authorial voice moves in both directions, for novelists seek to establish their cultural authority through a range of genres, while still promoting the central significance of fiction as their source of "knowledge." So, for instance, when in the wake of the London bombings in 2005, the *Times* publishes an opinion article by Salman Rushdie titled "Muslims Unite! A New Reformation Will Bring Your Faith into the Modern Era," surely the "authority" of his opinion rests upon the fact that he is the author of *The Satanic Verses?* This novel is one of the first examples of what I am calling contemporary omniscience, and, by virtue of the controversy it generated, is a touchstone for the way we understand the role of fiction in and as public discourse. Melanie Phillips went so far as to claim, in *Londonistan,* that the "Rushdie affair became a rallying call for Muslim consciousness," generating a radical Islamist presence in British public life which eventually resulted in the London bombings. The Rushdie affair also crystallized the paradoxical relation between artistic freedom and freedom of speech. One relates to the right for an artist's aesthetic decisions to be judged outside a moral framework; the other relates to a citizen's right to voice unpopular opinions without fear of persecution. In conflating the two under the banner of Western democracy, defenders of the novel are claiming Rushdie's right to voice an opinion in public, while asserting that the novel, as a work of fiction, cannot be taken as a literal opinion. This tension is mirrored by the formal distinction between author and narrator which *The Satanic Verses,* in its experiments with literary omniscience, deliberately complicates.

In 2005, Rushdie was ranked as number ten on *Prospect Magazine's* list of 100 global public intellectuals, and this is not on the strength of his nonfiction work. The contemporary novelist who aspires to influence cultural opinion can best be described as a form of public intellectual: a thinker and writer who is able to speak to a general audience on a range of public issues from a base of specific disciplinary expertise. So Martin Amis's nonfiction work, *The Second Plane* (2008) becomes an extension of his fictional exploration of masculinity into social commentary, in which jihadism is anatomized as the product of threatened masculinity. In the Author's Note to *The Second Plane,* Amis makes a bold bid for cultural authority based on this fictional work: "Geopolitics may not be my natural subject, but masculinity is" (x). As Amis said in an interview for *Vice* magazine: "When September 11 came along, I wasn't prepared for anything as interesting as that to happen in my lifetime. If I had to explain what my novels were about in one word it would be masculinity, and here was masculinity in a whole new form . . . The social history of man is simply sex" (Knight). In this sense, the cultural capital of novelists is determined by the extent to which their fiction is taken up as a contribution to both public debate and literary-critical scholarship, authorizing them to speak in other nonliterary modes of discourse.

Contemporary Omniscience and Narrative Theory

None of the foregoing questions and claims can be properly addressed without also examining what omniscient narration actually is. This is no easy task, for, despite the seeming unity of the term, trying to define it in a formal sense demonstrates the slipperiness of the concept it labels. Indeed, one of the central claims of this book is that investigating what constitutes contemporary omniscience will help us reconsider the formal category of omniscient narration itself. According to Gerard Genette, in *Narrative Discourse,* the paradox of poetics is that "there are no objects except particular ones and no science except of the general" (23). Existing theoretical accounts of omniscient narration derive largely from the study of classic nineteenth-century novels. While narrative theory acknowledges historical shifts in fashion, it operates with a synchronic understanding of omniscient narration as a static element of narrative, produced by the structural relationship between focalization and voice. A central premise of this book is that narrative authority is not a purely immanent feature of a text, to be recuperated from a formalist study of narrative conventions such as privilege or level. The authority of these conventions is historically contingent and must be granted by readers, as evidenced by this quote from Morton P. Levitt: "to criticize Trollope for being omniscient is ludicrous; to criticize Murdoch or Drabble for being omniscient is necessary" (7). A study of contemporary fiction will enable us to approach the category of omniscient narration as a mutable practice of novelistic craft sensitive to historical and cultural contexts.

In an instructive historical irony, a theoretical debate about omniscience has emerged in the first decade of the new millennium, at roughly the same time that a revival of omniscient narration has reached a critical mass in contemporary fiction. A dramatization of this debate would see Nicholas Royle and Jonathan Culler lined up for a concerted new millennium attack on literary omniscience, and Barbara K. Olson and Meir Sternberg carrying out a staunch rearguard defense. And yet, so far, besides terminological wranglings and abstract theorizing, the debate has not led beyond re-examinations of nineteenth-century fiction, such as William Nelles's 2006 article "Omniscience for Atheists: Jane Austen's Infallible Narrator" in which he claims that the godlike attributes of omniscience cannot be assigned to Austen's work. The debate, which I address in more detail in chapter 1, revolves around the viability of the analogy between author/narrator and God which the term omniscience presupposes, and its parameters are largely epistemological and theological: how and how much does an omniscient narrator "know" about the fictional world; and what sort of figure or entity can be considered omniscient?

By virtue of the fact that omniscience refers to the all-knowing quality of the narrator, and is typically associated with the privilege of "non-natural" access to characters' consciousness, it has tended to be discussed within the category of focalization. A major theoretical problem arising from this focus is the common understanding that all third-person (heterodiegetic) narrators are omniscient: they either have degrees of limitation on their access to knowledge about the fictional world; or they choose to reveal or withhold omniscient knowledge according to the dictates of the story. Literary omniscience is thus largely defined by the epistemological "privilege" of the narrator, and narrative authority becomes a manifestation of the amount of diegetic information this narrator possesses or wields. For instance, in *The Dictionary of Narratology*, Gerald Prince defines authority as: "The extent of a narrator's knowledge of the narrative situation and events. An omniscient narrator (*Tom Jones, The Red and the Black*) has more authority than one who does not provide an inside view of the characters" (9). In this sense, a narrator's authority refers to their capacity to tell a story, to the conventional reliability of their narration.

The authority of omniscient narrators, furthermore, is a product of their status as narrating agents ontologically distinct from the story world. In *Narrative Fiction* (1983), Shlomith Rimmon-Kenan writes: "It is precisely their being absent from the story and their higher narratorial authority in relation to it that confers on such narrators the quality which has often been called 'omniscience'" (95). If a narrator's formal status as heterodiegetic (i.e., not a character in the story being told) and extradiegetic (i.e., occupying the highest level of discourse outside the story) grants them the "quality" of omniscience, then we have limited methodological tools for distinguishing between different historical manifestations of omniscience.

My aim in this book is to investigate how the conventional authority of omniscient narrators over a fictional world relates to the cultural authority of their authors in the public sphere. This requires a different approach to literary omniscience from that which foregrounds epistemological concerns. Cultural authority refers to the status of authors in the public sphere, their visibility and capacity to influence public opinion through their fiction. It is thus contingent upon historical context and measured by critical standing. The very anxiety about a decline in the cultural authority of novelists is predicated upon the possibility of this contingency. The fact that omniscient narration fell out of favor as a viable narrative voice in literary fiction indicates that its formal narrative authority is also subject to the contingency of literary fashion and critical reception.

The first step, then, is to understand what has been considered problematic with the narrative authority of omniscient narration. While omniscience is typically characterized as a narrator's privileged access to the consciousness of characters, works of omniscient narration are criticized on aesthetico-moral grounds for overtly asserting an authorial presence in the telling of a story and thus breaking the mimetic illusion, dictating the response of readers, and denying the autonomous selves of characters. In these terms, the authoritative possession of knowledge is less of a concern than the assertion of power through overt rhetorical attempts at influence.

The next step is to consider what authorial image is modeled by omniscient narration. While the quality of omniscience is analogous to that of God, its conventional authority is established by the traditional equation of narrator and author. As Francine Prose remarks in *Reading like a Writer*: "The omniscient voice in Dickens always sounds far more like the voice of Dickens than the voice of God" (108). Likewise, William Nelles claims that "the model for Austen's infallible narrators is not God in heaven, but Jane Austen" (128). When one considers the broader questions of the institutional conditions of literary production and the prevailing discourses of anxiety over the cultural authority of the novelist which I outlined earlier, asking whether contemporary omniscient narrators are as godlike in their knowledge of a fictional world as their nineteenth-century forebears will yield little insight.

In contrast to the prevailing theoretical emphasis on narratorial knowledge, then, I approach omniscience as the rhetorical performance of narrative authority which simultaneously invokes and projects a historically specific figure of authorship. This theoretical move will establish a shift in analytical focus away from static concerns with narratorial privilege and toward a more dynamic study of narratorial performance, enabling an investigation of the discursive relationship between narrative voice and the extrafictional statements of authors in the public sphere. My use of the term performance here bears a relationship to the distinction in Chomskyan linguistics between a speaker's competence (a knowledge of language) and performance (the actual use of language). An omniscient narrator's competence (i.e., putative knowledge of the fictional world) is a theoretical postulation. Only in performing this knowledge, through a range of rhetorical strategies, does a narrator claim the authority of omniscience. Indeed, this rhetorical performance is how we determine a narrator's "competence."

To study the rhetorical performance of contemporary omniscient narrators, a more dynamic approach to narrative authority than the possession of knowledge is required. By narrative authority, I mean the status of narrating agents which emerges out of a relational exchange involving both the rhetorical assertion and the institutional conferral of authority. This relational exchange is not specific to omniscient narration; it is fundamental to the communicative act in all forms of narrative fiction. Likewise a figure of authorship can be projected by or inferred from any narrative voice, such as a first-person confessional narrative being paratextually framed and received as a fictionalized autobiography, the author's personal experience lending testimonial authenticity to the character narrator.

In the case of omniscient narration, the authority of the narrator over characters is not simply a convention of form granted by "third person" status, but rhetorically performed by "extranarrative" elements such as evaluative commentary and reflexive statements of creative control (of lack of it) over these characters, and by various modes of representing consciousness. The authority of the narrator over the narratee is not only a product of the omniscient narrator's mediating presence between narratee and characters, but again a rhetorical performance in the form of narratorial commentary, and particularly an apostrophic instantiation of the narratee via direct address.

These two formal features of narrative authority—the relation between narrator and character; and the relation between narrator and narratee—both establish the framework for a reader's encounter with the text and its author. Narrative commentary, such as an aphoristic statement with relevance to the extratextual world, has greater authority when uttered by an omniscient narrator rather than a character or first-person narrator, not simply because of that narrator's formal (extradiegetic-heterodiegetic) status but because it is most likely to be attributed to the author who must assume responsibility for that statement in a way they would not have to were it attributed to a character (which was the crux of the trial over Flaubert's *Madam Bovary*). With character narrators, authorial opinion involves what James Phelan calls "mask narration." Quoting passages from *A Farewell to Arms* and *The Big Sleep,* Phelan writes: "In these passages, Hemingway and Chandler use their respective character narrators to voice their own beliefs. Both authors, I daresay, would be comfortable with the idea of having these passages lifted from their novelistic contexts and put on posters attributing the thoughts to them rather than to their character narrators" (*Living* 202). In omniscient authorial narration, the intrusive commentary is more likely to be attributed directly to the author, without masking.

The narrator–narratee relation in omniscient narration establishes a model for the author–reader relation, but the key difference is that narrative authority at this extrafictional level is contingent upon a work's critical reception. Much narrative theory interested in reader response conceptualizes this response in terms of the "real" reader's private encounter with a text, their ethical judgments, their cognitive processing. I intend to approach author–reader relations in a discursive sense, by which I mean narrative voice is one discursive and generic mode by which an author utters statements in the public sphere, and the cultural authority of this voice is contingent upon its critical reception, rather than the private response of individual readers. The narrative authority of authors, as opposed to narrators, then, refers to the public assertion of authorial opinion via the narrative discourse of their fiction, and the granting of this authority by its public reception.

My argument is that contemporary omniscient narration is an overt attempt to parlay the conventional authority of a fictional narrator into cultural authority for the author, or, to put it another way, into cultural authority for narrative fiction itself. This does not mean that a narrator's knowledge of the storyworld is unimportant to the narrative act, rather that engaging the narratee's desire for knowledge of the storyworld becomes a way of engaging the reader's desire for cultural insight.[5]

The following chapters in this book are organized around the question of narrative voice and its relation to authorship. They take as their base the classical narratological concept of voice, what Genette calls the "narrating instance," and test the useful of this concept in the face of subsequent refinements, criticisms and rejections from the perspective of rhetorical, cognitive and feminist approaches to narrative theory. Throughout the book I analyze how the formal features of omniscient narration are deployed to rhetorically perform narrative authority in a broader cultural context framed by the anxiety of obsolescence. Each chapter demonstrates how the methodological requirements for investigating the nature of contemporary omniscient narration call for a reconsideration of key elements of narrative theory, from the relationship between voice and focalization, to the representation of consciousness, to the narrative communication model.

Chapter 1 anatomizes the main theoretical problems associated with literary omniscience: the theological (the viability of the analogy between author and god); the epistemological (the difference between omniscient narration and other modes of third-person or heterodiegetic narration); and the ontological (the division and overlap between narrator and author). I argue that one of the reasons for the theoretical instability of the concept is that definitions have shifted in response to historical developments in novelistic form and according to the prevailing critical climate of the time. I proceed to offer a genealogy of the term and chart its theorization in Anglo-American formalism and structuralist and postclassical narratology, before elaborating my approach to the narrative authority of omniscient narration in opposition to scholarly debates which have emerged in the new millennium.

The next four chapters identify and classify four modes of contemporary omniscience and the figures of authorship they project, especially through extranarrative or extrarepresentational statements, including direct addresses, intrusive commentary and self-reflexive statements. Each chapter focuses on a particular aspect of the narrating instance and how it facilitates narrative authority. Chapter 2 more fully elaborates how contemporary omniscience is situated within a turn to post-postmodern fiction before offering cases studies of the *ironic moralist* (Salman Rushdie, Martin Amis, David Foster Wallace, Adam Thirlwell). The most prominent aspect of this mode is the direct address to readers through which narrators self-consciously grapple with the "universal" moral authority of the authorial narrator in the wake of metafiction.

Chapter 3 discusses *the literary historian* (Gail Jones, Michel Faber, Edward P. Jones, David Lodge), an omniscient narrator who asserts the historiographic value of imaginatively reconstructing history in fictional form, both drawing upon and challenging the authority of scholarly approaches to the archive. The key aspect of this mode is the temporal distance of the modern "time of narrating" from the historical past, in which extratextual historical knowledge is drawn upon to legitimize proleptic commentary. Chapter 4 provides case studies of the *pyrotechnic storyteller* (Nicola Barker, Rick Moody, Zadie Smith, as well as Rushdie and Wallace). Drawing upon Richard Aczel's "qualitative" approach to narrative voice as the stylistic evocation of subjectivity it analyses the ways in which stylistic expressivity establishes the intrusive presence and linguistic control of the narrator. In chapter 5, I examine the *immersion journalist* (Tom Wolfe) and the *social commentator* (Don DeLillo, Jonathan Franzen, Richard Powers), a narrator whose "omniscience" operates in the hyperbolic sense of displaying polymathic knowledge. Typically these narrators offer a paradigm for explaining the conditions of human behavior, such as neuroscience, genomics, the forces of capitalism and history, manifested in commentary and internal analysis, which competes with the conventional authority of the novelist's insight into human nature.

Chapter 6 addresses the question of "double-voiced" language in contemporary omniscient narration, investigating how the conventional "privilege" of access to character thought operates through FID. My argument is that theoretical accounts of FID have established an interpretive frame of alterity which perpetuates aesthetic and ethical prejudices regarding the historical progression of novelistic form toward the liberation of characters from narratorial control. The chapter proposes a model of FID as a self-conscious narratorial performance of the process of character thought and point to the self-reflexive experimentation with FID across all four modes of contemporary omniscience. A feature of this experimentation is *shared linguistic habitus,* in which readers' assumptions regarding idiomatic attribution are challenged by a deliberate interplay between stylistic contagion (the "infection" of narratorial language by a character's idiom) and narratorial usurpation (the narrator's linguistic intrusion in a character's interior monologue). As well as interrogating the relation between speech and thought, this self-reflexive experimentation facilitates a post-postmodern concept of *characterological cognitive self-awareness,* in which characters not only think, but reflect upon their own cognitive processes, including their lexical choices, in the act of reflection.

In chapter 7 I address the question of omniscience in the context of a different voice, that of the first-person narrator. First-person omniscience is another prominent form in contemporary fiction, and typically has been seen as a parodic critique of the claims for authority made by classic omniscience. The chapter demonstrates how Genette's concept of paralepsis (an infraction of the dominant code of focalization in which a narrator provides more information than is licensed by this code) has become a synonym for omniscient character narration (a narrator saying more than he or she knows), and transformed into a cognitive frame by which this mode of narration can be described as "unnatural." This approach is criticized as a product of the *epistemological fallacy* in narrative theory. I draw upon David Herman's concept of hypothetical focalization as an alternative to paralepsis and argue that characters employ hypothetical focalization to perform omniscience in the narrative act, relying upon the imagination rather than unnatural knowledge to authorize their stories. By virtue of invoking the figure of the novelist, rather than that of the autobiographer or the memoirist, these narrators project an authorial desire for a more relativized mode of omniscience in contemporary fiction.

Chapter 8 elaborates the broader methodological ramifications of my investigation of narrative voice. Keeping in mind the relationship I have established between contemporary omniscience and cultural anxieties about the decline of literature and the diminished status of novelists, I propose a *discursive narratology,* a formalist study of narrative which is capable of addressing the nature of fiction as public discourse and the role of the author in the construction of narrative authority. The chapter offers a critique of the ways in which the "real" reader has been theorized in contemporary narratology and reader response theory, and argue for an approach to the author as a concrete textual agent in the structure of narrative communication. Drawing upon Susan Lanser's theory of an "extrafictional" voice, and Genette's theory of the paratext, I present a discursive reformulation of the narrative communication model. This approach emphasizes the public nature of fictional narratives and their reception, rather than the mechanics of private individual reading.

In my proposed model, the paratext is reconceptualized as a Foucauldian discursive formation, with the narrative *discourse* of fiction situated alongside other nonliterary discourses in the public sphere, from authorial statements to readers' textual responses. The typical agents of narrative communication are thus reconfigured as a series of textual sites within which subject positions can be adopted and articulated along a discursive plane (rather than an inside/outside conception of the fictional text), with narrative authority emerging from the relations between subject positions in this formation.

CHAPTER 1

Omniscience and Narrative Authority

> Omniscience is not simply a hyperbole, it is an incoherent and flawed plot device in a story that critics and theorists have been telling for a hundred years and more. Why retain the concept of omniscience at all?
>
> —Nicholas Royle, *The Uncanny* 206

IN THIS CHAPTER I elaborate my approach to narrative authority in contemporary omniscient narration by reconsidering existing theories of literary omniscience. My claim is that formalist accounts of omniscient narration have developed and altered in response both to different manifestations of the form in the history of the novel, and to the prevailing critical orthodoxies which have accompanied this history. I will begin with a brief discussion of self-reflexive references to omniscience in the following two extracts. The first is from Thackeray's *Vanity Fair* (1848):

> If, a few pages back, the present writer claimed the privilege of peeping into Miss Amelia Sedley's bedroom, and understanding with the omniscience of the novelist all the gentle pains and passions which were tossing upon that innocent pillow, why should he not declare himself to be Rebecca's confidant too, master of her secrets, and seal-keeper of that young woman's conscience? (171)

The second is from Martin Amis's *The Information* (1995):

> And I made the signs—the M, the A—with my strange and twisted fingers, thinking: how can I ever play the omniscient, the all-knowing, when I don't know *anything*? (63)

Both passages are examples of intrusive omniscient narration in which the narrators reflect on their own authority as storytellers, and present themselves not just as narrators, but as novelists, as the author of the book we are reading. I have chosen these two examples, of course, because both of them make specific reference to the function of literary omniscience as a form of knowledge. If we conduct a classic taxonomic study of these two novels, we will see that both narrators display all the knowledge of their respective fictional worlds that is characteristic of omniscience, in terms of access to consciousness and spatio-temporal freedom. So in terms of narrative perspective there is little difference, although the Amis novel is less panoramically ambitious, focalizing mainly through the protagonist, Richard. In terms of narrative voice, both novels are narrated in the third person by authorial narrators who are outside the frame of representation. So we can tick off the list of formal properties and classify synchronically the two novels as omniscient.

And yet there is surely a palpable difference between the performative stances which these two narrators adopt. In the Thackeray passage there is a confident and playful assertion of the novelist's privilege of omniscient knowledge, whereas in the Amis passage there is a manifest anxiety about the narrator's omniscient authority. In fact, Amis's narrator is not grappling with a failure of diegetic knowledge, but a failure of novelistic insight resulting from his own limitations as a person. He is reflecting scenically on his own experience in order to ask whether he can satisfy his role as an observer of human nature.

Both of these novels enact what for me is the key feature of literary omniscience: the performance of narrative authority through intrusive narratorial commentary, which "personalizes" the narrator. If there is a formal difference between these two examples, it lies in the way they engage the reader, in how they establish different modes of narrative authority as omniscient story tellers. These formal differences can productively be understood with reference to the historical shift in the cultural status of the novel, from the mid-nineteenth to the late twentieth century, which I discussed in the previous chapter.

In the passage from Thackeray's *Vanity Fair* cited above, the narrator follows up his rhetorical question about access to consciousness by providing an account of Becky's thoughts and of her social context required for the "history" being written. In describing Becky's regrets over turning down a marriage proposal which would have secured her a prosperous life and increased social status, the narrator engages the narratee directly:

> In this natural emotion every properly regulated mind will certainly share. What good mother is there that would not commiserate a penniless spinster, who might have been my lady, and have shared four thousand a year? What well-bred young person is there in all Vanity Fair, who will not feel for a hard-working, ingenious, meritorious girl, who gets such an honourable, advantageous, provoking offer, just at the very moment when it is out of her power to accept it? I am sure our friend Becky's disappointment deserves and will command every sympathy. (171)

Thackeray's narrator solidifies this ironic identification with Becky's plight with reference to his own experience, when he claims: "I remember one night being in the Fair myself, at an evening party" (171). In this breach of the story/discourse division, the narrator relates a first-hand observation of how impending marriage into a higher social rank will alter a person's standing: "If the mere chance of becoming a baronet's daughter can procure a lady such homage in the world, surely, surely we may respect the agonies of a young woman who has lost the opportunities of becoming a baronet's wife" (172).

This section is a good example of J. Hillis Miller's claim that the Victorian narrator is immanent rather than transcendent, possessed of an omniscience which moves within the community of the story being narrated. Miller draws attention to a quality of Thackeray's omniscient narrator which

> identifies him as a perfect example of a spokesman for the general consciousness of the community. This is his use of the editorial "we." The novel is punctuated by direct addresses to the reader in which he is encouraged to think of himself as one of a vast number of other readers who share similar experiences of life and similar judgments of it. We are asked to identify ourselves with one another and with the narrator who speaks for us until by a kind of magical sympathy we lose our identities, are drawn into the group, and taken all together come to form a ubiquitous chorus of judgement. (72)

Miller calls this a "rhetoric of assimilation" (72) which in "establishing the reader's participation in a community mind surrounding the individual minds of the characters in the story gives the strength of a universal judgment" (78).[1] So the diegetic authority, the omniscient knowledge, of Thackeray's narrator, established in the prefatorial chapter as "the Manager of the Performance" and a puppeteer, is supplemented by this extradiegetic appeal to a common reading public. This "community mind" is obviously a rhetorical construct rather than a sociological fact, and the judgments it endorses, as the preface intimates, are those of a "man with a reflective turn of mind" who will be in sympathy with the narrator's stance toward the characters.

The editorial "we" is largely absent from contemporary omniscience, as it is from Amis's *The Information*. Amis's narrator is as equally intrusive as Thackeray's but he cannot so readily invoke a community mind. He thus requires recourse to a different means of character evaluation. The protagonist, Richard Tull, is a failed writer, his dedication to avant-garde experimentalism heightened by the obscene popular success of his friend with a work of middlebrow fiction. "Essentially Richard was a marooned modernist," the narrator tells us. "Modernism was a brief divagation into difficulty; but Richard was still out there, in difficulty. He didn't want to please the readers" (170). Richard's struggle as a writer, which provides the narrative momentum of the novel, is in fact a struggle over the concept of the universal. "And writers *should* hate each other, Richard naturally believed. If they mean business. They are competing for something there is only one of: the universal" (312).

In an argument over when Richard will finish his novel, whether it will end up being published and earning money, his wife, Gina, says: "I don't know if you still really believe in it. Your novels. Because you never . . . Because what you . . . Ah I'm sorry, Richard. I'm so sorry" (87). This line of dialogue is followed by a brief paragraph of narration which completes Gina's unfinished sentence: "Because you never found an audience—you never found the universal or anything like it. Because what you come up with in there, in your study, is of no general interest. End of story. Yes, this is the end of your story" (87–88). This passage could be the narrator's rendering, via omniscient knowledge, of Gina's unvoiced thoughts, or the rendering of what Richard *thinks* are her unvoiced thoughts, doubling as an internal dialogue with his own self-doubts. It could also be the narrator's address to his character, for Richard's anxiety is echoed, both ironically and agonistically, by the narrator who struggles throughout the book with the "universal" authority of his own omniscience.

Richard's difficulties in finishing his book are paralleled by his diminishing sexual potency (at one stage using anxiety over "the death of the novel" as an excuse to his wife for his poor sexual performance) and much of the book deals with his experience of a midlife crisis. In one scene Richard experiences a spontaneous erection while his young son is moving about innocently on his lap:

> This used to cause him disquiet, and struck him as something he had better shut up about. But, again, he was enough of an artist to have faith in the universality of his own responses. He asked around among the dads and found that it was so. It was general—universal. It still struck him as essentially perverse. When you thought of all the other occasions which cried out for hard-ons that never came. And here you not only didn't need one. You didn't even want one. (195)

While Thackeray's narrator describes himself in the book as "an observer of human nature" (177), moving through Vanity Fair in person, drawing upon the novelistic convention of omniscient access to character thought to supplement his moral commentary, the observations of Amis's narrator are more introspective. The effect is not to undermine his authority, but to ground the legitimacy of his observations in his own experience. The passage I quoted at the beginning of this chapter, in which the narrator questions how he can be omniscient when he doesn't know anything, comes from a section of commentary which begins: "This whole thing is a crisis. This whole mess is a crisis of the middle years" (62). In what follows it becomes obvious that these lines refer not only to Richard's life, but to the book itself, perhaps its genesis if we wish to read it autobiographically, but more importantly its form.[2] The next line reads: "Every father knows the loathed park and playground in the unmoving air of Sunday morning (every mother knows it Friday evening, Tuesday afternoon—every other time)" (62). This "universal" comment about parenthood is personalized by the narrator's own account of a time in the playground when he was approached by a child who proceeded to spell out letters in sign language. The narrator believes the child is deaf and dumb and leans forward, attempting to decipher the letters, "suddenly braced for revelation, frowning, essaying, as if the boy could tell me something I really might need to know" (63). When the boy announces that he has spelled out his own name this precipitates the narrator's crisis of omniscience, a sense that he lacks the knowledge of human nature, the "information," necessary to write a novel. His strategy is not to build this sense of crisis into the structure of the novel in metafictional fashion, but to reassert his authority by a confessional identification with his character: "I wrote those words five years ago, when I was Richard's age. Even then I knew that Richard didn't look as bad as he thought he looked" (63). Amis's narrator, then, confesses to readers rather than engaging them in a dialogue. And rather than asserting the "universal" through detached observation and an assumption of collective agreement, he offers it provisionally through individual introspection (the line "Every father knows" echoing Richard's knowledge of universality derived from having "asked around among the dads"). This is what allows the narrator to claim: "Intimations of monstrousness are common, are perhaps universal, in middle age" (64).

It is clear that Amis's narrator is gendered, as his strategy is to identify with Richard's perspective. This strategy foregrounds the relativity of the narratorial commentary, which is replete with stereotypical statements about gender differences: "She was a woman. She knew so much more about tears than he did" (9). A gendered narrator uttering "perhaps" has less conventional authority than a nongendered one uttering unmoored extrapresentational statements. One can see at work here both a recognition and a disavowal of the role gender politics has played in rendering the concept of the "universal" untenable. Vera Nunning locates *The Information* within a trend of contemporary fiction which she describes as "a merging of realism and experiment" (249). According to Nunning, in this book Amis "parodies nearly all the characteristics of nineteenth-century authorial narration and refuses to conform to the dogmas of political correctness" (249). I would suggest that *The Information* is less a parody then an agonistic encounter with these characteristics, and that its refusal of "political correctness" is an element of this agon. For instance, after describing the beauty of Gina (focalized through Richard), the narrator offers this version of the editorial "we" in a search for universality:

> We are agreed—come *on:* we are agreed—about beauty in the flesh. Consensus is possible here. And in the mathematics of the universe, beauty helps tell us whether things are false or true. We can quickly agree about beauty, in the heavens and in the flesh. But not everywhere. Not, for instance, on the page. (15)

In the difference between the performance of narrative voice in these two novels, emblematic of the nineteenth and the late twentieth century, I encounter the need for a diachronic account of shifting modes of omniscient authority. This diachronic account would not be so much one of the historical decline and revival of a narrative convention (hence mapping onto the standard evolutionary model of the progression of the novel from authorial to figural narration), but one of the historical mutability of this convention. And if this mutability resides largely in the narrative function of commentary, then its relation to a certain figure of authorship becomes more important than the nature of narratorial knowledge. With this in mind I intend to revisit and reconsider the scholarship on literary omniscience, drawing attention to the historical mutability of the concept itself, and lay the groundwork for a contextual approach to omniscient authority.

The Problem of Omniscience

It is relatively easy to list the formal features of omniscient narration and offer the eighteenth-century novels of Fielding, and the novels of Victorian authors such as Thackeray, Dickens, and Eliot, as canonical exemplars. Many scholars have pointed out, however, that these novels don't always fit the mold of theoretical definitions. Wilhelm Fuger offered a prominent critique along these lines in his article, "Limits of the Narrator's Knowledge in Fielding's *Joseph Andrews*." Analyzing the functional limitations which Fielding's narrator places on his privileged knowledge, Fuger concludes that "there is no such thing as a fully omniscient narrator and that this spectral figure may only be a construct invented by literary theorists" (288). Once we attempt a rigorous definition of omniscient narration and its manifestation in particular works of fiction, once we attempt to theorize the form and its effects, we are presented with a number of difficulties which continue to be debated. These include: the viability of the comparison of authorial narrators to God; the relation between author and narrator; the difference between omniscient narration and other third-person modes; and the constitutive features of literary omniscience.

First, how important is the foundational analogy with divinity and the ensuing trope of a godlike storyteller? To what extent can this analogy be divorced from its theological implications without rendering the descriptive term redundant? As David Lodge ("The Uses") and Nicholas Royle point out, omniscience describes an author's relation to their creative product, and the narrator's relation to the fictional world, in religious, and specifically Christian terms. "To assume the efficacy and appropriateness of discussing literary works in terms of 'omniscient' narration," Royle argues, "is, however faintly or discreetly, to subscribe to a religious (and above all, a Christian) discourse and thinking" (260). God forbid! Whether or not this association with Christian thinking is an ideological problem, when the analogy is deployed as a theoretical paradigm for a certain type of narration it leads to the postulation of a supernatural narrator ontologically distinct from character narrators and the narrators of nonfiction. In *Authorial Divinity in the Twentieth Century,* Barbara K. Olson argues that the author/God analogy and the omniscient narrator/God analogy must be taken seriously for their theological implications. Her claim is that writers throughout history have been influenced by the implications of this analogy for their creative acts, celebrating or rejecting comparisons with God, or being troubled by the conceptions of divinity which follow from their artistic beliefs. Her argument is that we should not even be debating the analogy—we should be studying what sort of God is implied by both the testimonies and authorial experiences of writers, and the narrational acts they employ. There is no doubt this analogy has informed many writers and their fictional projects, but it does not follow that it ought to be the basis for a theoretical definition of narrative form.

The term and its applications certainly invite us to consider the relationship between author and narrator. Does literary omniscience refer to the act of writing and its genesis in authorial imagination, or to the act of narration and the knowledge of the author's storytelling proxy? While in previous centuries omniscient narration was understood as the method by which an author narrates in his or her own voice, formalist distinctions between the two assign creation to the author and knowledge to the narrator, begging the question of what sort of narratorial figure can claim omniscience. More importantly they divorce narratorial commentary from its provenance in an author's voice. As Meir Sternberg points out, in *Expositional Modes and Temporal Ordering in Fiction,* the term omniscient author is logically redundant, for if it refers to the creative power of authors it must apply to all works of fiction. For Sternberg, omniscient narration only makes sense when referring to the super-knowing qualities which the author has conferred upon the narrator as a storytelling delegate.

We are then led to the problem of what textual features are constitutive of omniscient narration: what are the minimal conventions necessary to a definition of literary omniscience which would enable us to label some narratives omniscient and others not? The "privilege" which omniscient narrators supposedly possess that other narrators do not is knowledge of characters' hearts and minds. The common distinction between "full" and "limited" or "restricted" omniscience to describe the amount of information a narrator provides about the fictional world and the interior lives of characters raises epistemological questions: how can a narrator be partially all-knowing? If they can reveal the thoughts of one character, why not all? These questions frame the problem of omniscience in abstract logical terms. The response, articulated most forcefully by Sternberg (*Expositional Modes*, "Omniscience"), is that an omniscient narrator is indeed in possession of full knowledge about the fictional world, but chooses to reveal or withhold information according to the dictates of the story. Such an approach effectively grants omniscience to all third-person narrators, although it does point to the fact that omniscience would be better understood as a rhetorical performance of knowledge.

From the omniscient author to the "omniscient author convention" to the omniscient narrator to omniscient *narration,* the range of cognate terms employed over the last century, along with the multiplication of narratological alternatives, manifest the historical changes in critical thought about novelistic form and the difficulty of explaining the concept of omniscience in a literary context. Most critics and theorists, however, continue to employ the term as an easy shorthand, a lingua franca across literary studies, while typically qualifying their usage with prefixes such as "so-called" or with scare quotes. Within the tradition of narratology, according to Wallace Martin, "[w]hen focalization is not treated as an independent category in the definition of point of view, 'omniscient narration' becomes a kind of dumping-ground filled with a wide range of distinct narrative techniques" (146). The diffuseness of literary omniscience might prove resistant to easy classification, but that doesn't make the term untenable as many have claimed. The necessary first step is to chart this range of techniques and ask how they have come to be grouped together.

This task cannot be approached in an abstract fashion because the theoretical instability associated with literary omniscience is a result of its historically shifting usage, from a metaphor of authorship to a formal category of narrative, with emphasis placed on different aspects at certain points in the history of criticism, depending on the prevailing novelistic aesthetic and theoretical climate, leaving us today with a series of sedimentary layers of meanings and functions. What is most vital is to investigate the reasons why certain works of fiction are labeled omniscient, and what characteristics are emphasized in this labeling. This will help us to understand different historical manifestations of the form.

A Genealogy of Literary Omniscience

A genealogy of the terms "omniscience" and "omniscient" in a literary context reveals the shifting preoccupations of theories of the novel and the histories of novelistic form which they tell, explicitly or implicitly. I will begin with the foundational metaphor. The constitutive feature of the analogy between author and God is not a narrator's perfect knowledge or absolute power, but an author's creativity. The analogy stems from the Renaissance comparison of the poet with God in which, unlike classical antiquity where he is inspired by God, the poet possesses a faculty of imagination like that of God. This concept was introduced to English criticism by Philip Sidney in "An Apology for Poetry" (1595). According to Sidney: "the poet, disdaining to be tied to any such subjection, lifted up with the vigour of his own invention, doth grow in effect another nature, in making things either better than Nature bringeth forth, or, quite anew, forms such as were never in Nature" (7). Sidney's "second nature" is what we would call a heterocosm. The idea of an all-knowing author is a secondary product of this theory of creativity.

Dorrit Cohn and Nicholas Royle both point to Friedrich von Blanckenburg's 1774 *Essay on the Novel* as the earliest critical application of this analogy to the novel, quoting this line: "A writer, lest he wish to dishonor himself, can not hold to the pretense that he is unacquainted with the inner world of his characters. He is their creator: they have received from him all their character traits, their entire being, they live in a world that he himself has fashioned" (qtd in Royle 256). Robert Ellis Dye points out that this passage refers to the authorial construction of character, an author's ethical responsibility to develop a convincing interior life, and is not tied to a particular narrative voice or the qualities of a narrator: "Blanckenburg is talking, then, about the author-creator of any literary work, and not specifically about the narrator's field of vision in the novel" (132).

Henry Fielding claims this analogy for the novelist in *Tom Jones* (1749). "This Work, may, indeed," the self-reflexive omniscient narrator claims, "be considered as a great Creation of our own" (459). The narrator goes on to condemn any "little Reptile of a Critic" who finds fault with parts of the book before having finished reading the whole. "The Allusion and Metaphor we have here made use of, we must acknowledge to be infinitely too great for our Occasion; but there is, indeed, no other which is at all adequate to express the Difference between an Author of the first Rate, and a Critic of the lowest" (459). The allusion to God, then, is founded on the metaphor of creation, used to separate the artist's capacity for invention from the critic's parasitic reliance on older arbitrary rules of judgment.

If the concept of literary omniscience can be seen as emerging from a theory of creativity, the analogy with God need not be retained when we see how the theory of creativity develops in literary criticism. The analogy, considered blasphemous before the sixteenth century, was the first step in internalizing earlier theories of inspiration, leading to the Romantic ideal of the original genius. Coleridge's "secondary imagination" becomes a mental faculty designating not only the reproductive imagination described by neoclassical critics and supported by the philosophy of Locke and Hobbes, but the poet's creative power, which is an echo of the primary imagination, itself "a repetition in the finite mind of the eternal act of creation in the infinite I AM" (167). This concept leads eventually to a secularized democratization of creativity in twentieth-century theories of the unconscious as the source of creativity.[3]

When it comes to English theories of the novel, omniscience is first mooted as a method of storytelling among others. In her "Life of Samuel Richardson" (1804), Anna Laetitia Barbauld assesses Richardson's work in relation to the "three modes of carrying on a story" (xxiii): the narrative or epic, in which "the author relates himself the whole adventure"; the memoir, "where the subject of the adventures relates his own story"; and a third way, "that of *epistolary correspondence,* carried on between the characters of the novel." Barbauld describes the narrative or epic mode as "the manner of Cervantes in his Don Quixote, and of Fielding in his Tom Jones. It is the most common way." She describes the method in this way:

> The author, like the muse, is supposed to know everything; he can reveal the secret springs of actions, and let us into events in his own time and manner. He can be concise, or diffuse, according as the different parts of his story require it. He can indulge, as Fielding has done, in digressions, and thus deliver sentiments and display knowledge which would not properly belong to any of the characters. (xxiii)

Although she does not use the word "omniscient," instead making an analogy with the muse to explain the all-knowing qualities of the author (which indicates that the author's creative power is the source of knowledge which animates the narrative), Barbauld elaborates the familiar range of conventions, from the author's own voice, to access to consciousness ("the secret springs of action"), to the freedom to shift from scene to summary ("concise, or diffuse"), to the provision of commentary. The point here is that only when the author narrates in his own voice, rather than the voice of a character, does he have license (according to the laws of realism) to reveal all that he knows of the fictional world he has created.

The earliest use of the word omniscience in a literary context that I have found in English appears in 1848 in Thackeray's *Vanity Fair,* which I quoted at the beginning of this chapter. It is clear that Thackeray uses omniscience to denote the privilege of knowing the secret thoughts of characters, and in declaring himself master of these secrets the comparison with God is clear (for he searcheth the heart and knoweth the mind). It is also clear that Thackeray understands this privilege purely as a convention of authorship, for the narrator draws attention to the fact that he is a writer and a novelist, indicates the arbitrariness of shifts in point of view, and even describes his omnipresence in terms of pages, not the spatio-temporal coordinates of the fictional world. In short this passage is a rhetorical performance of omniscient authority, for the "privilege" of the novelist is not only access to the thoughts of characters but the capacity to assert an authorial presence by speaking directly to the reader in his own voice. The relation between these two features largely dictates the way in which omniscience is understood throughout the centuries.

Barbauld's taxonomy of storytelling methods is carried through by Walter Raleigh in *The English Novel* (1894), where he explicitly uses the term omniscient to describe authorial voice. In classifying the three methods of telling a story, Raleigh writes:

> The first and most usual way is that the author should tell the story directly. He is invisible and omniscient, a sort of *diable boiteux,* who is able to unroof all houses and unlock all hearts, and who can never be questioned as to how he came to a knowledge of the events he narrates. There are stories that can be told in no other way than this; the favourite way of Fielding, Scott, Dickens, and Thackeray. At a slight sacrifice of dramatic force the events of the story are supplied with a chorus, and at any time that suits him the author can cast off his invisible cloak and show himself fingering the "helpless pieces of the game he plays." (148)

There are similarities with Barbauld here, the capacity to unlock all hearts, the convention of infinite knowledge, but there is less emphasis on techniques than on a particular figure of authority, one which appears to be immanent in the fictional world, invisible, yet always able to assert his presence. One could argue here that the difference in emphasis stems from the fact that while Barbauld had only Cervantes and Fielding as examples, Raleigh had the whole range of Victorian fiction. Again, although using the word omniscient, Raleigh does not invoke an analogy with God. His description of the *diable boiteux* (meaning "lame devil," or Asmodeus, demon king) recalls an earlier instance of the term in Dickens's correspondence. In an 1865 letter discussing the origins of his periodical, *Household Words,* Dickens writes of the necessity to "get a character established as it were which any of the writers may maintain without difficulty." This character would be "a certain SHADOW," a "kind of semi-omniscient, omnipresent intangible creature" whose knowledge is granted not by creative power but by its capacity to inhabit the private spaces of the urban world, to "go into any place" and "be in all homes," and thus able to articulate "the spirit of the people and the time," to speak as a general voice, not just that of the author (qtd in Forster 511).

According to David Pike, "the 'Asmodean flight' was a common emblem for the problematic power of the omniscient narrator" in the nineteenth-century realist novel. "On the one hand the term lays claim to supernatural knowledge on the part of the novelist; on the other hand it intimates the moral taint that could become associated with a fictional overreaching and revelation of things perhaps better left hidden" (85). The Asmodean desire to unroof houses continues to be referenced in contemporary omniscience, self-consciously in this passage from Michel Faber's neo-Victorian novel, *The Crimson Petal and the White:* "All of the household, except for William, is under the sheets, like dolls in a doll's house. If the Rackham house were such a toy, and you could lift off its roof to peek inside, you would see William in shirt-sleeves at his desk, working on correspondence: nothing to interest you, I promise" (200). Similarly, Amis's book, set in modern London, opens: "Cities at night, I feel, contain men who cry in their sleep and then say Nothing. It's nothing. Just sad dreams. Or something like that. . . . Swing low in your weep ship, with your tear scans and your sob probes, and you would mark them" (3).

Another early appearance of the word "omniscience" is in an 1874 review of Thomas Hardy's *Far From the Madding Crowd* by Henry James, who writes: "the author has evidently read to good purpose the low-life chapters in George Eliot's novels: he has caught very happily her trick of seeming to humour benignantly her queer people and look down on them from the heights of analytic omniscience" (85). Here an immanent, roving, all-knowing narrator is not emphasized so much as one who is able to analyze and judge from on high. An understanding of omniscience as the psychological investigation of character motivation became more prominent as a result of the influence of George Eliot. Susan Lanser claims that classic realism, exemplified by Eliot's novels, emerges from the contradictory "narrative imperatives" of "knowing and judging, or representation and ideology" (*Fictions of Authority* 85). From the late nineteenth century "omniscient" and "analytic" were often used interchangeably. This can be seen in Brooks and Warren's *Understanding Fiction* (1943), which outlines various types of narration, including where "the story may be told by the omniscient author, or analytic author, the author who does undertake to present the working of the mind of one, or more, of the characters, and who may investigate and interpret motives and feelings" (659).

An important shift in the way novelistic method was approached in English literary criticism, and hence how omniscience was theorized, is indicated by Vernon Lee's 1895 essay "On Literary Construction." For Lee, "the most important question of all" (19) when considering novelistic construction is that of point of view, indicating growing interest in how readers are oriented to the consciousness of characters. Drawing on the analogy of perspective in painting, Lee writes:

> This supreme constructive question in the novel is exactly analogous to that question in painting; and in describing the choice by the painter of the point of view, I have described also that most subtle choice of the literary craftsman: choice of the point of view whence the personages and action of a novel are to be seen. For you can see a person, or an act, in one of several ways, and connected with several other persons or acts. You can see the person from no particular body's point of view, or from the point of view of one of the other persons, or from the point of view of the analytical, judicious author. (20)

Here we find an anticipation of narratological theories of focalization, from the spatial orientation of characters, to access to consciousness, to ideological perspective, with "the point of view of the analytical, judicious author" (again with George Eliot as the exemplar) situated as one perspective among others in a novel. It is an important conceptual shift from modes of telling to modes of perception which will later become elaborated in James's famous "house of fiction" metaphor in his preface to the *Portrait of a Lady*.

The twentieth-century concept of omniscience as a type of authorial intrusion in the form of excess narrative information rather than scenic dramatization is anticipated by George Gissing in an 1885 letter:

It is fine to see how the old three-vol. tradition is being broken through. One volume is becoming commonest of all. . . . Thackeray & Dickens wrote at enormous length, & with profusion of detail; their plan is to tell everything, to leave nothing to be divined. Far more artistic, I think, is this later method, of merely suggesting; of dealing with episodes, instead of writing biographies. The old novelist is omniscient; I think it is better to tell a story precisely as one does in real life,—hinting, surmising, telling in detail what *can* so be told, & no more. In fact, it approximates to the dramatic mode of presentment. (166)

Gissing offers an early argument for the redundancy of omniscience resulting from new methods of narration which have coincided with changes to the book publishing industry. This is a sentiment which James himself would agree with and, of course, James famously eschewed the heights of analytic omniscience—"the mere muffled majesty of irresponsible 'authorship'" (*Art of the Novel* 328)—in his own fiction as he sought to apply the principle of dramatization not only to the action of the story, but the consciousness of his characters. According to Joseph Warren Beach in his 1918 book, *The Method of Henry James:* "Mr. James is seldom or never, in his later work, the 'omniscient author.' He has a great scorn for this slovenly way of telling a story. It is only in his earlier work that he sometimes allows himself to step in and give special information to the reader,—information which he could not have had from the person or persons who are for the moment most concerned" (57). With the increasing prominence of new modes of third-person narration, omniscience became a problem for critics of the novel to address.

Point of View and the Omniscient Author Convention

When comparing the methods of telling employed by English novelists, both Barbauld and Raleigh described the value of the epistolary mode as combining the intimacy and immediacy of a character narrator with the freedom of the authorial narrator. The arguments which Barbauld and Raleigh make about the relative merits and disadvantages of authorial omniscience and character narration are still in circulation today, but we will no longer encounter claims that epistolary fiction is the more dramatized and hence mediating position between these two modes. From the early twentieth century this privileged technical solution has been firmly associated with third-person narration limited to a character's perspective, which Norman Friedman described as "to have the story told as if by a character in the story, but told in the third person" (1164). This critical formulation, of course, is a response to the development of modernist fiction and its impulse toward "dramatization" for which Henry James was the most vocal champion and, in English fiction, pioneering exemplar.

There is no need to rehearse in great detail here what is common knowledge: that James's prefaces to the New York Edition of his collected work, in which he elaborates in autobiographical fashion his fascination with locating a center of consciousness for his narratives, necessitating a rejection of many aspects of omniscience (such as overt commentary and exposition and multiple points of view), became the basis for a poetics of fiction codified by Percy Lubbock's *The Craft of Fiction* (1921).[4] In this book, Lubbock claims: "The whole intricate question of method, in the craft of fiction, I take to be governed by the question of the point of view—the question of the relation in which the narrator stands to the story" (251).[5]

Lubbock's study of point of view in the novel is inseparable from an historical conceptualization of novelistic method as an artistic evolution: a dynamic struggle of authors to rid their fiction of their own presence as omniscient storytellers. This progressive development of point of view, for Lubbock, culminates in James's *The Ambassadors,* and from James's ideas he elaborates an evaluative aesthetic criterion of showing rather than telling. The significance of *The Craft of Fiction* for theories of omniscience is twofold: first, it describes, through detailed analyses of Tolstoy, Thackeray, Flaubert, and James, the formal features of omniscient narration in operation in specific texts, only to register it as a technically outmoded point of view, and thus provides an historical and critical framework for condemning the use of omniscient narration in the twentieth century. Secondly, in doing so, it highlights the paradox of presence and absence which has animated later theoretical debates about literary omniscience. On the one hand, the means by which the novel is able to move beyond omniscience is the effacement of authorial presence; on the other hand, the resulting orientation of "point of view" to character consciousness manifests precisely the privilege of omniscience: laying bare the secret recesses of character's minds and hearts.

It is interesting to note that whenever Lubbock uses the term "omniscience" it is not in reference to character consciousness, but all the techniques which display authorial presence, that is, an author telling rather than showing. For Lubbock, as for Vernon Lee, point of view concerns the means by which readers can be supplied with their own point of view, without the mediating presence of authorial consciousness. In Lubbock's poetics, the omniscient author tells a story from his point of view, interposing his mind between that of the reader and the character: "He tells it as he sees it, in the first place; the reader faces the story-teller and listens" (251). Omniscience, then, is manifested in certain elements of a narrative, from "intrusive" commentary to exposition, the pictorial summary of events instead of the dramatic rendering of scenes, anything which does not place readers in a character's center of consciousness and thus betrays a mediated authorial point of view, a panoramic picture of how the author "sees" the world. "By convention," Lubbock writes, "the author is allowed his universal knowledge of the story and the people in it. But still it is a convention, and a prudent novelist does not strain it unnecessarily" (115).

Besides the dissenting voice of E. M. Forster's *Aspects of the Novel* (1927), Lubbock's work set the terms for subsequent critical works which reinforced the modernist aesthetic in formalist criticism. Joseph Warren Beach's *The Twentieth Century Novel: Studies in Technique* (1932) is a good example of the critical industry which developed from Lubbock's pioneering work. To introduce the chapter titled "Exit Author" Beach writes:

> In a bird's eye view of the English novel from Fielding to Ford, the one thing that will impress you more than any other is the disappearance of the author. In Fielding and Scott, in Thackeray and George Eliot, the author is everywhere present in person to see that you are properly informed on all the circumstances of the action, to explain the characters to you and insure your forming the right opinion of them, to scatter nuggets of wisdom and good feeling along the course of the story, and to point out how, from the failures and successes of the characters, you may form a sane and right philosophy of conduct. (14)

It can be seen here how the emphasis on authorial intrusion becomes a critique not just of breaking the mimetic illusion, but of asserting a moral control over the reader by virtue of obscuring the character. In the 1950s, critical accounts of the trajectory of novelistic experimentation toward authorial effacement were updated by Robert Humphrey's *Stream of Consciousness in the Modern Novel* and Leon Edel's *The Modern Psychological Novel*. "In the old novels," Leon Edel wrote, "the omniscient author was nearly always present and nearly always addressing an audience" (138). Edel and Humphrey install *Ulysses* rather than *The Ambas-*

sadors as the high point of the development of the novel. In *The Rhetoric of Modernist Fiction* (2006), Morton P. Levitt extends this tradition into the new millennium when he reiterates modernist experiments with point of view as a specific rejection of omniscience: "Tracing the movement out of omniscience is surely, as I understand it, the most useful clue to the emergence of the Modernist novel" (125).

And yet Flaubert and Joyce provide the touchstone of modernist aesthetics in two famous comments which make specific reference to the author/god analogy. "The author in his book," Flaubert wrote in correspondence with Louise Colet, "must be like God in the universe, everywhere present and nowhere visible. Art being a second nature, the creator of this nature must employ analogous procedures" (319). This is echoed in the dialogue of Stephen Dedalus, hero of Joyce's *A Portrait of the Artist as a Young Man:* "The artist, like the God of the creation, remains within or behind or beyond or above his handiwork, invisible, refined out of existence, indifferent, paring his fingernails" (233). In *The Rhetoric of Fiction* (1961), his corrective to what he considered the damaging aesthetic dogma of showing rather than telling, and the evasion of ethical questions inherent in the privileging of authorial impersonality, Wayne Booth engages with the paradox of omniscience which I pointed out earlier:

> There is a curious ambiguity in the term "omniscience." Many modern works that we usually classify as narrated dramatically, with everything relayed to us through the limited views of the characters, postulate fully as much omniscience in the silent author as Fielding claims for himself. Our roving visitation into the minds of sixteen characters in Faulkner's *As I Lay Dying,* seeing nothing but what those minds contain, may seem in one sense not to depend on an omniscient author. But this method is omniscience with teeth in it: the implied author demands our absolute faith in his powers of divination. We must never for a moment doubt that he knows everything about each of these sixteen minds or that he has chosen correctly how much to show of each. In short, impersonal narration is really no escape from omniscience. (161)

Booth argues that modernist impersonality is not an escape from "authorial presence," which Lubbock and his followers claimed, because he locates omniscience in the implied author, the norms and values of the author's second self which inform the text, and not in a set of narrative conventions. In other words, omniscience is a moral as well as a technical choice, and Booth's counterargument indicates that critiques of authorial intrusion are never purely aesthetic. It is clear, though, that Booth is describing omniscience in terms of privileged access to character's consciousness. The effect of this is to foreground this conventional privilege, rather than overt authorial presence, as the constitutive feature of literary omniscience, thus licensing use of the term to cover virtually all narratives in the third person.

This is evident in Norman Friedman's 1955 essay, "Point of View in Fiction: The Development of a Critical Concept," in which he undertook to provide a synoptic overview of theories of point of view and addressed the problem of omniscience by expanding it to include precisely those modernist novels which had been deemed to have eschewed it. Friedman provides a taxonomy of various points of view along a scale from telling to showing, understood in relation to the degree of presence of a narrator, whether the narrator is the author or a character. At one end of this scale is "Editorial Omniscience," in which "'omniscience' signifies literally a completely unlimited—and hence difficult to control—point of view" (1171). This point of view is characterized by the preponderance of summary over scene in which the author's voice dominates. According to Friedman: "The characteristic mark, then, of Editorial Omniscience is the presence of authorial intrusions and generalizations about life, manners, and morals, which may or may not be explicitly related to the story at hand" (1171). Here we have the typical account of omniscient narration as the intrusive presence of the analytic judicious author: "it is a natural consequence of the editorial attitude that the author will not only *report* what goes on in the minds of his characters, but he will also *criticize* it" (1172). Friedman goes on to classify increasing limitations on this originary mode of storytelling, from "Neutral Omniscience" to "Multiple Selective Omniscience" to "Selective Omniscience." The only form of third-person narration which is not described as a type of omniscience is "The Dramatic Mode" in which no mental states are reported (1178).

Narratology: Who Sees and Who Speaks?

The Anglo-American study of novelistic method and the pedagogy of creative writing, which emerged from it, are distinguished by their concern with authorial craft, with the aesthetic decisions authors make in constructing a work of narrative fiction, and with evaluating the efficacy of those decisions. As I have pointed out, this tradition is virtually predicated on the assumption that omniscient narration is a technically outmoded method of storytelling, and an aesthetic which by default sees the key features of omniscience as impediments to the mimetic illusion necessary for realist fiction. I have also shown how this critical tradition emerged out of an encounter with the modernist novel and the preoccupation with "point of view."

In the second part of the twentieth century, this critical tradition is all but subsumed by the development of narratology, which stems from structuralist linguistics and seeks to identify a grammar of narrative fiction of which novels are particular manifestations. In classical narratology, exemplified by Gerard Genette's *Narrative Discourse,* we are not presented with an account of the methods of storytelling available to an author, but with an taxonomy of discrete elements of narrative discourse. This tradition, too, emerges out of an encounter with modernism (for Genette, his touchstone is Proust, rather than James or Joyce) but eschews interpretation and evaluation.

In Genette's work, the formal elements traditionally unified under the category of the omniscient author convention become dispersed across multiple taxonomies: spatio-temporal freedom is understood in terms of order (analepses and prolepses); scene and summary are understood in terms of duration (or narrative speed) as well as mood (distance); narratorial knowledge and access to consciousness are understood in terms of focalization; and authorial voice is in understood in terms of the narrating instance (time of narrating, person, level, and the functions of the narrator).

Two key methodological distinctions provided by Genette, which separate his work from earlier studies of novelistic method, complicate a unified narratological account of omniscient narration: the separation of author and narrator (divorcing the narrating instance from the instance of writing); and the analytic distinction between voice (who speaks) and focalization (who sees). Genette's claim that a narrator such as Balzac's "knows" about the fictional world he is reporting in the narrative, while Balzac himself only imagines the events of the narrative he has invented (214), means that we cannot understand narratorial knowledge as the product of an author's creative power. We may accept by convention the authoritative knowledge of a heterodiegetic (third-person) narrator, but we are left with the epistemological question of how to account for that narrator's knowledge. Genette's claim that we must separate narration from perception means that we have to find ways to divide the perceptual and ideological features of point of view amongst these two categories. However, Genette refers specifically to omniscience only in his section on focalization. Furthermore, in defining focalization as the regulation of narrative information, but classifying types of focalization according to degrees of access to character's consciousness, Genette is demonstrating that revealing character's thoughts had become the prevailing definition of literary omniscience.

With focalization defined as the regulation of narrative information based on a principle of degrees of restriction, Genette outlines a tripartite typology which includes: non- or zero focalization, internal (variable, fixed or multiple) focalization and external focalization. Following Todorov, Genette defines zero focalization as a case of the narrator saying more than any of the characters knows, which becomes the narratological alternative to the omniscient point of view.[6] He points out that "the division between variable focalization and nonfocalization is sometimes very difficult to establish . . . and yet on this point no one could confuse Fielding's manner with Stendhal's or Flaubert's" (192). This point should indicate that the difference between the work of these novelists is not one of focalization so much as voice, and it is furthermore not a difference which can be accommodated by the idea of person, since they are all heterodiegetic.

Some basis for understanding the relationship between focalization and voice is provided by the last, least developed, and little discussed aspect of voice in Genette's method: the function of the narrator. Here Genette identifies a foundational *narrative function,* that is to tell the story, and then posits four extranarrative functions which a narrator can perform: the *directing* (referring to the organization of the narrative itself); the *communicative* (engaging the narratee); the *testimonial* (referring to the relationship the narrator has with the story); and the *ideological* (commentary on the action which establishes the authority of the narrator's presence) (255–59). This last function seems most pertinent to omniscient narration: "the narrator's interventions, direct or indirect, with regard to the story can also take the more didactic form of an authorized commentary on the action" (256). In *Narrative Discourse Revisited* Genette further points out that "the use of commentarial discourse is somewhat the privilege of the 'omniscient' narrator" (130).

It can be seen here that the more hazy ideological features of point of view have been assimilated into the function of the narrator, while the perceptual aspects are retained in the category of focalization. Genette declines, however, to establish a typology of these functions which would relate back to his other categories of voice and mood. Narrative theory since Genette has sought to clarify the relationship between focalization and voice, and typically the emphasis has been on expanding the concept of focalization or perspective.

The most significant revision of Genette's work was offered by Mieke Bal, who asserted the theoretical necessity for a further division between the focalizer (the subject of perception) and the focalized (the object of perception). The focalizer, or "agent" of perception, can be attached to a narrator who is external to the storyworld, or to a character who is within the story world. Furthermore, focalization can be from without, centering on observable action, or from within, centering on character's thoughts. In this typology, omniscient narration can be correlated with an external narrator or narrator-focalizer who has the capacity to focalize from without or from within.

Bal's reformulation of focalization theory has the tendency to be largely visual in its orientation, which is one reason why Genette avoided the term "point of view." Shlomith Rimmon-Kenan, in *Narrative Fiction*, sought to further develop Bal's theory by adding a range of "facets" of focalization. These facets are divided into the following categories: the *perceptual (space and time)* in which the external focalizer has a bird's eye or panoramic view and can focalize simultaneously on events in different places; the *psychological (cognitive)* in which the external narrator has unrestricted knowledge of the represented world; the *psychological (emotive)*, referring to the narrator's detached objectivity and capacity to focalize from within to penetrate the consciousness of characters; and the *ideological,* which reveals the authoritative norms of the text through which characters and other ideologies can be evaluated.

In this version of narrative theory, the "focalizer" is called upon to explain a lot of features, but ultimately none of them can be adequately understood without its relation to the external narrator. In her discussion of narrative voice in a separate chapter, which retains Genette's concept of level and person, Rimmon-Kenan writes:

> The extradiegetic narrators of *Tom Jones, Père Goriot,* and *Sons and Lovers* are in no sense participants in the stories they narrate (hence they are both extradiegetic and heterodiegetic). It is precisely their being absent from the story and their higher narratorial authority in relation to it that confers on such narrators the quality which has often been called "omniscience." (95)

So on the one hand all the features of omniscience are dispersed throughout separate facets of focalization, on the other hand they are unified under the category of narrative voice, which provides the authorization for the focalization. In response, Seymour Chatman rejected the idea of a narrator who can focalize, arguing that the analytic distinction between story and discourse means narrators can never see the storyworld, they can only report it ("Characters and Narrators"). In Chatman's formulation, then, we would understand omniscient point of view as the narrator providing an ideological slant on the filtered events of the narrative.

Postclassical Narratology

Narrative theory since Genette has been far more concerned with focalization than with voice, or, more accurately, it has been concerned with discussing the relation between voice and focalization in the broader context of narrative perspective or mediation. This is evident from the many post-Genettian reformulations of focalization theory, some of which I have discussed, to the number of books which continue to be devoted to the topic, to the whole orientation of postclassical narratology grounded in cognitive science, from possible worlds semantics (Herman), to the scripts and schemata of frame theory (Jahn, Fludernik), to the psychonarratological empirical study of reader response (Bortolussi and Dixon), Theory of Mind approaches (Palmer, Zunshine), and neurobiological accounts (Young), all of which build upon the concerns latent in Vernon Lee's and Percy Lubbock's discussion of point of view as the means by which readers' minds are oriented to the perspective of fictional minds.

The reasons for the relative lack of attention to voice in narrative theory are several: a general critical climate of skepticism about voice as the stylistic expression of authorial identity; the influence of deconstructive critiques of the metaphysics of presence, of logocentric approaches to writing as speech embedded in the metaphor of voice (see Gibson); and a general impulse, consistent with a modernist aesthetic, to demonstrate that narrative fiction need not possess a narrator, from Chatman's "non-narrated" narratives to Banfield's "empty deictic centre" to critiques of the narrator as an anthropomorphic construct of readers. These come together in the general theoretical and critical orientation across literary studies and within narratology toward investigating the role of readers in the construction of narrative meaning.

My argument is that we will not arrive at an adequate understanding of omniscient narration unless we assimilate focalization, or perspective in the broader sense, into the category of voice and approach it as a rhetorical strategy of the narrator. Monika Fludernik claims that the narratological distinction between voice and focalization is theoretically untenable, because "[t]he linguistic clues for determining focalization . . . are the same clues as those employed to determine voice" ("'New Wine'" 633). She goes on to reject the concept of voice as an interpretive illusion. And yet she recognizes that, in practical terms, "readers" rely upon this illusion to make sense of a narrative: "It then turns out to be a useful strategy to hypostasize the existence of a narrator figure who is telling us the story and whose presence and existence seem to be vouchsafed for by the stylistic features of authorial diction" (623). I would suggest that the concept of narrative voice is an interpretive strategy of reading precisely because it is a rhetorical strategy of authorship, and that focalization is constructed from voice in the way that story is constructed from discourse.

The separation of author from narrator, the narrowing of omniscience to access to consciousness, and the focus on reception have all served to inform the postclassical emphasis on omniscience as "unnatural" or "nonnatural" knowledge. The most influential work in this regard is Fludernik's *Towards a "Natural" Narratology*, which proceeds from the basis that narrative fiction is modeled on, and "narrativized" in terms of, cognitive frames derived from naturally occurring oral storytelling situations. "Authorial narration," Fludernik claims,

> performs the naturally impossible by yielding to the human narrator the authority of a quasi-godlike historian of human affairs. This contradiction, the very non-naturalness of the historian's omniscience, is, however, naturalized in the frame of empirical enquiry which authenticates a scientific metaphor for the narrator's exercise of omniscience. (167)

She argues that the reason why access to consciousness, or "mind reading," is at the forefront of discussions of omniscience is that it "violates expected natural frames" (167).

In the introduction to *New Perspectives on Narrative Perspective*, Willie van Peer and Seymour Chatman argue there is a need for narratology to move beyond product analysis to process analysis, which "changes the basic research model from the question, *What* is the perspective in this story? to *How* is perspective in this story brought about?" (7). Contemporary narratology approaches this question largely in terms of how readers process perspective. For my purposes, I think we need to harken back to prenarratological concerns with novelistic *method,* and ask how authors bring about perspective in a story. We can then ask the question *why*:

For what broader cultural purpose do authors construct narrators who employ different types of focalization as part of a rhetorical assertion of narrative authority?

Developing a methodological approach to this question will gain more from the other significant movement in postclassical narrative theory: that of rhetorical narratology. James Phelan provides a neat *précis* of this approach in *Experiencing Fiction:* "The first principle is that narrative can be fruitfully understood as a rhetorical act: somebody telling somebody else on some occasion and for some purpose(s) that something happened" (3). The phrase "on some occasion" can be taken as a rough equivalent of Genette's narrating instance. If, for Genette, voice is understood as where (level) and when (the time of narrating) in relation to the story the narrator (person) is narrating from, rhetorical narratology suggests the need for greater attention to the functions of the narrator: to whom and why is the narrator narrating? Furthermore, Phelan emphasizes the doubled communicative situation of narrative fiction, with twin communicative tracks between author/reader and narrator/narratee, which readers must negotiate as part of their "experience" of fiction. This approach, while also oriented toward the way readers engage with narratives, and particularly the aesthetic and ethical judgments which readers make, is grounded in a study of the relation between narratorial voice and (implied) authorial intention, which invokes certain readerly stances. These rhetorical considerations, for me, are the basis of an approach to the narrative authority of contemporary omniscience. Before outlining my approach, I will address the debate about omniscience which has emerged in the new millennium.

Contemporary Debates

According to William Nelles, Jonathan Culler, "will-he-nil-he, appears to be a lightning-rod in the current debate over omniscience" (128). In his 2004 article "Omniscience," Culler undertakes the task of clearing up the problem of omniscience, from an explicit position of disdain for its theological overtones. He asserts that omniscience "is not a useful concept for the study of narration, that it conflates and confuses several different factors that should be separated if they are to be well understood—that it obfuscates the various phenomena that provoke us to posit the idea" (184). For Culler, there are four textual "phenomena" that produce effects generally understood as omniscience: the performative authority of reliable narrative declarations about the fictional world; the reporting of character's private thoughts; overt self-reflexive statements which draw attention to the invented nature of the fictional world; and the synoptic overview of events as a means of producing a kind of universal wisdom.

Culler carefully sifts through each phenomenon, explaining how the term omniscience is inadequate to describe its effects, and concludes by suggesting the need for an alternative vocabulary. It is hard to argue with his dissection of these phenomena, but ultimately Culler's essay seems to prove nothing except what most narratologists accept: that omniscience is an imperfect analogy. Narrative theory has of course long employed a range of alternative or near-alternative terms, from "extradiegetic heterodiegetic narration with non or zero focalization" (Genette) to "authorial narration" (Stanzel) to "narrator-focalizer" (Rimmon-Kenan), to "psychonarration" (Cohn). The term "omniscient narrator" still persists in the wider scholarly community and in the public sphere, however, and its continued traction is presumably the occasion for Culler's essay. I am happy to continue using the term with its attendant narratological imprecisions, for it is embedded in our critical lexicon and none of the existing alternatives quite manages to encompass the narrative freedom (in terms of panoramic scope and narratorial judgment) which the trope of a "godlike" narrator suggests.

One alternative to omniscience which Culler favorably invokes, in order to bypass the traditional analogy with God, and more accurately explain at least one of his phenomena, is "telepathy." This term is proposed by Nicholas Royle in his 2003 book *The Uncanny*. Royle argues, in fact, that omniscience, focalization, and point of view are all critical fallacies, part of an institutionalized metadiscourse of narrative theory which does not attend to the complexities of actual literary works. Royle wants to do more than abolish an unproductive critical term, though; he wants to reconceptualize our approach to literary history, and our understanding of modern narrative fiction. For Royle, the disappearance of God, or should we say, the authority of God, in the eighteenth century, can be read in the hyperbolic appropriation of the term "omniscience" to denote human knowledge.

He further argues that in the late nineteenth century, at the moment when omniscience becomes a common term in literary criticism, the concept of telepathy emerges in the discourse of psychology. "Telepathy," Royle claims, "is both thematically and structurally at work in modern fictional narratives, and calls for a quite different kind of critical storytelling than that promoted by the religious, panoptical delusion of omniscience" (261). From brief readings of Dickens, George Eliot, and Virginia Woolf, Royle moves to an examination of Salman Rushdie's 1981 book, *Midnight's Children*, where, in the character and narrative voice of Saleem Sinai, "the telepathic here accedes to a new level of explicitness" (269), demonstrating that the structure of fictional narration is fundamentally telepathic rather than omniscient.

> What the novel instead offers is the metadiscursive trope of "omniscient third-person" reconfigured as "telepathic first-person"—in other words, it demonstrates in a new, even unprecedented way the fundamentally telepathic (rather than omniscient) structure of fictional narration more generally. (269)

As evidence, Royle cites an interview in which Rushdie admits he began writing *Midnight's Children* in an omniscient third-person voice before abandoning it. What, then, I find myself asking, are we to make of Rushdie's 1988 book, *The Satanic Verses,* where surely *omniscience* accedes to a new level of explicitness? Where the narrator self-consciously addresses us as god, or the devil, the creator of a magic realist world? Where the protagonist is visited by this God, who happens to look like Rushdie himself? In the first chapter of this novel Gibreel Farishta and Saladin Chamcha float safely to the ground after falling from a plane which has been blown up by terrorists. Toward the end of this chapter we find this passage:

> I know the truth, obviously. I watched the whole thing. As to omnipresence and—potence, I'm making no claims at present, but I can manage this much, I hope. Chamcha willed it and Farishta did what was willed.
> Which was the miracle worker?
> Of what type—angelic, satanic—was Farishta's song?
> Who am I?
> Let's put it this way: who has the best tunes? (10)

God's visitation to Gibreel later in the novel is described in these terms: "He saw, sitting on the bed, a man of about the same age as himself, of medium height, fairly heavily built, with salt-and-pepper beard cropped close to the line of the jaw. What struck him most was that the apparition was balding, seemed to suffer from dandruff, and wore glasses. This was not the Almighty he had expected" (318). The link between God, the narrator, and the author is made clear when the narrator admits late in the novel that he visited Gibreel, despite a noninterventionist policy:

I'm saying nothing. Don't ask me to clear things up one way or the other; the time of revelations is long gone. The rules of Creation are pretty clear: you set things up, you make them thus and so, and then you let them roll. Where's the pleasure if you're always intervening to give hints, change the rules, fix the fights? (408)

The Satanic Verses, for me, is in fact a convenient historical marker of the moment where, critical fallacy or not, omniscient narration, uncannily, like the return of the repressed, returns in serious literary fiction, but in a different form. In saying this, I mean that *The Satanic Verses* requires critics of the novel to engage with the way Rushdie plays with the conventions of omniscient narration. The same holds true for the number of prominent novels published in the two decades since *The Satanic Verses* that employ omniscient narration.

In asking whether the term "omniscience" is useful for understanding the effects of particular phenomena of narrative fiction, Culler's essay raises the question of whether any narrative can usefully be classified as omniscient, and thus whether the formal category proposed by critics actually exists in literary practice. In response, I would suggest that the idea of omniscience does not "confuse and conflate" different factors for which the term is used as a dumping ground. Rather, that certain works of narrative fiction produce the overall effect we have labeled omniscience by combining all four phenomena Culler identifies (and others, such as temporal range). So, once they have been separated for the purposes of analysis, the relation between these phenomena needs to be understood.

Culler's first two phenomena—authoritative reportage of the story world and of characters' thoughts—also hold true for internally focalized heterodiegetic narratives (and the first for external focalization). Culler himself points out the difficulties of considering these narratives in terms of "limited" omniscience or of narratorial reticence: it effectively confers omniscience on all extradiegetic heterodiegetic narratives. The last two phenomena, however—narrators who self-consciously claim authorship of the work, and narrators who dispense universal wisdom—which are more specific to a typical understanding of omniscient narration (i.e., telling rather than showing), draw upon the epistemological surety of the first two for the authority of their claims. In classical narrative theory, these first two phenomena can be understood in terms of focalization, while the latter two can be understood in terms of narrative voice.

Meir Sternberg provides a lengthy riposte to the challenges mounted by Royle and Culler in his 2007 article, "Omniscience in Narrative Construction: Old Challenges and New." He argues that, according to Genette's own understanding of focalization as a means of regulating narrative information, heterodiegetic narrators cannot possess restricted knowledge; they merely display a restricted performance of knowledge.

> Thus the focalizings called "internal," whether "fixed" (*The Ambassadors*), "variable" (*Madame Bovary*), or "multiple" (*Rashomon*), and "external" (Hammett's *The Glass Key*): all typically exhibit an all-knowing (mind reading, omnitemporality, omnipresence) that keeps the given "focalized" information short of what its power makes accessible and might reveal at will to the last "nonfocalized" detail. (757)

For Sternberg, who takes umbrage to Culler's anti-theism, the author is by definition omniscient and the narrator is the author's super-knowing delegate: "the narrator is constructed in God's image to perform the required discourse job with authority, epistemic at least" (763). This narrator's divulgence of omniscient knowledge ranges from omnicommunication to free suppression, depending on the artistic strategy required. In one sense, accepting Sternberg's claim that all heterodiegetic narrators are omniscient would neutralize epistemological considerations, and allow us to focus on the more important rhetorical function of narratorial performance. I'm inclined, though, to use the term omniscient narration as a label only for certain types of fiction, rather than as a general category of narrative: those works which actualize a panoramic intrusive narrator, which perform omniscience, rather than those narratives which report without comment, or in which commentary does not reveal a sense of the narrator's personality.

In his follow up to Culler's article, "Omniscience for Atheists: Jane Austen's Infallible Narrator," William Nelles provides the most thorough and strict test of omniscience as a paradigm for literary narratives. "Discussions of omniscience," Nelles argues, "assign it a broad and variable range of characteristics, many of which have little to do with omniscience per se" (120). He defines omniscience as a toolkit which authors employ to produce narrators with the godly powers of omnipotence, omnitemporality, omnipresence and telepathy, or mind reading. Nelles's claim is that because these four features "are denied real human beings" they "are uniquely reserved to omniscient narration" (121). As a result, exposition cannot be included because it often conveys information which is common knowledge to characters, and commentary on a character's thoughts is excluded because once these thoughts are known, a narrator does not require omniscience to comment upon them.

Nelles thus excludes the key feature of intrusive commentary from a definition of omniscient narration. And yet surely commentary, in the form of judgment of characters, is an important "privilege" of God? As Susan Lanser writes in her account of nineteenth-century classic realism: "It is only a slight exaggeration to suggest that upon this narrator rested the demands and powers of divinity itself, trusted at once to know all and to judge aright. . . . Realist 'omniscience,' then, means far more than a narrator's privileged knowledge of fictional facts" (*Fictions of Authority* 85–86). Furthermore, if literary omniscience is "pretend omniscience," as Nelles says, why could a human narrator not assume the "qualities" of omniscience in the act of narration? Whether or not the narrators of these novels are sufficiently godlike to warrant the description omniscient is not my concern. They obviously display a constellation of formal qualities which produce an effect that must be named, and named as distinct from other modes of heterodiegetic narration.

Omniscience and Narrative Authority

The broader claim which I intend to elaborate is that omniscient authority needs to be located in the function of the narrator, and that we need to approach the narrating instance in terms of how it invokes a historically specific figure of the author. The overriding effect which the various formal elements of omniscient narration both enable, and are underpinned by, is that of a specific rhetorical performance of narrative authority. By this I mean the heterodiegetic narrator's authority to pass judgment on the fictional world, and the authoritative resonance of these judgments in the extradiegetic or public world of the reader. Essential to this authority is a coherent narrative persona who serves as a proxy for the author. Contemporary narrative theory has generally been reluctant to engage with this effect because it is at odds with recurring assertions that third-person narratives need not possess a narrator. This is the essence of Culler's critique of omniscience: that we posit a narrator to explain unnatural knowledge and then are left to explain what sort of narrator could possess this knowledge.

My understanding of omniscient narration, then, is that the term is a trope, a figure of speech denoting a particular type of narratorial performance, not simply a quality of narratorial knowledge.[7] We need not take the notion of an "all-knowing" narrator literally. We could enter into an epistemological debate about how and how much a narrator knows, whether limited omniscience is logically possible, but I don't think this would be of much use for textual analysis. The debate over what sort of narrator could possess omniscient knowledge also strikes me as unnecessary. The Anglo-American study of novelistic method may have used the term omniscience, but it never posited a divine or superhuman narrator: it simply accepted the convention of the "omniscient author" telling the story directly. Narratology has productively complicated this conflation of author and narrator, but it has also created problems with accounting for narratorial knowledge. In *The Rhetoric of Fictionality*, Richard Walsh challenges several central concepts of narrative theory by presenting "a number of attempts to vindicate rather old-fashioned ideas in new terms" (1). One of Walsh's challenges is to the concept of the narrator, arguing that all fictional narratives are narrated either by a character or by the author. As a result, omniscience "is not a faculty possessed by certain class of narrators but, precisely, a quality of authorial imagination" (73).

I would qualify Walsh's argument only by suggesting that authors can imagine a personalized "second self" to narrate their story, effectively establishing themselves as extradiegetic characters. For if, as Walsh points out, character narrators, such as Humbert Humbert or Huck Finn, "are at least as strongly characterized in the telling of their tales as they are in the role of protagonist" (71), then surely the same must apply to authorial narrators. This effect of authorial "characterization" is achieved most overtly by commentary which asserts the omniscient narrator's superior knowledge to the characters in terms of his or her moral sagacity, intellectual breadth, and psychological and social insight. With this commentary, Wayne Booth argues in *The Rhetoric of Fiction*, "the narrator has made of himself a dramatized character to whom we react as we react to other characters" (212). Booth describes this dramatized narrator as a companion and guide to readers, encouraging them to establish a relationship with the author's "second self." The term omniscient narration, then, is best used to describe a certain type of narrative in which a heterodiegetic narrator, by virtue of being an authorial proxy, functions as an extradiegetic character, setting up a communicative rapport with the reader in order to rhetorically highlight the value of the narrative to a broader extraliterary public sphere.

The value of understanding omniscience in terms of narrative authority is evident when examining the grounds on which the concept and examples of the form are criticized. Omniscient narration is never taken to task for providing access to characters' consciousness, for this is seen as one of the distinguishing features of fiction itself, but it has long been attacked, on aesthetic, ethical and ideological grounds, for foregrounding the presence of the author-narrator. Consider this quote from W. J. Harvey's 1979 essay on George Eliot's omniscience: "I take it as axiomatic that the omniscient author convention becomes objectionable only when the author intrudes" (88). Furthermore, it is "the intrusive moral comment" (98) which is of most concern. This chief characteristic of omniscience, authorial presence, is a performance of narrative authority over both characters, in the moral judgment of them, and readers, in assuming their complicity with this judgment. The narrative authority which arises from judgment is central to denunciations of the religious associations of omniscience. It is the basis of Culler's atheistic disdain for authors "playing God"; it is at the heart of Sartre's famous attack on Mauriac; it underpins Bakhtin's critique of the monologic novel; and it is figured as the source of repressive panopticism by theorists such as Mark Seltzer and D. A. Miller, who link narrative omniscience with Michel Foucault's concept of modern disciplinary surveillance.

By virtue of referring both to authorial creativity and narratorial knowledge, literary omniscience cannot be understood in purely formalist terms, and narrative authority cannot be a product simply of formal conventions. This is because the performance of authority is bound up with the author's cultural status and the circulation of the novel in the public sphere. Understanding what historically specific figure of cultural authority omniscient narrators project to assert the importance of their fictional narratives, and fiction in general, to public discourse is the most important aspect of this study.

Scholes and Kellogg provide a history of this figure when they approach the ways in which "point of view" developed from ancient narratives to modern fiction in terms of "the problem of the authority of the narrator" (242). They offer an early criticism of the analogy with God presupposed by omniscience, and demonstrate how Fielding, building upon the influence of Cervantes, offers a model of omniscient narration which draws upon the authority of three figures: the bard, the *histor,* and the maker. The bard draws its lineage back to the Homeric epic, in which the epic poet appeals to the inspiration of the muse rather than tradition to authorize his performance (242). The *histor* draws its lineage back to ancient historians, Herodotus and Thucydides, where again, rather than tradition, the narrative is authorized by the critical spirit with which he approaches his sources. The "intrusive" commentary offered by the *histor* "is simply the *histor* going about his business" (266). In his novels, Scholes and Kellogg argue, Fielding's "narrative persona" (267) models his authority on the epic bard and the *histor,* while also drawing attention to the fictitious nature of his narratives: "in practice he sometimes adopts the role of histor (there are things he cannot find out), of bard (he can reveal unspoken thoughts when he wants to), and of maker (he admits he is making things up)" (268).

Scholes and Kellogg thus provide an excellent model for linking the various formal features of omniscience to particular figures of narrative authority. What must be noted is that the development of this mode in Victorian fiction, while still demonstrating the relevance of these figures, presents in the omniscient narrator a different kind of authority: that of the novelist, and especially the novelist as ethical guide. As Susan Lanser writes, the Victorian omniscient narrator possesses a "self-authorizing authority" grounded in, "not, as it was a century earlier, the illusion of empirical evidence, but (tautologically) the narrative voice itself" (*Fictions of Authority* 85–86). Which is to say, narrative authority is the function of a certain kind of cultural capital for the novelist.

Authority, Gender, and Authorship

To develop an approach to narrative authority which understands omniscience as an historically contingent and culturally located mode of narration, feminist narratology offers the most productive resources. Here I turn to Susan Lanser's *Fictions of Authority*. In this book Lanser develops a feminist poetics of narrative voice centered on attempts by women writers to assert their cultural authority in a gendered public sphere. By positing a link between "social identity and narrative form" Lanser emphasizes that the rhetorical strategies authors employ to establish the authority of their narrative voices must be understood in the social context of their reception:

> Discursive authority—by which I mean here the intellectual credibility, ideological validity, and aesthetic value claimed by or conferred upon a work, author, narrator, character, or textual practice—is produced interactively; it must therefore be characterized with respect to specific receiving communities. (6)

The social identity which has traditionally carried the most discursive authority is that of white educated men, and hence the status of a narrator is received in relation to this dominant power. For Lanser, then, the question of narrative authority cannot be separated from the discursive formations which produce what Foucault called the author function, generating modes of authorship which can be adopted or challenged by various narrative strategies. As such, she claims:

> the emphasis of this book is on the project of self-authorization, which, I argue, is implicit in the very act of authorship.... [T]he act of writing a novel and seeking to publish it—like my own act of writing a scholarly book and seeking to publish it—is implicitly a quest for discursive authority: a quest to be heard, respected, and believed, a hope of influence. (7)

In the course of her book, Lanser discusses the historically shifting negotiation of masculine authority by women novelists through their strategic deployment of narrative voice, and articulates three "narrative modes" which she calls authorial, personal, and communal voice. "Each mode," Lanser explains, "represents not simply a set of technical distinctions but a particular kind of narrative consciousness and hence a particular nexus of powers, dangers, prohibitions and possibilities" (15). This approach requires Lanser to reconfigure some of the categories of classical narratology to investigate particular figures of authorship which emerge from them. One of these is Genette's distinction between extradiegetic and intradiegetic, which Lanser reframes, not so much in terms of level, but in terms of the connection of these levels to the narratee. This leads her to make a "distinction between private voice (narration directed toward a narratee who is a fictional character) and public voice (narration directed toward a narratee 'outside' the fiction who is analogous to the historical reader)" (15). Given that the capacity to speak with authority in public discourse has traditionally been a male privilege, Lanser's introduction of the public voice enables her to make considerations of gender a vital contextual complement to formalist discussions of level and to narrative authority in general.

The narrative mode which Lanser calls the authorial voice is the most relevant to this book because this is her term for the authority vested in omniscient narration. Where Rimmon-Kenan had accounted for the authority of omniscient narration in purely formalist terms, produced by the extradiegetic and heterodiegetic status of the narrator, for Lanser, the relation between narrator and narratee established by this status must be correlated with the public relationship between author and reader which it invokes:

> The mode I am calling authorial is also "extradiegetic" and public, directed to a narratee who is analogous to a reading audience. I have chosen the term "authorial" not to imply an ontological equivalence between narrator and author but to suggest that such a voice (re)produces the structural and functional situation of authorship. (16)

For Lanser, the "privilege" of the omniscient authorial voice resides in a rhetorical invitation for readers to equate the narrator with the author, speaking directly to them. In discussing the textual specificities of this act of self-authorization, Lanser makes what I think is a key distinction between omniscience as the narratorial performance of authority and other forms of heterodiegetic narration in which access to consciousness is at the fore. This distinction is between narratorial acts of representation (reporting the fictional story) and extrarepresentation, which involves "reflections, judgments, generalizations about the world 'beyond' the fiction, direct addresses to the narratee, comments on the narrative process, allusions to other writers and texts" (17). Lanser employs the term "authoriality" to refer to the extrarepresentational practices of "heterodiegetic, public, self-referential narrators," arguing that these narrators make greater claims to discursive authority than more reticent narrators, because they "expand the sphere of fictional authority to 'nonfictional' referents and allow the writer to engage, from 'within' the fiction, in a culture's literary, social, and intellectual debates" (17). So here Lanser is giving more weight to what Genette called the ideological function of the narrator in order to understand the narrative authority of omniscience in terms of the gendered and public nature of voice.

Having established that narrative authority must be understood as emerging from the relationship between narrative voice and a particular figure of authorship, I will turn, in the following chapters, to the manifestation of this relationship in contemporary omniscient narration. An important question to consider is the extent to which the modes of narrative authority and the figures of authorship which constitute contemporary omniscience must be understood in terms of gender. The first observation to make is that contemporary omniscient narration seems to be largely a phenomenon of male writers. A. S. Byatt has been a vocal defender and dedicated practitioner of omniscient narration, citing

George Eliot as her model. But the practice of asserting discursive authority through an intrusive third-person narratorial presence founded on the conventional "privilege" of zero focalization has, to my knowledge, been taken up by far fewer female than male novelists. Hence, of the fifteen authors whose work I will be classifying and providing cases studies of, only three of these are women: Gail Jones, Zadie Smith, and Nicola Barker. The next step is to consider the extent to which this gender imbalance carries methodological implications.

In her earlier work, *The Narrative Act,* Lanser offers a series of claims regarding the conventional assumptions readers make about the gender of authors and narrators. First, that "in the absence of textual information to the contrary, a certain degree zero of narrator identity is presumed," and that "the unmarked case for both writing and narration is the male case: writers and narrators are presumed male unless the text offers a marking to the contrary" (166). She also points out that, despite this degree-zero assumption, readers will conventionally equate the unmarked voice of a heterodiegetic public narrator with the social identity of the author. So if readers note that the author of the book they are reading is female, this "signals a female narrative voice in the absence of markings to the contrary" (167). These claims strike me as uncontroversial, and are clearly relevant when considering the long held practice of female authors adopting male or androgynous pseudonyms to take advantage of a default assumption of normative male authorship.

It would seem important to note, then, that if omniscient narration by convention has the highest narrative authority, this authority must be gendered male. We might then think about the formalist definition of the "privilege" of omniscience. Traditionally this privilege has been equated with the "godlike" capacity to know the interior lives of characters, and one could easily extend the implications of the metaphorical comparison to the ultimate "male" authority of god. However, I have argued that epistemological and theological approaches to omniscient narration are less important than considerations of the rhetorical performance of omniscient authority. In which case, the key "privilege" of omniscience is the authority to speak with influence in public discourse, particularly through what Lanser calls "extrarepresentational acts."

This enables a productive link between Lanser's contextual narratological approach to authorship and narrative authority and the broader accounts of a crisis in literary authority which I have argued underpins the emergence of contemporary omniscience. Kathleen Fitzpatrick's claim for the gendered nature of the anxiety of obsolescence proves salient in this regard. For Fitzpatrick, public lamentations over the loss of the novelist's cultural authority in the face of electronic media can be correlated with white male authors simultaneously appropriating a disingenuous position of marginality and figuring the mainstream as feminine. Toward the end of her book, Fitzpatrick claims that underneath the anxiety of obsolescence "lies a concern about the continuing role of the white male subject in contemporary society" (230), an "overwhelming cultural theme, which may appropriately be called, after Nina Baym, a melodrama of beset white manhood" (231). For Fitzpatrick, the disinvitation of Jonathan Franzen from Oprah Winfrey's Book Club is a key example of a conflict between an embattled white manhood equated with literary culture and the feminized space of popular mass media: "the otherness of the electronic media to the 'higher' art of the novel parallels the otherness of women and racial and ethnic minorities to the experience of white men" (232). The anxiety of obsolescence, then, is not animated so much by an attempt to reclaim a broad cultural authority in the form of attracting more readers, as it is by a desire to protect an elitist masculine literary culture from the threat of otherness.

Here we might find a useful hypothesis for why male authors are predominantly the ones who have renovated omniscient narration—typically regarded as the voice in fashion at the high point of the novel's cultural authority—but inscribed this narrative voice with a more relativized and agonistic mode of narrative authority, as in the case of Martin Amis with which I opened this chapter. Returning to Lanser's claims about the gendered nature of narrative voice, then, in the case studies of the modes of contemporary omniscience which follow, I will endorse Lanser's claim that the degree zero of narrator identity is male, and draw attention to the occasions when narrators explicitly mark their gender to facilitate the link with authorial voice which I am claiming is essential to narrative authority. The textual marking of gender occurs precisely through the extrarepresentative narratorial intrusions which perform an omniscient narrator's authority. I will also show how, in approaching fiction as a mode of public discourse, the conventional equation between a narrator's and an author's "social identity" in Lanser's terms enables an author's nonfictional statements to be read as extrarepresentative commentary on the same discursive, rather than diegetic, level. Hence my claim that narrative authority arises out of relations between author and reader which are also governed by extratextual relations. Understanding the contingency of authority as an appeal to the public authority of the author we can start to theorize the different functions of omniscience in specific historical periods.

CHAPTER 2

The Direct Address and the Ironic Moralist

> The contexts, the great forms of the eighteenth- and nineteenth-century sagas, have been exhausted; realism and experimentation have come and gone without seeming to point to a way ahead. The contemporary writer, therefore, must combine these veins, calling on the strengths of the Victorian novel together with the alienations of post-modernism.
>
> —Martin Amis, *The War against Cliché* 78–79

ALTHOUGH book reviews and scholarly articles on individual works of fiction may mention their use of omniscient narration, general accounts of the phenomenon of contemporary omniscience are virtually nonexistent. The few attempts to distinguish between classic and contemporary omniscience that I have found have come from teachers of creative writing. In *The Power of Point of View: Make Your Story Come to Life* (2008), Alicia Rasley argues that "classical omniscient" has "attitude and persona," an "ironic, all-wise, witty voice commenting on events" (14), whereas "contemporary omniscient" "eliminates the narrative persona, though not the narrative control" (140). This formulation replicates the standard distinction between overt Victorian omniscience and covert modernist omniscience (or editorial and neutral omniscience in Friedman's terms) and hence is at odds with the phenomenon I am concerned with here.

In the previous chapter I argued that literary omniscience must be understood as more than a narrator's complete knowledge of the fictional world, evidenced by access to the consciousness of characters. I also argued that the narrative authority of omniscience cannot be understood in purely formalist terms as a narrator's possession of this knowledge (focalization), by virtue of his or her ontological distinction from characters (voice). If we take access to consciousness as the defining feature of omniscience, then virtually all third-person narrators are omniscient, and we become mired in epistemological debates about full or partial omniscience. In my approach, omniscient narrators are distinguished from other heterodiegetic narrators by the extent to which they rhetorically perform this conventional authority. That is, we cannot assume omniscience as a default quality of authorial narrators; it must be manifested in overt displays of zero focalization (saying something no character could know) and extranarrative statements which establish the intrusive presence of the narrator. Approaching narrative authority less as the capacity to report reliably on the story world, and more as a type of narratorial status produced by a relational exchange between agents in the communication model, I have argued that the authority of omniscient narrators, by virtue of their function as a proxy for the author, is contingent upon a particular figure of authorship. The reason the intrusive omniscient narrator of Victorian fiction is said to have fallen out of favor in the twentieth century was that its narrative status lost cultural authority in an age of relativism. The authorial figure projected by omniscient narrators in contemporary fiction can thus be archaic or (post)modern depending on the rhetorical performance of this voice.

On this basis, the distinction I am making between classic and contemporary omniscience is not simply a periodizing one between novels written before the twentieth century and novels written since the 1990s. The fact that a novel has been published recently does not necessarily make it contemporary. I am mindful here of John Barth's claim in his 1967 essay, "The Literature of Exhaustion," that a "good many current novelists write turn-of-the-century-type novels, only in more or less mid-twentieth-century language and about contemporary people and topics; this makes them considerably less interesting (to me) than excellent writers who are also technically contemporary" (30). Even Barth's classic metafictional short story "Lost in the Funhouse" (1968) cannot be considered a technically contemporary example of metafiction in comparison to David Foster Wallace's "Octet," which introduces extra levels of irony as it self-consciously wrangles with the legacy of postmodernism.

By contemporary omniscient narration, then, I mean works of fiction in which intrusive third-person narrators demonstrate an awareness of the influence of postmodernism on the figure of authorship which their narrative voices project. In this sense, there may be works written today which employ omniscient narration but are not contemporary in their use of the form. Vikram Seth's *A Suitable Boy* (1993) would be one such example of classic omniscience, modeling its form on the Victorian novel. Richard Russo's defense of omniscience suggests that it has always been the unacknowledged mainstream of narrative fiction in the twentieth century. This may be true if we accept third-person narratives with multiple perspectives and an unobtrusive voice, such as Russo's *Empire Falls* (2003), as omniscient. However, I have established greater emphasis on the performance of omniscience through intrusive presence and zero focalization to clarify the term and delimit the field, and my focus here is on novels whose omniscience differs from classic omniscience as a result of their aesthetic and intellectual relation to the legacy of postmodernism.

Russo's defense stems from the assumption by writers, literary critics, and theorists that omniscient narration is an outmoded relic of the Victorian novel; an assumption which has exerted tremendous influence on the production and reception of literary works for the past century, from the history of decline which I mapped out in the previous chapter, to the prevailing aesthetic prejudice which underpins the "practical" advice against the form dispensed in writing programs, to the professional advice of agents and publishers, to the response of reviewers. In other words, in the same way that the anxiety of obsolescence, as Kathleen Fitzpatrick describes it, operates discursively to enable certain statements about the state of the novel, the critical narrative of the obsolescence of omniscience constructs a blind spot in which omniscient narration is not recognized as an element of contemporary literary culture. When contemporary works of fiction are discussed, their use of omniscience is not considered important, or it is seen to complicate the contemporaneity of the work. For instance, Matthew Paproth claims, in "The Flipping Coin: The Modernist and Postmodernist Zadie Smith":

> The problem with classifying Smith's fiction, then, is its determinedly straightforward, traditional presentation of narrative and its relatively uncomplicated narrative voice. Rather than presenting us with the kind of tortured unremitting narratives that Beckett presents us with, or with the kind of mixed-up chutnified narrative that Rushdie presents us with, Smith's narratives are leisurely paced, elegantly structured, and written from the perspective of a confident omniscient narrator. (14)

Again we have the assumption that omniscience is a form of narration and an authorial posture so encrusted with Victorian sensibilities that any use of its conventions can only be understood as nostalgic conservatism or ironic critique. The books I am concerned with here may demonstrate some kind textual self-consciousness of the form but are neither nostalgic revivals (in an unreflective or ironic fashion) or parodic metafictional critiques, so much as they are hyperbolic or agonistic searches for new modes of narrative authority. The novels I have chosen to study, furthermore, are embedded in the governing institutions of literary fiction. They possess cultural capital by virtue of being objects of discussion around which a discursive formation or a paratext accumulates, and exert some pressure on the way in which the novel circulates as an art form and cultural artifact in public life. In other words, I'm interested in the contribution of omniscient narration to current debates on the status of the novel as an art form in the wake of postmodernism and on the function of authors in public discourse.

Omniscience, Metafiction, and Postmodernism

I want now to briefly sketch the ways in which postmodern experimentation has influenced contemporary omniscience. Invoking the term "postmodern" is inevitably fraught with problems of definition, and I follow critical custom in asserting that its deployment in relation to fiction can only ever be provisional. The commonly accepted features of postmodern fiction include self-reflexivity, parody, irony, playfulness, pastiche, nonlinearity, and a general tendency for formal experimentation which challenges what Catherine Belsey, in *Critical Practice*, called "expressive realism" (7–14). Some prominent definitions of postmodern fiction include: metafictional subversions of the relation between fiction and history (Hutcheon); fiction in which the generic dominant is a narrative foregrounding of ontological questions—as opposed to the epistemological dominant of modernism (McHale, *Postmodernist Fiction*); a tendency to favor diegesis over mimesis (Lodge, "Mimesis"); and, in a critique of formalist approaches, the global expansion of English language fiction in the wake of colonialism (Berube).

If we accept "postmodernism," at the very least, as a periodizing term marking the cultural sensibility and general aesthetic accompanying the condition of postindustrial late capitalism, I will define postmodern fiction, for the purposes of this book, as an aesthetic move beyond the "exhaustion" of modernist experimentation without returning to traditional realism, and a cultural response to a perceived crisis of authority for the novel as a mode of public discourse, dramatized in the phrase "the death of the novel." David Lodge's important 1969 essay, "The Novelist at the Crossroads" is a good starting point here, for it identifies three genres which emerged from the anxiety of writers faced with this situation. These genres are fabulism, or what became known as magic realism; the nonfiction novel, now sometimes called "faction," or grouped under the broader term of "creative nonfiction"; and the problematic novel, now known as metafiction. What I would like to suggest is that Lodge's three genres are examples of postmodern experimentation with narrative voice which opened up the possibility for reintroducing omniscient narration in literary fiction.

The privileged mode of postmodern fiction is without doubt metafiction. As Patricia Waugh claims: "Although metafiction is just one form of postmodernism, nearly all contemporary experimental writing displays *some* explicitly metafictional strategies" (22). Metafiction itself takes a variety of forms, but many examples, such as Barth's "Lost in the Funhouse," overtly assert the presence of an omniscient narrator by virtue of the characteristic authorial intrusions which draw attention to the act of writing: "The boy's father was tall and thin, balding, fair-complexioned. Assertions of that sort are not effective; the reader may acknowledge the proposition, but. We should be much farther along than we are; something has gone wrong; not much of this preliminary rambling seems relevant" (79). As Wenche Ommundsen claims, in *Metafictions?:* "The ostentatious, intrusive narrator or author-figure, interrupting the story to air his or her preoccupations with the processes of fiction-writing, is perhaps the most explicit way of expressing a reflexive awareness" (7–8).

It is precisely the intrusive presence of the author in Victorian omniscience which modernist poetics reacted against. Henry James, of course, famously excoriated Trollope for the reflexivity of his authorial voice, for parading his creative omnipotence in direct addresses to the reader. "In a digression, a parenthesis or an aside," James laments,

> he concedes to the reader that he and this trusting friend are only "making believe." He admits that the events he narrates have not really happened, and that he can give his narrative any turn the reader may like best. Such a betrayal of a sacred office seems to me, I confess, a terrible crime. ("The Art" 71)

If omniscient narration can be defined as an authorial narrator's rhetorical performance of narrative authority manifested most overtly in self-reflexive, intrusive commentary, then postmodern metafiction which does the same is surely omniscience with teeth in it. Furthermore, the attention drawn to the armature of fiction by the self-reflexivity of the form establishes a link between author and narrator.

Barth's postmodern manifesto "Literature of Exhaustion" is the key document here, suggesting that technically contemporary novelists could reclaim the pleasures of plot and narrative as long as they built an ironic awareness of this reclamation into the narrative. John Fowles's metafictional classic, *The French Lieutenant's Woman,* is a good example of how this postmodern stance might relate to omniscient narration and its association with the Victorian novel. After twelve chapters in which the authorial narrator of Fowles's novel diligently mimics the voice of a Victorian novel, we have this famous confessional intrusion:

> I do not know. This story I am telling is all imagination. These characters I create never existed outside my own mind. If I have pretended until now to know my characters' minds and innermost thoughts, it is because I am writing in (just as I have assumed some of the vocabulary and "voice" of) a convention universally accepted at the time of my story: that the novelist stands next to God. He may not know all, yet he tries to pretend that he does. But I live in the age of Alain Robbe-Grillet and Roland Barthes; if this is a novel, it cannot be a novel in the modern sense of the word. (85)

The French Lieutenant's Woman is typically characterized as a metafictional parody of the Victorian novel. However, it can also be seen as a self-conscious attempt to revive the pleasures of the form. In his "Notes on an Unfinished Novel" Fowles wrote: "We suspect people who pretend to be omniscient; and that is why so many twentieth-century novelists feel driven into first person narration. . . . But in this new book, I shall try to resurrect this technique" (153). Of course, the narrator of *The French Lieutenant's Woman,* as we are told in a direct address to the reader, has the problem of dealing with omniscience in "the age of Barthes and Robbe-Grillet" (85). In other words, an omniscient narrator in the twentieth century cannot be the same as an omniscient narrator in previous centuries. An awareness of this fact is what underpins contemporary omniscience.

After Postmodernism

The same period that I have identified as marking the return of omniscience in contemporary fiction, from the 1990s to the present, has also been described as the period in which postmodern literature gave way to the post-postmodern, or at least another iteration of postmodernism. For instance, in *The Routledge Companion to Postmodernism* Barry Lewis clearly demarcates 1990 as the end of postmodernist writing as the dominant mode of literature (95). Post-postmodern literature has typically been defined as fiction which owes some debt of influence to, or at least demonstrates a textual awareness of, the major works and characteristics of postmodernism, but which attempts to put this legacy of experimentation in the service of more humanist concerns. If metafiction was the privileged genre of postmodernism, its critique forms the engine of what is now being called post-postmodernism: characterized as an attempt to move beyond the "exhausted" form of metafiction and the dead-end of formal experimentation which was its legacy (McLaughlin, Burn). This impulse has informed a return to or reworking of traditional forms and narrative (Hoffmann); a less fraught engagement with popular culture, such as embracing the language of the everyday or drawing inspiration from comic books, rather than operating within an anticapitalist mode of critique (Hoberek); and a more humanistically oriented exploration of the self, rather than a critique of the subject, including the ethical questions this involves (Timmer). These accounts of post-postmodernism share three features: the periodizing (from the 1990s); the generational (a younger group of writers who came to prominence in this period); and the combinatorial (a synthesis of classical realist form with elements of postmodern experimentation).

The features of post-postmodernism have all been described in both British and American fiction, by Vera Nunning, in "Beyond Indifference: New Departures in British Fiction at the Turn of the 21st Century," and Stephen J. Burn in "The End of Postmodernism: American Fiction at the End of the Millennium." Burn describes how throughout the last decade of the twentieth century a critical mass of artists and theorists prosecuted claims for the demise of postmodernism as a movement, partly because its continued semantic diffuseness lacked explanatory force, and partly because it failed to adapt to the contemporary media ecology, with its characteristic self-reflexivity losing its avant-garde dynamism when metafictional strategies became absorbed and co-opted by mainstream popular culture and marketing.

My argument for locating contemporary omniscience within this broad concept of the post-postmodern, indeed for suggesting it is the exemplary voice of this impulse, is predicated on two claims. First, if postmodernism, by foregrounding the presence of an author-narrator (the metafictionist, the fabulist, and the journalist) self-reflexively revived the omniscient narrator, then this became the point of departure for contemporary writers. Secondly, this authorial presence can be read as symptomatic of the post-postmodern novelistic anxiety over the cultural relevance of fiction produced by the institutional conditions of literary culture which I outlined in the introduction. Two common critiques of postmodernism, its empty formal experimentation and its rejection of the concept of character, are founded on the claim that these features render the novel irrelevant to public discourse. Contemporary omniscient narration emerges from an attempt to engage with the insights of postmodernism while reconfiguring the authority of the novelist in the public sphere.

In suggesting that contemporary omniscience can be characterized as post-postmodern, I don't want to argue that this marks the end of postmodernism as a literary enterprise, a cultural sensibility, or a mode of critical and philosophical thinking. But I do want to show how some of the forms identified as postmodern have been further extended by contemporary writers, regardless of whether these writers are given generational labels of postmodern or post-postmodern. I propose, then, four permeable and overlapping modes of narrative authority which contemporary omniscience relies upon, and whose postmodern lineage can be traced back to Lodge's genres: (1) the *Ironic Moralist;* (2) the *Literary Historian;* (3) the *Pyrotechnic Storyteller;* and (4) the *Immersion Journalist* and *Social Commentator.*

In analyzing these four modes I will pay attention to two aspects of narrative voice: first, the formal manifestations of "authorial" presence from evaluative commentary on characters, to aphoristic statements about "human nature," to self-relexive addresses to the reader; and secondly, how this commentary configures the narrative voices around modes of authority different from that of the novelist in classic omniscience. In many cases I will draw upon some of the nonfictional extra literary statements of authors to demonstrate their vital role in establishing the narrative authority of their fiction in the public sphere.

The Ironic Moralist

The first mode of contemporary omniscience, the *ironic moralist,* grapples self-reflexively with the legacy of the "universalizing" moral authority of classic omniscience, and it does so in the shadow of metafiction. The self-reflexivity in this mode, in which the narrator's intrusive authority is constantly paraded, is less concerned with exposing the artifice of fiction, than with the problem of how to assert the universal in relation to the particular. The narratorial direct address is the main device used to engage with this problem: demonstrating an anxiety over the extent to which moral commentary can be taken as authoritative. Any discussion of contemporary omniscience must begin with the direct address, one of the key features of classic omniscient authority, and the feature most criticized for working against dramatization. To recall Leon Edel's claim: "In the old novels the omniscient author was nearly always present and nearly always addressing an audience" (138). I have already discussed Martin Amis's *The Information* in this context. The other examples I will examine here are David Foster Wallace's story "Octet" and Adam Thirlwell's *Politics*.

The narrator of Rushdie's *The Satanic Verses* can also be classified as an ironic moralist. As I pointed out in the introduction, this narrator self-consciously asserts his omniscient status, indeed literalizes the metaphor of a godlike narrator by claiming to be God. At the same time, he complicates his moral authority by virtue of presiding over a magic realist world in which he hints that he may also be the devil: "Who am I? Let's put it this way: who has the best tunes?" (10). There has been some debate about the nature and function of narrative voice in this novel, with scholars such as James Harrison and Keith M. Booker identifying what they call a satanic narrator at play. Roger Clark provides an overview of this debate in his book, *Stranger Gods: Salman Rushdie's Other Worlds,* before arguing: "While it is something of a simplification to say that the text has *only two* narrative voices, I would argue that it has a conventional, omniscient narrator as well as an otherworldly satanic narrator" (134). Clark characterizes the satanic narrator as an insidious covert presence in the novel, a puppeteer who wields an omnipotent hand at the diegetic level: "the satanic narrator possesses Chamcha then uses him to manipulate Gibreel" (144). At the same time, his satanic pride compels him to announce his presence at the extradiegetic level, surfacing in various direct addresses which undermine the unity and control of the conventional omniscient narrator: "I know; devil talk. Shaitan interrupting Gibreel. Me?" (93).

Certainly Rushdie's narrator encourages readers to entertain doubts about his nature, and the purposes of his narration. In a broader sense, however, the "satanic" narratorial intrusions are ludic distractions from a desire to assert universal statements about human nature, even as the narrator performs postcolonial critiques of the empire. While the title refers to the apocryphal story of the devil reciting passages of the Koran to Muhammed, this reference is given a more quotidian parallel in the form of Saladin Chamcha's desire to gain revenge on Gibreel Farishta for abandoning him to the authorities when they first fell from their burst plane to the shores of England. Chamcha inflames Gibreel's murderous jealousy through a series of anonymous phone calls in which he whispers lines of doggerel intimating sexual knowledge of Gibreel's wife: "and then it was time for the return of the little satanic verses that made him mad" (445). This leads Gibreel to murder his wife and kill himself. Recognizing that the story is "the echo of a tragedy," a "burlesque for our degraded, imitative times" the narrator asserts: "Well, then, so be it.—the question that's asked here remains as large as ever it was: which is the nature of evil, how it's born, why it grows, how it takes unilateral possession of a many-sided human soul. Or, let's say: the enigma of Iago" (424). In framing his question this way, the narrator is implicitly recognizing the perennial relevance of Shakespeare's tragedy, even after having reported earlier Chamcha's echo of Thomas Babington Macaulay's famous *Minute on Indian Education* (1835), which called for an educational system in India to create a class of anglicized Indians, when he tells his future wife "that *Othello*, 'just that one play,' was worth the total output of any other dramatist in any other language" (398).

The narrator goes on to ask rhetorically whether Gibreel and Saladin represent "two fundamentally different *types* of self" (427). Gibreel "has wished to remain, to a large degree, *continuous*" whereas Saladin "is a creature of *selected* discontinuities, a *willing* re-invention; his *preferred* revolt against history being what makes him, in our chosen idiom, 'false'" (427). This is complicated by the fact that:

> Such distinctions, resting as they must on an idea of the self as being (ideally) homogenous, non-hybrid, "pure,"—an utterly fantastic notion!—cannot, must not, suffice. No! Let's rather say an even harder thing: that evil may not be as far beneath our surfaces as we like to say it is.—That, in fact, we fall towards it naturally, that is, not against our natures.—And that Saladin Chamcha set out to destroy Gibreel Farishta, because, finally, it proved so easy to do so; the true appeal of evil being the seductive ease with which one may embark upon that road. (427)

Here we have an intrusive narrator discussing his characters with his readers, as could be found in classic omniscience. The moral commentary includes what could be a claim for original sin, our natural state arising from the Fall, but it is made hesitantly with the awareness of postcolonial and postmodern critiques of an essentialized self.

David Foster Wallace, "Octet" (1999)

In both his fiction and nonfiction, David Foster Wallace has deliberately framed his intellectual and aesthetic project as an encounter with the legacy of metafiction. In his 1993 essay, "E Unibus Pluram," Wallace locates himself within a class of "fiction writers as a species," and locates this class in "a literary territory that's gone from Darwinianly naturalistic to cybernetically post-postmodern in eighty years" (151). According to Wallace this new generation of American fiction writers must contend with two interrelated phenomena: the literary influence of postmodern metafiction, and the cultural power of television. The link between the two, for Wallace, is the corrosive power of self-conscious irony and its rebellious critique of any position of authority and sincerity.

Postmodern fiction, Wallace points out, developed at the same time that television assumed cultural ascendancy in America. "For postmodern fiction—written almost exclusively by young white males—clearly evolved as an intellectual expression of the 'rebellious youth culture' of the sixties and early seventies," made possible by the homogenizing effects of television on national culture (182). The failure of postmodern fiction to grapple with the challenge of television, Wallace argues, lies in its inability to transcend a position of ironic distance which television had already adopted: "The fact is that for at least ten years now television has been ingeniously absorbing, homogenizing, and re-presenting the very cynical postmodern aesthetic that was once the best alternative to the appeal of low, over-easy, mass-marketed narrative" (173).

Irony, Wallace's chief target, is a way of "heaping scorn on pretensions to those old commercial virtues of authority and sincerity" (179), while protecting oneself from this scorn and making the receiver complicit in this stance. So if fiction writers are to reclaim cultural authority from television they must eschew the irony they have become complicit with; the contemporary fiction writer must risk charges of banality and sentimentality in order to separate fiction from its mutually implicated relationship with television fostered by postmodern metafiction. Wallace concludes by arguing that: "The next real literary 'rebels' in this country might well emerge as some weird bunch of 'anti-rebels,' born oglers who dare to back away from ironic watching, who have the childish gall actually to endorse single entendre values" (193).

In this way, like John Barth, he is claiming the need to move beyond an "exhausted" form of experimentation and reclaim some of the traditional territory of authors. However, he understands this as an ethical rather than technical challenge, and the exhausted form of experimentation he is referring to is not modernism, but the postmodernism championed by Barth. While his long story, "Westward the Course of Empire Takes Its Way," with its clear intertextual reference to Barth's "Lost in the Funhouse," is typically seen as the prime example of this project, I would suggest that Wallace's short story "Octet" is by far more important and successful. Like "Lost in the Funhouse" and Fowles's *The French Lieutenant's Woman,* this story stages an agonistic encounter with the process of writing, but ultimately is less concerned with a formalist interrogation of the architectonic structure of fictional narrative and its realist aspirations, than with the nature of fiction as communication. In fact, I suggest, "Octet" can be read as a self-reflexive exploration of the key device of omniscient authority: the authorial narrator's direct address to the reader.

By virtue of the fact that the narratorial direct address is extranarrative in its function, that is, a pause in the narrative, it has been condemned as breaking the illusion of reality. This is why the direct address, in the form of self-reflexive authorial intrusions, became the most important device of postmodern metafiction and its critique of realist fiction. Wallace's strategy, in a sense, is to recuperate the sincerity and intrapersonal efficacy of the direct address from its deployment in metafiction as a laying bare of the artifice of fiction. If this artifice, the craft of writing, is laid bare, the story asks, what can be revealed: an empty fictional structure, or the fibrillating self of the "real" author?

While "Octet" is not a typical example of omniscient narration, its authorial narrator experiments with some key features of omniscient authority: reflexively demonstrating his creative power by drawing attention to the fictive nature of the story, addressing readers and discussing characters with them. However, this narrator, as a writer and proxy for the author himself, does not "know" his characters, and the struggle to provide universal commentary or write the story he envisaged eventually takes over the narrative. The story is structured as a series of "pop quizzes," self-contained but interrelated vignettes in which complicated scenarios of interpersonal relations are presented (the relationship between two drug addicts, between work colleagues, a wife and her son, and between a man and his wife's family). The questions at the end of each section employ the pop quiz format as a direct address inviting readers to make ethical judgments about the characters' actions or to surmise their motivations. For instance, the first section, "Pop Quiz 4" about two "late stage terminal drug addicts" concludes with: "Q: Which one lived" (111). Readers are thus encouraged to provide the moral evaluation of characters which is normally the preserve of the omniscient narrator. The third section, "Pop Quiz 7," about a "lady" who walks away from a custody battle with her wealthy ex-husband to ensure their child retains access to a Trust Fund, concludes with "Q: (A) Is she a good mother" (114). The fourth section "Pop Quiz 6(A)," about "X" who feels disconnected from his wife's family because he loathes her dying father whom everyone else worships, concludes with "Evaluate" (123).

The quizzes, however, read like sketchy works in progress, with no character names and operating largely through summary. The second section, entitled "Pop Quiz 6," makes this provisional nature of the story overt, as it is full of hypotheticals and hesitations. It begins: "Two men, X and Y, are close friends, but then Y does something to hurt, alienate and/or infuriate X" (111). What follows is a narrative based on speculations about what this "something" was, concluding with: "In fact the whole mise en scene seems too shot through with ambiguity to make a very good Pop Quiz, it turns out" (113). "Pop Quiz 6 (A)" proceeds to make reference to the "abortive PQ6" (120). Here the narrator is both speaking to himself as he works through the problems of the story and aware of the reader's "presence.'

In *Towards a Natural Narratology,* Monika Fludernik discusses traditional omniscience in these terms: "To the extent that the authorial narrator exemplifies the laws of human nature on the basis of illustrative case studies of a few human subjects (the protagonists), 'his' uncanny ability to know other people's minds becomes backgrounded and hardly noticeable as an infraction of real-life frames" (124). "Octet" is occasioned by the narrator's anxiety over his inability to provide these "illustrative case studies," resorting to the performance of his own anxiety as the exemplification of human nature.

The last section, "Pop Quiz Nine," becomes an extended metafictional examination of the failure of the piece to realize the writer's original intention. The authorial intrusion, however, takes the form of a second-person address which simultaneously establishes the narrator of the previous pieces as the narratee and protagonist and, by virtue of its grammatical form, invites the reader to adopt this position. It begins: "You are, unfortunately, a fiction writer. You are attempting a cycle of very short belletristic pieces" which are "supposed to compose a certain sort of *'interrogation'* of the person reading them" (123). This phrase, "a fiction writer," echoes Wallace's references in "E Pluram Unibus" to a subspecies of voyeuristic humans who are representative of the inability to form meaningful relationships which television fosters. Of course the person reading this cycle of belletristic pieces is the writer himself, who thus becomes a surrogate for the reader. "There are right and fruitful ways to try to 'empathize' with the reader," the authorial narrator opines, "but having to try to imagine yourself *as* the reader is not one of them" (129). The implication is that readers are asked to imagine themselves as the writer. A distinction between narrator and narratee is established in a footnote in the first person: "All I can do is be honest and lay out some of the more ghastly prices and risks for you and urge you to consider them very carefully before you decide. I honestly don't see what else I can do" (133). This narratee is clearly a fictional version of the authorial narrator—"You're still going to title the cycle 'Octet'" (129)—yet it is also clear that the narrator is attempting to address readers through his self-directed apostrophe.

In turning over the problems of the existing pop quizzes, the narrator writes that referring to the aborted Pop Quiz 6 has

> the disadvantage of flirting with metafictional self-reference—viz. the having "This Pop Quiz isn't working" and "Here's another stab at #6" within the text itself—which in the late 1990s, when even Wes Craven is cashing in on metafictional self-reference, might come off lame and tired and facile, and also run the risk of compromising the queer *urgency* about whatever it is you feel you want the pieces to interrogate in whoever's reading them. (124)

Here we find the same critique of metafiction which Wallace articulates in his essay on American fiction and television: its own sense of "used-upness" (to use Barth's phrase). Can meta-metafiction revive this used-up postmodern experiment? We, the reader, are a constant presence in this last section, with phrases such as "whoever's reading them" referencing the subject position of the reader, while the second person instantiates the narratee.

In *Dear Reader: The Conscripted Audience in Nineteenth-Century British Fiction*, Garrett Stewart argues that reconstructing a sense of the nineteenth-century reading public can begin with a formal study of how novels "conscript" their readers through rhetorical invocations of the act of reading. The "Dear reader" trope, he claims, is a "synecdoche for a nineteenth-century literary public initially made available to us through the inferences of fictional reading" (6–7). For Stewart, reading is an "event" enacted in classic realist fiction through two interrelated strategies which "together establish the discursive situation of the reader" (15): the direct address to readers which textually locates them; and scenic descriptions of characters reading which parallel and analogically dramatize the reader's act. "As independent reading agent outside the story, your relegation by text to a delegate of attention within it converts you to either a second or a third person, either an addressee or a character, even if, in the latter case, only 'the reader'" (8).

Stewart traces the "Dear reader" trope from its epic origins to its high point in Victorian fiction, and then its obsolesence as it is outlawed by modernism before it "flares up again in the postmodern involutions of the *nouveau roman*" (33). In this lineage, the direct address is given a new articulation in second-person narration, and in a novel such as Italo Calvino's *If on a Winter's Night a Traveler* which marks "how the epic stretch toward tribal consolidation through narrative is inverted by a postmodern textual circuitry that processes—and so pulverizes—all traces of social space into textual space" (34).

The occasion Stewart offers for his investigation is the decline of literary reading as a cultural activity in the late twentieth century. If the direct address became dated after the "glory days" (5) of the novel in the nineteenth century, then its fate, he implies, parallels that of literary reading itself. An attendant irony is that critical theories of reading emerge at the same time. "Both a vanishing pastime, indeed vanishing craft, and a fading cultural stance, fictional reading has thus been ever more insistently theorized—as if with a certain unsaid urgency, if not elegiac plangency—during its gradual eclipse by other media" (5). Stewart's book was published in the same year as Jonathan Franzen's lament in *Harper's* for the loss of a reading community, and three years after Wallace's essay. "Octet," published three years after Stewart's book, can be placed within his trajectory of the "Dear reader" trope, both addressing the reader and dramatizing the reader by analogy: a second-person address to the writer reading his own draft and wondering how to directly address readers. A footnote in the final pop quiz sets up the story's metafictionality as a problem of the direct address:

> Though it all gets a little complicated, because part of what you want these little Pop/Quizzes to do is break the textual fourth wall *and kind of address (or interrogate?) the reader directly,* which desire is somehow related to the old "meta"-device desire to puncture some sort of fourth wall of realist pretense, although it seems like the latter is less a puncturing of any sort of real wall and more a puncturing of the veil of impersonality or effacement around the writer himself, i.e. with the now-tired S.O.P "meta"-stuff it's more the dramatist himself coming onstage from

the wings and reminding you that what's going on is artificial and that the artificer is him (the dramatist) and but that he's at least respectful enough of you as reader/audience to be honest about that fact that he's back there pulling the strings, an "honesty" which personally you've always had the feeling is actually a highly rhetorical sham-honesty that's designed to get you to like him. (125, emphasis added)

There is a reference here to the diminished capacity of the (postmodern) direct address to challenge the (modernist) "impersonality" and "effacement" of the writer. Its reference to Thackeray's puppet master ("pulling the strings") also indicates a desire to avoid the ironic distancing of this narrative voice. The only way to salvage the story, the narrator tells the protagonist (himself/the reader), is to rescue the direct address from the sham honesty of metafiction. "In other words what you could do is you could now construct an additional Pop Quiz—so the ninth overall" (131). You could "address the reader directly and ask her straight out whether she's feeling anything like what you feel" (131). The irony, however, is that the reader is only addressed indirectly, through a version of what Brian Richardson calls the autotelic second person, the "defining criterion" of which "is the direct address to a 'you' that is at times the actual reader of the text and whose story is juxtaposed to and can merge with the characters of the fiction. It is a narrativization of a form of address" (30). Italo Calvino's *If on a Winter's Night a Traveler* (which begins: "You are about to begin reading Italo Calvino's *If on a Winter's Night a Traveler*") is posited as the exemplar. "Autotelic texts," Richardson claims, "have the greatest share of direct address to the actual reader and superimpose this onto a fictional character designated by the 'you' that tends to be treated from an external perspective as if in the third person" (32).

So Pop Quiz 9 becomes a metafictional reflection on the failed octet which doubles as a direct address to readers asking them whether they think this last pop quiz is enough to salvage the whole piece. Employing the second person encourages the reader to adopt the subject position of narrator who wants to

> demonstrate some sort of weird ambient *sameness* in different kinds of human relationships, some nameless but inescapable *"price"* that all humans are faced with having to pay at some point if they ever want truly "to be with" another person instead of just using that person somehow. (132)

This puts the universal comment about "all humans" upfront by performing that "price," the exposure of the self, in the act of narration.

This attempt at direct communication between writer and reader is compared to the "universal" problem of human relations, the desire for recognition by others: "In fact one of the very last few interpersonal taboos we have is this kind of obscenely naked direct interrogation of somebody else. It looks pathetic and desperate" (131). For metafiction to have any purchase in this goal it must run the risk of desperation. This is the crux of the story, the source of its anxiety as well as its rhetorical gambit:

> It may well be that all it'll do is make you look like a self-consciously inbent schmuck, or like just another manipulative pseudopomo Bullshit Artist who's trying salvage a fiasco by dropping back to a metadimension and commenting on the fiasco itself. (135)

The last paragraph of the story reads like this:

> Rather it's going to make you look fundamentally lost and confused and frightened and unsure about whether to trust even your most fundamental intuitions about urgency and sameness and whether other people deep inside experience things in anything like the same way you do . . . more like a reader, in other words, down here quivering in the mud of the trench with the rest of us, instead of a *Writer,* whom we imagine to be clean and dry and radiant of command presence and unwavering conviction as he coordinates the whole campaign from back at some gleaming abstract Olympian HQ.
> So decide. (136)

The narratee as writer is being asked to decide whether he will risk an honest, desperate direct address to the narratee as reader, who is thus being asked whether she actually feels the "queer nameless ambient urgent interhuman sameness" (133) which the author-narrator-narratee does. The final pop quiz then, which asks readers to decide whether the narrator is being sincere, also self-reflexively poses the question of whether postmodern metafiction can be put to service in fiction in the wake of its redundancy. At the same time, the reference to the "Olympian HQ" of the writer is an obvious invocation of a particular figure of authorship associated with omniscient narration, establishing this narrative voice as an exemplar of the ironic moralist. The rhetorical function of this narrator, then, is to ask whether the universal authority of the author to comment meaningfully on human nature can survive the postmodern critique of this authority.

In *Gendered Interventions,* Robyn Warhol provides a study of the rhetorical strategies by which the narrators of Victorian novels establish relations between readers and narratees, specifically through the direct address to a "you." In doing so, Warhol distinguishes between "distancing" and "engaging" narrators. A distancing narrator employs the direct address to specifically characterize the narratee, with the effect of discouraging readers from identifying with the subject of the narratorial address. This strategy, which generates an ironic stance from the narrator in relation to the reader, operates by referring to the reader as "a third party," whether through specific names or the more general term "reader." The strategy inscribes the narratee as a "flawed" reader by anticipating or warning against misinterpretations, thus establishing variant reading positions which a reader must be careful to adopt or reject; and playfully drawing attention to the narrator's creative control over the characters and the story being told. Conversely, the engaging narrator seeks to close the gap between reader and narratee, typically addressing a generalized "you," or collective entities, which readers are more likely to identify with, guiding them to a sympathetic response to the plight of characters, and earnestly asserting the connection between the fictional world and the actual world of the reader. These "interventions" in the narrative discourse are, for Warhol, gendered, with distancing strategies most common in novels by men (Fielding, Thackeray, Trollope), and engaging strategies most common in novels by women (Gaskell, Stowe, Eliot), although she is careful not to claim any essentialist link between the two, and demonstrates overlaps between the strategies.

For Warhol, "all narrative interventions must, at some level, interfere with the illusion of reality" (41), but the over-arching irony of distancing strategies move the realist novel toward metafiction, whereas the interventions of an engaging narrator encourage the verisimilitude of the fictional world in an earnest attempt to effect social change by drawing attention to the social inequalities represented in the novel. Seen in these terms, the use of (in)direct address in "Octet" carries the dramatic and thematic tension of the story: self-reflexively pondering whether the engaging narrator, who is earnest and addresses a public reader, can be regained from the ironic metafictional excesses of the distancing narrator. Of course, in doing so this narrator performs both engaging and distancing functions, moving from isolated direct addresses to readers, inviting their judgment of characters, to the autotelic second person in which the reader and narratee are collapsed into the subject position of the authorial narrator, inviting judgment of the act of narration. The question is whether these narratorial strategies can be read as culturally gendered in the way Warhol argues they are in the Victorian novel.

It will be recalled that in his essay Wallace equates metafiction with the white male authors of postmodernism. His claim that the post-postmodern writer must risk the charge of sentimentality, the exposure of the self, in a desire for authorial sincerity might then be seen as a gendered critique of the ironic distancing narrator, something which he follows up in "Octet" when the narrator discusses the danger of using "words like *relationship* and *feeling*" (133) in an attempt to engage the reader. The implication is that the writer who steps out from the cover of irony risks feminization. The narrator in fact takes care to refer to the narratee not only as "you," but, when a third-person reference is syntactically required, as "she." This replicates the decision many writers take to undermine the universalizing assumption of "he" as the default gender of readers. In this context, though, it also has the effect of gendering the reader:

> And then you'll have to ask the reader straight out whether she feels it, too. . . . Right there while she's reading it. Again, consider this carefully. You should *not* deploy this tactic until you've considered what it might cost. What she might think of you. (133)

The analogy used to explain this cost is instructive: "It might very well make you (i.e. the *mise en scène*'s fiction writer) come off like the sort of person who not only goes to a party all obsessed about whether he'll be liked or not, but actually goes around at the party and goes up to strangers and *asks* them whether they like him or not" (134). The figure of the writer is gendered male, while the figure of the reader is gendered female, so when the story concludes by stating the only way to save itself from metafictional irrelevance is to be "more like a reader" we can assume that the "Olympian HQ" of the *Writer* is a threatened position of male cultural authority. The final injunction "to decide" is thus freighted with the gender implications of multiple subject positions in the narrative communication model.

In canvassing the possibility of a direct communication between author and reader, the story is designed to provide precisely the sort of "universal" comment on human nature associated with the omniscient narrator: in this case about the fundamental human need for connection and the simultaneous fear of this connection. Rather than asking readers to identify with the situation of the characters in the story, and guiding their responses, the narrator enacts this "universal" anxiety about human relations at the level of the discourse, so the act of writing fiction, the instance of writing conflated with the narrating instance, becomes the exemplification, in the form of an extradiegetic character, of the universal desire for interpersonal relations.

In her book *Do You Feel It Too? The Post-Postmodern Syndrome in American Fiction at the Turn of the Millennium*, Nicoline Timmer characterizes post-postmodern fiction as the attempt by a generation of writers influenced by postmodernism to reconfigure or transform the concept of self inherited from anti-humanist critiques of subjectivity. Locating this impulse in a general move toward the "rehumanization" of the subject in contemporary theory, particularly through the influence of cognitive psychology on theories of narrative, Timmer argues that Wallace is a "key figure in the development of a new ethic and aesthetic in fiction" (23).

Timmer describes "Octet" as one of Wallace's "fictionalized manifestoes for a new direction in fiction writing, a form of writing that can no longer be adequately labelled 'postmodern'" (102). In this story, I would add, Wallace experiments with possibilities for recovering the authority of narrators to comment. If third-person metafiction was an ironic revival of the intrusive omniscient author, "Octet" is an agonistic recuperation of the direct address for the purpose, not of moral commentary on human nature, but earnest communication, the author's desire to speak in his own voice. Yet, the legacy of metafiction for Wallace meant this direct address was still layered in levels of reflexive irony, operating as a dialogue with himself as writer and reader of his failed story.

Adam Thirlwell, *Politics* (2004)

> Thirlwell's insistent narratorial interjections begin to acquire the ring of an over-assiduous tour guide, whose determination to ensure that no detail goes unnoticed removes your liberty to enjoy the view.
>
> —Alfred Hickling, "Actually, I Don't Like It" 22

A similar anxiety about authorial communication can be found in Adam Thirlwell's *Politics*. In *The Twentieth Century Novel*, Joseph Warren Beach asserted that there are "three major tendencies of the Victorian novel which have, for good or ill, gone largely out of fashion in the twentieth century" (20). According to Beach:

There is the disposition to be edifying in a moral way. There is the fondness for talking the characters over with the reader, taking sides, and letting the reader know what attitude he should take. And there is the scientific passion for explaining the character, making us understand how the particular phenomenon before us illustrates the laws of human nature in general (20).

Thirlwell, who was included as one of *Granta*'s Best Young Novelists for 2003, on the basis of his then unpublished first novel, employs all three tendencies in *Politics*. And it is obvious that in doing so he is grappling with the legacy of metafiction, with the direct address appearing as persistently as a nervous tic as the authorial narrator urges readers not to misinterpret his evaulative commentary: "This is another moment in my novel where you must not let your own private theories affect how you read" (266). The irony of this line is that the narrator offers his own theories on topics from romance to nationalism throughout the novel.

The novel opens with a sex scene in which the protagonist, Moshe, is excruciatingly self-conscious about his performance: "As Moshe tried, gently, to tighten the pink fluffy handcuffs surrounding his girlfriend's wrists, he noticed a tiny frown" (3). Immediately following this opening line, the narrator forcefully asserts his presence through a direct address: "I think you are going to like Moshe. His girlfriend's name was Nana. I think you will like her too" (3). During this opening scene, Moshe's concern about what he thinks "must be the most nervous scene in the history of sex" (10) is interrupted by two pages of narratorial commentary which begins: "I am going to expand a little on Moshe's problem. It is a universal problem. It is the universal insecurity that one is not universal" (11). The narrator offers an opinion that the genre of the novel can provide solace precisely for readers with this sort of anxiety—"To get over the problem of vanity and other cases of illusion, we have novels" (11)—and asserts that "If Moshe had read this novel, then I think he would have been happy" (12). The narrator then invites readers to compare Moshe's "universal problem" to their own experiences, before expressing an anxiety regarding his own capacity to provide this solace:

> My idea is that you are like this too. Maybe, just maybe, you are not. But I reckon that, at some point in your life, something almost identical to this has happened to you.
>
> Of course it has! This book is meant to be reassuring. This book is universal. It is a comparative study. The last thing I want is for this to be just me. (12)

In these comments we find both a brazen display of diegetic authority and an agonistic lament for extradiegetic authority. The doubt about the capacity of his novel to be universal is a doubt about his capacity to influence readers, later invoking this doubt as a problem of genre: "I know you are not convinced by this. You are unpersuaded. Where is the realism? you say. Where is the accuracy of the European novel. Where is the truth to nature of Balzac or Tolstoy?" (131). The self-reflexivity facilitates an appeal to the subjective personality of the individual writer, relativizing the "universal" authority of the narrator's omniscience, and personalizing himself as an extradiegetic character to the extent of discussing his own life. "Personally, I think it was a good thing. This is not because I think blowjobs are intrinsically a good thing. Well no, I do think blowjobs are a good thing. I am rarely averse to a blowjob, but that is not why I think that a blowjob was the right thing here" (54).

The narrator is at pains to remind us that his novel is about goodness and kindness, constantly anticipating possible responses to the characters or his comments before replying defensively, most commonly with the qualifying phrase "I think," oscillating between hesitancy and assertiveness:

> Sometimes I think that this book is an attack on sex. Sometimes I think it is prudish. It might be. And if it is, then some people, maybe even a lot of people, will think that this is wrong. They will think that being prudish is indefensible.
> But me, I do not think that prudishness is indefensible. I really don't. (182)

There is no confident appeal to a general consciousness, but a rhetorical performance of doubt, the need to argue a position, as if unsure of the extent to which readers will be able to enter what Peter Rabinowitz dubbed the authorial audience, defined by James Phelan as: "The hypothetical, ideal audience for whom the implied author constructs the text and who understands it perfectly" (*Living* 213). While Phelan makes a distinction between the authorial and narrative audiences, the authorial narrator of *Politics* collapses any interpretively meaningful distinction. The omniscient narrator knows the interior lives of his characters, but as a proxy for the author he can only speculate about his readers. Often this doubt relates to how readers might respond to the explicit sexual nature of the novel: "I am not sure what the general attitude to pissing is. I do not know how most people view pissing as a sexual manoeuvre" (156).

Politics is centered around a "romance" between two young Londoners, Moshe and Nana, and particularly their self-conscious sexual experimentations, which develop into a ménage à trois with one of Moshe's friends, Anjali. The "comparative study" which the narrator promises works by comparing the situations of his characters to the private lives of real historical personages, from artists such as Andre Breton and Greta Garbo, to political figures such as Hitler and Mao. The ontological plane of the narrator is clearly the same as that of flesh and blood readers, which means that his "knowledge" of the characters must be a product of his fictional invention, rather than a divine quality of omniscience.

For instance, building upon Moshe's anxiety about his sexual performance, the narrator cites a conversation about sex between key figures of the Surrealist movement in 1928 (the acknowledgements referring to a book called *Investigating Sex: Surrealist Research, 1928–1932*). He then comments that: "I really do not think that Moshe needed to be so flustered by his performance. André Breton, the founder of the Surrealist movement, came in twenty seconds maximum" (60). Commenting on the fact that Nana contracts thrush from Moshe, the narrator points out that Chairman Mao did the same to multiple women:

> But maybe there is a more human side to Chairman Mao. Maybe he was just embarrassed.... It is not easy admitting to your doctor that you are the carrier of a sexually transmitted disease. Even Moshe found it difficult, and Moshe is a much less public person than Mao. (93)

The narrator also seeks to "universalize" his narrative by drawing elaborate parallels between the sexual politics of the ménage à trois his characters are involved in and real world geopolitical situations. Discussing Moshe's concern about how the threesome is developing, his need for "more positive signs," the narrator digresses to state: "In August 2000, the Italian police intercepted some conversations in Arabic between Al Qaeda members" (177). He goes on to express sympathy for those police who did not read these conversations as signs of an impending attack: "It is not easy, spotting clues. In retrospect, everything is so much clearer" (178).

In another chapter, the narrator elaborates Nana's desire to discontinue her involvement in the relationship by comparing it to the relationship between nation states:

> In 1995 the Nobel Peace Laureate, Sir Joseph Rotblat, called for a treaty among nuclear-weapons states. Each state would agree not to be the first

to use nuclear weapons in any conflict. On 5 April 1995, a No First Use Policy of the Declared Nuclear Weapons States was duly signed.

I know that Nana and Moshe and Anjali were not nuclear-weapons states. They were obviously not states at all. So this might seem a little melodramatic and irrelevant. But it is not melodramatic and irrelevant. (228)

He goes on to explain the theoretical flaw of Mutually Assured Destruction: "This type of agreement only works if everyone is feeling threatened" (228). On this basis he establishes a parallel with Nana's decision to leave the ménage: "Their tacit agreement to stay together had no longer any binding force. It would be no worse for Nana to leave than to stay" (228).

The audacity of the narrator's self-conscious attempts to universalize the characters' situations through a "comparative study" is most evident in the parallels he makes with actual historical personages. In one instance, the narrator quotes from a letter Mikhail Bulgakov wrote to the government of the Soviet Union in 1930 before writing: "But, you say, that is entirely different. Bulgakov was living in Stalinist Russia. What is the connection between the pathos and courage of Bulgakov's letter, and the relationship of Nana and Moshe? Surely I am not saying that the relationship of Nana and Moshe and Anjali was equivalent to living under Stalinism?" (132). He goes on to make a distinction between "totalitarian aggression" and "the use of friendliness as a coercive technique," concluding that "in terms of friendliness, I cannot see a difference between the individual behaviour of Nana and Mikhail Bulgakov and Moshe and Anjai and Stalin" (134).

The thread of these digressive comparisons is that they establish the political conditions under which people live in Communist states from Stalinist Russia to the Czechoslovak Socialist Republic, to Maoist China, inevitably highlighting the conditions under which his fictional characters live. "Moshe's problem was entertainingly similar to the problem of dissent in a capitalist society. As many left-wing critics have pointed out, it is very difficult to object to capitalism" (206). He goes on to describe Gramsci's theory of hegemony before asserting: "I, however, have a different theory why no one cares when someone attacks capitalism. You always look like a poseur. . . . Similarly, if Moshe complained that a threesome was not ideal, you would assume he was being hypocritical" (207).

Drawing attention to the moral conundrums at play in a threesome, the narrator asks: "But what is infidelity?" He goes on to discuss the arrest of the poet Osip Mandelstam in Stalinist Russia in 1934 before commenting: "I am not getting at Osip. Honestly, I like him. Because I like him, I do not want to idealise him too much" (176). Here we see Thirlwell's intrusive omniscient narrator discussing the motivations of real historical personages in the same way he discusses those of his fictional characters. He does not make these personages characters in the story, they resist fictionalization, yet his evaluation of them exists on the same discursive plane as that of the fictional characters. As a result he self-consciously seeks to parlay the conventional authority of the narrator (complete knowledge of his characters) into cultural authority for the author through the rhetorical performance of universalizing commentary. For instance, the narrator discusses a sexual encounter between Adolf Hitler and the film actress Renée Muller in 1936, in which she was asked to play the role of dominatrix: "Adolf and Renée had just encountered a central human predicament. It is this. Sex is not specific. It is not original. You might think your perversions are all your own, but no. Perversion is general. Perversions are universal. You have to make them specific" (212).

In a review of the novel in *The Independent* Henry Sutton writes that ongoing references to historical situations "are used to highlight various conundrums Thirlwell's characters are going through. For instance, should Nana be a little less altruistic and a little more self-serving?" Matt Thorne, also in *The Independent,* writes: "the most interesting question his novel poses is whether Moshe, Nana and Anjali are representatives of a generation which has yet to be depicted in fiction." For me the most interesting question is why Thirlwell's omniscient narrator so doggedly and self-consciously performs an agonized bid for the universality of his moral commentary. I would argue that the novel in fact is striving to work in the opposite direction: it is an attempt to use the fictional situation of the characters as a parallel to the political situation in the actual world, to explore the inner lives of characters not as the basis for universal commentary about human nature, but as a mode of metaphorical commentary on twentieth-century politics. It is an attempt to assert the authority of the novelist to offer political commentary. "I am not interested in anything so small as the history of the USSR. I am not writing anything so limited. No, what I am interested in is friendliness" (133).

In the last few pages of the novel, the narrator tells us: "And Moshe would come back to her. Of course he would. I know everything. I know Moshe very well" (277). So if the narrator knows everything about the characters, can this be parlayed into knowledge of the world? "This book is universal. I said that at the start. Because it is universal, it is ambiguous. It has something for everyone." (278). Here is the "moral" of the story: "I do not think people are very intelligent about selfishness. I do not think they see how moral it can be. Because it is moral, refusing to be self-destructive. It is a perfectly moral position" (278). The narrator's selfishness here, his resistance to the "self-destructive" posture of narrative impersonality, is a self-conscious claim for the moral authority of omniscient narration, albeit an authority relativized by an acknowledgement that a general consciousness cannot be invoked. It is an overcompensating direct address.

CHAPTER 3

Prolepsis and the Literary Historian

THE SECOND MODE of contemporary omniscience, which I will call the *literary historian*, relies upon the authority of the historical record and the possibilities of imaginatively recovering private or occluded moments in history opened up by postmodern theory and explored in "factional" works such as Thomas Keneally's *Schindler's Ark*. Unlike "historiographic metafiction"—a form which Linda Hutcheon claims the term postmodern fiction should be reserved for (40)—this mode displays a faith in the literary imagination to supplement the historical record, rather than undermine the narrative "truth" of history. Some examples would be stories from Gail Jones's two collections of short fiction, *The House of Breathing* and *Fetish Lives*; Michel Faber's *The Crimson Petal and the White*; Edward P. Jones's *The Known World*; David Lodge's *Author, Author*, and my own short story, "Thomas Pennington's Fetich."

In these works, the traditional metaphor of the novelist as historian, established by the prototypical omniscient narrator of Henry Fielding's *Tom Jones*, becomes literalized in the figure of the contemporary narrator as historian engaged in historical and historiographic debate. Like contemporary historical fiction in general, this mode of omniscience stresses that the inner lives of protagonists (the purview of the novelist), and the lived experience of everyday people or of historical personages, is important to our understanding of earlier periods and past events (the purview of the historian). There are different manifestations of this literary historian, from the biographical narrator of Lodge's *Author, Author* (which I will discuss in the final chapter), which is modeled on the nonfiction novel exemplified by *Schindler's Ark* (winner of the Booker Prize for fiction), to the fantastic historians of magic realism in which the fictionality of an imaginative intervention in history is made palpable. For instance, Patrick Süskind's *Perfume* (1986) opens with this line:

> In eighteenth-century France there lived a man who was one of the most gifted and abominable personages in an era that knew no lack of gifted and abominable personages ... forgotten today ... because his gifts and his sole ambition were restricted to a domain that leaves no traces in history: to the fleeting realm of scent. (3)

Similarly, Isabelle Allende's "Phantom Palace" (1992) charts the fate of native Indians in Latin America who "lived in peace since the dawn of time" before the arrival of the Spanish Conquistadors, and who "came to be so skilful in the art of dissimulation that history did not record them, and today there is no evidence of their passage through time" (201).

Formally speaking, the most significant aspect of contemporary historical fiction is the way it establishes a quantifiable temporal gap between the modern narrating instance and historical past of the story. The effect is that the narrator's omniscient authority is simultaneously heightened and problematized by their distance from the events of the story. Contemporary historical fiction thus exploits the implications of the aspect of narrative voice which Genette called the time of narrating. According to Genette:

> The use of a past tense is enough to make a narrative subsequent, although without indicating the temporal interval which separates the moment of the narrating from the moment of the story. In classical "third person" narrative, this interval appears generally indeterminate, and the question irrelevant, the preterite marking a sort of ageless past. (*Narrative Discourse,* 220)

In the mode of the omniscient literary historian, the "temporal interval" is not only determinable (spanning the years between the historical period which the story is set in and the present day of the narrative discourse, which by convention we could date as coterminous with the book's publication), it is crucial to the function of the narrative as a form of history: the preterite marking a datable past. Furthermore, the rhetorical effects of the time of narrating employed in this mode cannot be understood in purely narratological terms, for the temporal interval between story and narration is established by reference to historical facts which are not only posterior to the events of the story, but are referable to the actual world of the reader, and hence falsifiable as narrative "report." The narrating instance invokes the extrafictional historical record to establish a temporal distance unyoked from tense structures, with contemporary historical fiction often employing the "immediacy" of the present tense without being simultaneous narration. This sense of history, rather than the panchronic omnitemporality of divinity, is the temporal model of contemporary omniscience.

One device for drawing attention to the narrating instance is the direct address to modern readers, as in this line from Süskind's *Perfume:* "In the period of which we speak, there reigned in the cities a stench barely conceivable to us modern men and women" (3). Another is the use of prolepsis, defined by Genette as "any narrative maneuver that consists of narrating or evoking in advance an event that will take place later" (40). For Genette, this means interrupting the present moment of the story to make room for an account of the future, and he uses the term "reach" to measure the temporal distance between the narrative present and the proleptic event. More specifically, the omniscient literary historian employs *external* prolepses, that is, reference to events beyond the duration of the story, such as this line from Michel Faber's *The Crimson Petal and the White:* "Of Jack the Ripper she need have no fear; it's almost fourteen years too early, and she'll have died from more or less natural causes by the time he comes along" (7). These external prolepses can then be said to be *extratextual* because they reference the actual world of the historical record. In my story, "Thomas Pennington's Fetich" (2004), the opening paragraph contains the line "An epidemic of syphilis festers in the unspoken limbs of polite company, and will continue until the discovery of Salvarsan in 1909" (200). The "reach" of this reference is one year beyond the protagonist's contraction of syphilis at the chronological "end" of the story in 1908.

This temporal model underpins the narrator's capacity to parade the archival research of the author through a number of narrative strategies. There is expositional summary linguistically indistinguishable from biographical or historical nonfiction, such as this passage from A. S. Byatt's

The Children's Book (2009): "The year 1881 was a year of beginnings. A number of idealist, millenarian projects and groups were founded. There were the Democratic Federation, the Society for Psychical Research, the Theosophical Society, the Anti-Vivisection movement. All were designed to change and reinvent human nature" (45). There are references to contemporaneous publications, such as in David Lodge's *Author, Author:*

> Mr Gladstone himself was moved to write an immensely long article about it in the May issue of *The Nineteenth Century,* entitled *"Robert Elsmere* and the Battle for Belief," describing it as "brilliant but pernicious," which gave a huge further boost to sales. (97)

And there is a welter of descriptive detail which would not be found in fiction set in the present. All these narrative strategies are designed to establish verisimilar authenticity, while simultaneously offering a narrative predicated on the assumption that the omniscient narrator "knows" something about history which the historical record cannot. This knowledge is the product of the authorial imagination, either through fantasy or through sympathetically reconstructing the private side of history via the available archival evidence.

Gail Jones, "On the Piteous Death of Mary Wollstonecraft" (1992)

The opening two paragraphs of the short story "On the Piteous Death of Mary Wollstonecraft," by the Booker Prize–longlisted Australian writer Gail Jones, exemplify the mode of the literary historian. The story begins with a lyrical present-tense account of the protagonist's consciousness: "She arises momentarily from the deepsea of unconsciousness, trawls up her drowned mind through fluid dimensions" (105). It is an intimate imagining of the character's mind in a moment of distress: childbirth as we later discover. The next paragraph signals an abrupt shift to an impersonal authoritative voice with the foreknowledge of history. It reads like a biographical encyclopedia entry, with the exception that it is rendered in the future tense: "She is about to die, this Mary Wollstonecraft. Born in the year 1759, she will die at thirty-eight of post-partum complications. She is the controversial and august author of *A Vindication of the Rights of Woman.* Both famous and feminist in her own uncongenial time" (105). The two key features of omniscience—access to consciousness and intrusive authorial presence—are sharply juxtaposed, with the biographical information lending authority to the fictional imagining of the character's interior. In foregrounding the gap between the historical record and the private lives of historical personages, Jones's story both highlights its fictionality and seeks to legitimate fictional speculation as a form of historiographic enquiry.

After the opening two paragraphs there are a series of fragmentary sections which I take to be instances of Wollstonecraft's life flashing before her as she dies. There are the immediate events leading up to her death, that is, the birth of her daughter Mary, and then a series of memories relating to her husband, William Godwin, and her lover, Gilbert Imlay. The focus, however, is on Wollstonecraft's state of mind in the last hours of her life. There are two overt instances of zero focalization—of the narrator saying more than the characters know—which establish the difference between classic and contemporary omniscience in the mode of the literary historian. The first occurs after Wollstonecraft has given birth:

> "A daughter," she whispers. "Once more a daughter."
>
> Mrs Blenkinsop notices the ambivalence in her mistress's voice. Mrs Blenkinsop fails to notice, however, that here are evident the symptoms of another subsidence, that Mary Wollstonecraft is busy sliding back into her own body, a body in which, at this very moment, some torment of the womb, some organic agitation, tricks her into thinking that she has not yet delivered. (107)

Here the narrator tells us not only what Mrs Blenkinsop doesn't know but what Mary herself doesn't know about her own body. In the next overt performance of omniscience, the narrator relativizes her "impossible" knowledge by appeal to the proleptic voice of history. We have a paragraph which begins: "Mary closes her eyes and knows, as mothers are reputed instinctually to know such things, that the baby will die" (109). The next paragraph undercuts this maternal instinct:

> Had she been better clairvoyant Mary Wollstonecraft would have known that her daughter Mary would live for fifty-three years and achieve a fame ratified in the twentieth century by that most pompous and preposterous of all institutions, Hollywood. "The Rights of Women" will historically prove a difficult concept; her daughter's "Frankenstein," however, is a convenient cultural nightmare. (109)

The irony of this passage is generated not by the narrator's impossible knowledge of the "future," but by reference to the historical record, and by a form of cultural commentary only possible from the narrating instance of the present day. This external anachrony is unnecessary to the story: its extranarrative function is designed purely to establish the narrative authority of the contemporary narrator in relation to the historical record, setting up the rhetorical purpose of the story, which is made explicit in the final section. This section shifts from a present-tense account of Wollstonecraft's death to a past-tense denouement in which the ill-considered memoir which Godwin wrote after her death is blamed for the reputation of "Villainous Depravity" which Wollstonecraft gained.

> Foolishly confounding Virtue and Truth, William Godwin wrote a memoir of his deceased wife's life. In it he hoped to memorialise the Excellent Woman. He spoke of Imlay, of Fuseli, of suicide attempts, illegitimate birth, sexual passion and intellectual voluptuousness. "Mary Wollstonecraft" became synonymous with Villainous Depravity. (119–20)

So in a sense Jones is trying to set the historical record straight by writing a piece of fiction, to inhabit the cracks of biographical knowledge, to transgress the epistemological limits of historiography. If Wollstonecraft's life became the source of salacious biography, what Jones is trying to do is recover this life, provide it with some dignity by imagining the moment of her death. The rhetorical function of the narrator, then, is to achieve this approach to Wollstonecraft's life by negotiating the shifts between external commentary and internal focalization made possible by literary omniscience.

Omniscient Narration and Neo-Victorian Fiction

Given that the omniscient narrator is commonly seen as synonymous with Victorian fiction, any account of contemporary omniscience must address its manifestation in the popular genre of neo-Victorian fiction. As most scholars in this field would note, the temporal relation between narrating instance and story is crucial to the effects of the fictional encounter with history. On this basis, Christian Gutleben's *Nostalgic Postmodernism: The Victorian Tradition and the Contemporary British Novel* distinguishes between subversive and nostalgic invocations of Victorianism in contemporary fiction: those which erase the temporal gap or at least do not specify it are typically nostalgic; while those which maintain a temporal distance from the past are typically subversive. In the case of historical novels set in the Victorian past, Gutleben makes a distinction between serious reconstruction (in the form of mimetic pastiche) and ludic parody. In this latter category he includes omniscient narration, for parody "seems particularly relevant for the retro-Victorian novel's use of the omniscient narrator" (102). This claim is based on the common assumption in neo-Victorian studies that historical fiction dealing with this period "uses" a Victorian model of omniscience, rather than employing contemporary omniscient narration to explore the Victorian past.

Drawing upon Margaret Rose's definition, Gutleben claims that parody operates by inviting then disappointing generic expectations from readers. Omniscient narration in neo-Victorian fiction is then said to be parodic because it includes elements we would not expect in Victorian fiction. Gutleben's chief example of the ludic reworking of omniscience is at the level of focalized content provided by the narrator, evidenced in explicit sexual descriptions which violate the codes of decorum employed in nineteenth-century fiction. Discussing the novel *Ark Baby,* Gutleben writes: "the text subverts this anticipation by violating one of the most sacred taboos in Victorian fiction: sexual explicitness. The principle of omniscience is retrieved but pushed to the limits which traditional fiction was not ready to explore" (103). The juxtaposition of a Victorian setting with "the sauciness of the narrative instance," Gutleben claims, means that "what is at stake here is not the parody of a text but of a literary convention, i.e. the omniscient narrator" (104). Even if we accept that the omniscient narrator's discussion of sexuality is a ludic parody of Victorian conventions, it simply tells us that neo-Victorian fiction is another mode by which omniscient narration finds its way into contemporary fiction. However, defining this omniscience almost exclusively in terms of parody strikes me as formulaic and inaccurate.

In discussing A. S. Byatt's Booker Prize–winning novel *Possession,* Gutleben argues that "Byatt organizes her narrative apparatus so as to playfully question the Victorian novelistic conventions" (108). So when Byatt's narrator, who must occupy a contemporary narrating instance in order to tell the modern day story of two academic biographers, takes up the nineteenth-century story and describes the romance of the two Victorian protagonists, "a strictly Victorian voice could not have accounted for" the sexual thoughts and actions of these characters. As a result, "the narrative instance who decides to reveal these indications, although it mimics traditional omniscience, realistic trait-connoting descriptions and decorous Victorian language, can consequently only adopt a parodic stance towards its Victorian referent" (108–9). If this a parody of Victorian omniscience, it is not necessarily a parody of omniscient narration itself.

"Byatt's final (ab)use of the God-like omniscient narrator" (110), Gutleben claims, occurs in the postscript to the novel. Here the narrator provides information about the past (an illegitimate child produced by the affair between two Victorian writers) which the modern academic biographers of these writers will never know. For Gutleben, this revelation puts readers in possession of information which enables them to see the limitations of the biographical enterprises of the academic characters. For me, however, this revelation is not an "abuse" of omniscience. It demonstrates again an attempt to employ the convention of omniscience to establish the authority of the novelist in relation to that of the biographer, not to undermine this convention. Byatt herself wrote: "My instinct as a writer of fiction has been to explore and defend the unfashionable Victorian third-person narrator—who is not, as John Fowles claimed, playing at being God, but merely the writer, telling what can be told about the world of the fiction" ("True Stories" 102).

Michel Faber, *The Crimson Petal and the White* (2002)

> The narrative voice of *The Crimson Petal and the White* is an enigmatic one. Is she a Trollopean guide? Or just a trollop, a prostitute who seizes the reader's hand and won't let go? I leave you in that voice's care.
>
> —Michel Faber, "Tale of a Street Walker"

In a book chapter that identifies *The Crimson Petal and the White* as a "classic" of the contemporary neo-Victorian novel, Georges Letissier claims that "the double temporal perspective, with the twenty-first century looking back on the nineteenth century, with the benefit of hindsight, as it were, leads to what could be called *hyperomniscience*" (119). This hyperomniscience, which I call the "proleptic voice of history," is established by the narratorial direct address which draws attention to a contemporary narrating instance. The novel opens with this paragraph:

> Watch your step. Keep your wits about you; you will need them. This city I am bringing you to is vast and intricate, and you have not been here before. You may imagine, from other stories you've read, that you know

it well, but those stories flattered you, welcoming you as a friend, treating you as if you belonged. The truth is that you are an alien from another time and place altogether. (3)

For Maria Teresa Chialant this opening establishes the omniscient narrator as an "urban flâneur in the Dickensian mode," recalling the "certain shadow" of Dickens's Asmodean narrator. For John Mullan it establishes an "intrusive author" modeled on George Eliot's Victorian omniscient narrator; and for Mary Ellen Snodgrass, it implies "a metafictional I-thou relationship with the postmodern reader" (112). It is also a claim for narrative authority, the authority to tell a story, based on the narrator's assertion that this work of historical fiction will provide a more authentic account of Victorian London than other stories. Here we have a rhetorical performance of omniscient authority in which the narrator highlights the spatio-temporal gap between modern narrating instance and historical story before claiming to overcome the epistemological limitations of this gap by taking the reader back in time. The narrator performs this "time travel" with the metaleptic trick of encouraging readerly identification with a narratee, and then situating the narratee within the fictional world via the autotelic second person. The third paragraph establishes a metaphorical conflation of the reader seduced by the narrative promise of a book and a customer seduced by the sexual promise of a prostitute:

> And yet you did not choose me blindly. Certain expectations were aroused. Let's not be coy: you were hoping I would satisfy all the desires you're too shy to name, or at least show you a good time. Now you hesitate, still holding on to me, but tempted to let me go. When you first picked me up, you didn't fully appreciate the size of me, nor did you expect I would grip you so tightly, so fast. (3)

This is by way of introducing readers to the lowest rung of Victorian society, and one of the minor characters, Caroline, a prostitute who lives in Church Lane. According to narratologists who draw upon possible worlds and deictic shift theory, readers engage with fiction by cognitively relocating to the storyworld. The direct address of Faber's narrator is a self-reflexive strategy designed to locate readers on the same ontological level as the characters: "From where you stand you can actually see the shiver of distaste travelling down between Caroline's shoulder-blades" (11). This immersion of readers in the fictional world simultaneously maintains the narrator's intrusive presence as the guarantee of its authenticity. By virtue of referring only to a generalized "you," the narrator is, in Robyn Warhol's terms, an engaging one, even to the extent of ensuring it enables different genders to participate in the role of narratee: "Yes, it's alright. She's sleeping now. Lift the blankets and ease your body in. If you are a woman, it doesn't matter: women very commonly sleep together in this day and age. If you are a man, it matters even less: there have been hundreds here before you" (8).

Although the story is narrated in the present tense, the time of narrating is retrospective rather than simultaneous, designed to highlight the fact that the narrator's capacity to immerse readers in a fictional world is a product of the author's knowledge of history: "Apart from the pale gas-light of the street-lamps at the far corners, you can't see any light in Church Lane, but that's because your eyes are accustomed to stronger signs of human wakefulness than the feeble glow of two candles behind a smutty windowpane. You come from a world where darkness is swept aside at the snap of a switch" (5).

The novel follows the path of Sugar, a prostitute, from a brothel in Church Lane to mistress then governess in the employ of William Rackham, aspiring man of letters who becomes a business magnate when he inherits his father's perfume-manufacturing company. As Kathryn Hughes writes, in a review for *The Guardian*: "Michel Faber has produced the novel that Dickens might have written had he been allowed to speak freely. All the familiar tropes of high-Victorian fiction are here—the mad wife, the cut-above prostitute, the almost-artist, the opaque governess—but they are presented to us by a narrator with the mind and mouth of the 21st century."

The novel's explicit descriptions of sex—"Minute upon minute she lies on his thigh, milking him, slyly inserting her middle finger into his anus, deeper and deeper, pushing past the sphincter" (116)—is said to be what sets it apart from Victorian omniscience and hence makes it a parody of the form, demonstrating that the all-knowing narrator of nineteenth-century fiction had many social limitations on what could be said. However, the novel can also be said to use the convention of omniscience to supplement its historical reconstruction of the Victorian period. The ultimate example of zero focalization is this:

> In Agnes's head, inside her skull, an inch or two behind her left eye, nestles a tumour the size of a quail's egg. She's no inkling it's there.... No one will ever find it. Roentgen photography is twenty years in the future, and Doctor Curlew, whatever parts of Agnes Rackham he may examine,

is not about to go digging in her eye-socket with a scalpel. Only you and I know of this tumour's existence. It is our little secret. (218–19)

Here the narrator shares his omniscience with readers to establish trust and to demonstrate that what may have been narrated as madness or hysteria in a Victorian novel could have been the result of not possessing the hyperomniscience of this novelist.

The omniscience is on occasion coy, or "deliberately suppressive" in Sternberg's terms, about the psychology of characters, but supplements this reticence with historical knowledge:

Ah, to know that you'd have to get deeper inside her than anyone has reached yet. I can tell you the answers to simpler questions. How old is Sugar? Nineteen. How long has she been a prostitute? Six years. You do the arithmetic, and the answer is a disturbing one, especially when you consider that the girls of this time commonly don't pubesce until fifteen or sixteen. (34)

These regular narratorial intrusions supplement the welter of descriptive detail, the Jamesian solidity of specification, which operate historiographically, with scenic construction building up layers of ethnographic thick description: "Like many common women, prostitutes especially, her name is Caroline, and you find her squatting over a large ceramic bowl filled with a tepid mixture of water, alum and sulphate of zinc" (6). Descriptions such as these also constitute what Michael Riffaterre calls "diegetic overkill," the "representation of ostensibly insignificant details, the very insignificance of which is significant in a story as a feature of realism" (30). The significance in this regard is that they declare the factual research underpinning the fictionality of verisimilitude, as well as distinguishing this as a modern rather than contemporaneous account of the period. The foundation of this omniscient narrator's authority, then, resides not in a postmodern parody of the convention (its overt sexuality, the key Victorian figure of the governess being a prostitute, the resistance to closure similar to Fowles's multiple possible endings), or in a nostalgia for the certainties of the past encoded in the form itself, but in the figure of the contemporary historian whose research licenses evaluative commentary: "Morally it's an odd period, both for the observed and the observer: fashion has engineered the reappearance of the body, while morality still insists upon perfect ignorance of it" (66).

The acknowledgments page, with its references to historical sources, and Faber's public statements about the endorsement of his research by professional historians are designed to highlight the extratextual historical authority of these narratorial observations. Faber begins an essay titled "Eccentricity and Authenticity: Fact into Fiction," with a reference to how the book "has generally been praised for its period authenticity," culminating in an invitation to write this article for the *Victorian Institute Journal* (101). Faber's article, then, is an attempt to claim the extratextual authority of the historian to underpin the authenticity of his work as "a highly convincing time-travel experience" (101). In doing so, Faber distinguishes his work from postmodern encounters with history, describing the process of composition as a move away from the influence of postmodernist fiction. Faber reveals that in the course of writing his novel he discovered a number of historical inaccuracies. In the early draft, "my response to my error was not to remove it, but to flaunt it" (101), adding a footnote in which he acknowledges the error but dismisses it for the sake of the story:

> This disclaimer, simultaneously cloying and arrogant, makes me cringe now, but it arose naturally out of the late-1970s literary climate I grew up in. Post-Modernism encouraged me to assert my freedom to do whatever I pleased. I was The Author; I was in charge. The reader must be reminded that this story was an artificial construct. Text must be playful, must discard the shackles of bogus mimesis, must define itself against the pointless inhibitions of the 19th century bourgeois novel. The very notion of "history" was rotten to the core; all "fact" was falsification. (102)

Faber suggests that his arrogance diminished when he realized that "the deconstructionist desire to expose the apparatus of narrative was nothing new" (102). In other words, as many critics have pointed out, self-reflexivity has long been a part of the novelistic tradition. He then set about to make his novel as historically accurate as possible. According to George Letissier:

> *The Crimson Petal and the White* illustrates the classical format of the neo-Victorian novel, which has now discarded the postmodernist, deconstructionist stance of earlier post-Victorian fictions, such as *The French Lieutenant's Woman, Possession,* or *Poor Things,* to quote but a few, to

embrace the more traditional form of the three-decker, or "large, loose, baggy monster" of its Victorian forerunners. (113)

This reinforces my point that postmodern metafiction self-reflexively reintroduced omniscient narration, enabling this voice to be absorbed into the mainstream, and that post-postmodern fiction demonstrates a textual awareness of this legacy. Faber may have rejected postmodern playfulness in favor of a return to the realist novel, but he did not dispense with the intrusive omniscient narrator who was the instrument of this playfulness, evidenced by a line such as this: "If you are bored beyond endurance, I can offer only my promise that there will be fucking in the very near future, not to mention madness, abduction, and violent death" (190). The novelistic authority he asserts in relation to history is not one which seeks to demonstrate the essential fictionality of historical writing, but one which claims fiction can contribute to a knowledge of history. Rather than estranging the reader from immersion in the fictional world, the narratorial direct address is designed to engage the reader's belief in the authority of the author's historical knowledge, his capacity to invent a possible world.

Edward P. Jones, *The Known World* (2003)

> I always thought I had a linear story. Something happened between the time I began the real work in January 2002 of taking it all out of my head and when I finished months later. It might be that because I, as the "god" of the people in the book, could see their first days and their last days and all that was in between, and those people did not have linear lives as I saw all that they had lived.
>
> —Edward P. Jones, "An Interview"

> Edward P. Jones writes as God might, were He to publish fiction. Specifically, Jones mobilizes a relatively unusual verb tense to embed the future in the past, making every incident in his characters' lives simultaneously present to the stories' omniscient narrator–cum–celestial census taker.
>
> —Jenny Davidson, "Great Jones"

Edward P. Jones's Pulitzer Prize–winning novel *The Known World* has a more complicated relationship between its omniscient narration and its exploration of history than my previous examples of the literary historian, one which throws open for debate the connection between authenticity and authority in the public sphere. *The Known World* is set in antebellum Virginia, and centered on free blacks who owned slaves in the fictional county of Manchester. The narrator's ideological position is clear in this comment on the black plantation owner, Henry Townsend: "He did not understand that the kind of world he wanted to create was doomed before he had even spoken the first syllable of the word *master*" (64). The title refers to a tapestry of America hung on the county sheriff's wall, and constant references to the characters' perspectivally circumscribed "worlds" are a motif of the book, with lines such as: "the eating of it tied him to the only thing in his small world that meant almost as much as his own life" (2); "Mildred made him see that the bigger Henry could make the world he lived in, the freer he would be" (113); and "there was a whole world off to the right that the photograph had not captured" (189).

The title is particularly resonant in a formalist and historiographic sense: what sort of narratorial knowledge is required to explain this fictional world, and what can be known about this aspect of American history in the actual world? The crux of the book's treatment of slavery is found in this passage of internal focalization: "Moses had thought that it was already a strange world that made him a slave to a white man, but God had indeed set it twirling and twisting every which way when he put black people to owning their own kind. Was God even up there attending to business anymore?" (9).

In formalist terms, the narratorial "god" of this strange world (as Jones refers to himself in the above-quoted epigraph) exemplifies the unrestricted information of zero focalization. The omniscient narrator maps out a panoramic perspective of Manchester County, with a spatio-temporal range beyond the knowledge of any character, proleptically reaching as far forward as the late twentieth century to explain the outcome of events, and revealing the interior lives of multiple characters, including what they do not know about themselves: "So he rode on, not even knowing that he just wanted some peace, and not knowing, until much later, that he wanted back all that he had lost" (227). The narrative structure is relentlessly anachronous, opening with the death of the black slave owner, Henry Townsend, in 1855 and shuttling back and forth in time. The temporal reach is established by historical coordinates, with the narrator referring to an "1806 act of the Virginia House of Delegates" which "required that former slaves leave the Commonwealth within twelve months of getting their freedom" (15) and employing external anachrony to mark the story as anterior to the modern narrating instance. The narrator refers beyond the limits of the story to inform readers that in 1909 the colored people of Richmond unofficially named a street after a deceased slave, and then: "In 1987, after a renewed drive for renaming led by one of Delphie's great-granddaughters, the city of Richmond relented, and it put up new signs all along the way to prove that it was official" (205).

The most striking quality of the narrator is again the persistent use of prolepsis, with the action regularly interpolated with brief accounts of the ultimate fate of even the most minor characters:

> As the crowd made its way back down to the lane, some of the children were at the front, and at the head of those children was Elias and Celeste's oldest, Tessie. She began skipping but an adult told her that a human being had died and skipping should be left off to another day. Tessie would soon be six years old and being the child of her parents that she was, she listened and stopped skipping. Tessie would live to be ninety-seven years old, and the doll her father was making for her would be with her until her last hour. She and the doll, long missing the cornsilk hair her father had put on it, would outlive two of her children, and the doll would outlive her. (67)

The proleptic comments are so profuse that rather than plot-motivated advance notice (they anticipate events which will not be later narrated, although often still within the temporal reach of the story), they create a sense of past and future being narrated simultaneously with the narrative present. Here is part of a scene featuring Sheriff Skiffington and another character, Clara, discussing Clara's slave, Ralph, as the sheriff prepares to depart:

> "I'll take your word that everything will be fine"—and she tipped her head in the direction of the back of the house where Ralph was. They, Clara and Ralph, would live another twenty-one years together. Long before then he became a free man because the War between the States came and found them. Skiffington got into the carriage. (162)

What the narrator tells us about the future of these minor characters is generally not significant to the plot, and, indeed, the violent death of major characters at the end of the novel is never proleptically anticipated. The significance lies in how these recurring prolepses not only authoritatively perform the narrator's complete knowledge of the fictional world, but project a conception of the omniscient narrator as a kind of empathetic local historian who invests peripheral slave characters with a life as much worth knowing as their white owners or the central protagonists:

> Belle's second maid, who had never been sick a day in her life, would die the night after Belle did. Her name was Patty and she had had three children, one dead, two yet alive, Allie and Newby, a boy who liked to drink directly from a cow's teat. Those two children would die the third night, the same night the last of Belle's children died, the beautiful girl with freckles who played the piano so well. (33)

Coupled with the anachronous nonlinearity of the plot, the proleptic intrusions make it almost impossible to feel located in the "narrative present" for any length of time. For instance, when narrating Henry Townsend's 1855 death in the opening pages, the narrative anticipates a scene in which Henry's former teacher, Fern Elston, will discuss his life: "After the war between the states, Fern would tell a pamphlet writer, a white immigrant from Canada, that Henry had been the brightest of her students" (7). This scene is duly narrated later in the novel, in which the pamphlet writer is given a name, Anderson Frazier, and the conversation a date, August 1881 (107). Throughout the rest of the novel, the narrator constantly refers readers back to this conversation on "that day," even though it is still in the future for the characters:

> "Zeus," Fern said, "please ask Colley to come here. Tell Colley to bring the rifle and a pistol." When she married the second and third times, Zeus would be with her. *Indeed, as she talked to Anderson Frazier that day in 1881,* he was inside the house, occasionally looking through the curtain at the backs of their heads. He brought out lemonade to Anderson after Fern offered him some.
> "Yessum," Zeus said. (250, emphasis added)

This passage has an analeptic reference embedded in a proleptic statement. The effect is to frustrate the teleological conception of history as cause and effect. What the omniscient narrator knows about the history of Manchester County could not be known to historians. It is not only knowledge of the minds of characters, but of unrecorded and unrecordable information: "Had someone counted up what crops the fields had to give, it would have come to more than $325 a slave" (226). In *The Known World*, the omnitemporal freedom of omniscience is deployed to model a form of historical writing which would be possible if historians could transcend epistemological limitations and attain complete access to the world of the past.

Ultimately, given the subject of the book, a little known aspect of the history of slavery, the question raised for readers must be not how does the narrator know about the fictional world and minds of characters, which is accepted as a convention of fiction, but how much does the *author* know about this aspect of history in the actual world being referenced? That is, the authority this narrator claims is not based purely on the formal techniques of omniscient narration, or on the "unnatural" powers of a quasi-divine consciousness, but on the figure of the author as a literary historian. The narrator's "quality" of omniscience is supplemented by a rhetorical deployment of the apparatus of historiography in the service of this claim for authority. First there is reference to contemporaneous "primary sources." One of these is the pamphlet, *Curiosities and Oddities about Our Southern Neighbours,* written by the Canadian pamphlet writer, Anderson Frazier, after his meeting with Fern Elston:

> The pamphlet on slaveowning Negroes went through ten printings. Only seven of those particular pamphlets survived until the late twentieth century. Five of them were in the Library of Congress in 1994 when the remaining two pamphlets were sold as part of a collection of black memorabilia owned by a black man in Cleveland, Ohio. That collection, upon the man's death in 1994, sold for $1.7 million dollars to an automobile manufacturer in Germany. (106)

This "extrarepresentational" information lends the impression that the narrator's knowledge of the storyworld relies upon the archival research of the author. The "impossible" knowledge of the narrator, however, highlights the limitations of knowledge derived from primary sources: "Had Anderson not been white and a man, had the day not started out hot and gotten hotter . . . Fern might have opened up to Anderson" (109). Another historiographic device is reference to scholarly histories of the period, enabled by the temporal distance of the narrating instance:

> The town and the county went into a period of years and years of what University of Virginia historian Roberta Murphy in a 1948 book would call "peace and prosperity." For the people who depended upon slaves, this meant, among other things, that not one slave escaped, not until after Henry Townsend died. The historian—whose book was rejected by the University of Virginia Press—would also call Skiffington "a godsend

for the county." . . . In the history of the county, the chickens, all of which managed to live until 1856, were a momentous event ten places below the tenure of John Skiffington as sheriff, according to this one historian, who became a full professor at Washington and Lee University three years after her book was published. (43–44)

The first sentence gives the impression of the authorial narrator quoting scholarly sources to establish the authenticity of his narrative. What follows, however, is a stinging ideological critique of the scholarship of "this one historian." The novel's exploration of the question of history is thus manifested in the rhetorical strategy of the narrator to employ regular intrusions such as these which explicitly pit the unfettered knowledge of literary omniscience against the epistemological constraints of historiography. The narrative authority which emerges from this strategy is paradoxical: on the one hand the apparatus of historiographic scholarship is drawn upon to discursively establish the authenticity of the narrative, and on other hand this scholarship is shown to be misguided and inaccurate. Anderson Frazier's pamphlet, as well as Roberta Murphy's book, and that of the other historians referenced, such as K. Woodford from Lynchburg College (207), are fictional. Clearly they serve the purpose of lending verisimilitude to the fictional world of Manchester County and highlighting the omniscient narrator's diegetic authority. The more complicated authenticating strategy is the recurring reference to documents we know to exist in the actual world: the U.S. Censuses from 1830 to 1860.

As Tim Ryan writes in *Calls and Responses: The American Novel of Slavery since Gone with the Wind*, *The Known World* is "continually sceptical about the ability of human discourse to adequately represent the past, and the novel persistently emphasizes the limitations of the discipline of history. For example, the narrative satirically draws attention to the problematic nature of antebellum censuses—sources frequently utilized by contemporary historians" (194). As early as page 7, this engagement with the census is established:

In 1855 in Manchester County, Virginia, there were thirty-four free black families, with a mother and father and one child or more, and eight of those free families owned slaves, and all eight knew each other's business. When the war between the states came, the number of slave-owning blacks in Manchester would be down to five, and one of those included an extremely morose man who, according to the U.S. census of 1860, legally owned his own wife and five children and three grandchildren.

> The census of 1860 said there were 2,670 slaves in Manchester County, but the census taker, a U.S. marshal who feared God, had argued with his wife the day he sent his report to Washington, D.C., and all his arithmetic was wrong because he had failed to carry a one. (7)

A phrase such as "according to the U.S. census of 1860" suggests the opening figures are based upon this primary source, while the next sentence asserts the inaccuracy of its data. The narrator presents no evidence to prove the failings of the census, or whether the original statement is produced from the census or not. Does this narrator know what the census does not because of access to historical fact? Is this access the result of sympathetic imagination? Here we see the fantasy of omniscience, indeed the fantasy of fiction, as a desire to correct or at least supplement the historical record.

The authority of this omniscient narration is nonetheless reliant upon a figure of the novelist as literary historian able to contribute to debates about history, rather than as maker "using" historical research to tell a story. The effect may be to undermine the authority of historians to know the past, but instead of a postmodern critique of history as fiction, we are presented with a fiction which purports to know the strange world of the past with greater authority. As Ryan argues, "while the novel constantly emphasizes that human experience is too complex to be captured in language and while it insists that histories are undependable and limited forms of discourse, it also acknowledges that there is a significant and concrete reality toward which such texts gesture" (196). It is the very reference to historical discourse which grounds the capacity of the narrator to project a concrete fictional world:

> Louis, the son, was also Robbins's slave, which was how the U.S. census that year listed him. The census noted that the house on Shenandoah Road where the boy lived in Manchester was headed by Philomena, his mother, and that the boy had a sister, Dora, three years his senior. The census did not say that the children were Robbins's flesh and blood and that he traveled into Manchester because he loved their mother far more than anything he could name and that, in his quieter moments, after the storms in his head, he feared that he was losing his mind because of that love. (21)

This passage draws attention not to the human error involved in census taking, but the limitations of data collection itself in capturing the unofficial relations between humans, the incapacity of the census to know the private lives of people. And yet despite pointing out the methodological flaws of the census, such as the 1840 census taker's inability to properly discern whether someone is full-blooded Indian or not, and his miscalculation of the square miles of Manchester County, the narrator uses the census to lend discursive authority to his own narrative statements: "On one page of the census report to the federal government in Washington, D.C., the census taker put a check by William Robbins's name and footnoted on page 113 that he was the country's wealthiest man" (23). These sorts of statements gesture outwards to lend the impression that the author has consulted the records in order to construct his figure of the omniscient literary historian. "While frequently subverting and satirizing the limitations of the discipline of history," Ryan points out, "*The Known World* also acknowledges that we have no choice but to rely upon it to some degree" (201).

The figure of the omniscient narrator as literary historian is pitted against other figures of authority, from census takers, to pamphlet writers, to academics, drawing attention to the unreliability of their methods. Race is also factor. Apart from Anderson Frazier being white, we have this reference to an historian: "In 1993, the University of Virginia Press would publish a 415-page book by a white woman, Marcia H. Shia, documenting that every ninety-seventh person in the Commonwealth of Virginia was kin, by blood or by marriage, to the line that started with Celeste and Elias Freeman" (352). While the narrator does not undermine these statistics, mention of this historian's race invites us to consider the obvious—that the history of slavery is written by whites—and to ponder the race of the narrator. Given Susan Lanser's default equation of the gender of omniscient narrators with the social identity of a book's author, the same could be said for race here, constructing a figure of reliable historical authority empathetic with his characters.

According to Michael Riffaterre, the paradox of fictional truth can be described as the generic function of verisimilitude, rather than accordance with factuality. However, if we approach fiction as a mode of public discourse the reliability of this narrator's omniscient knowledge is ultimately dependent upon the narrative's discursive contribution to history in the public sphere, as opposed to the scholarly archive. According to a review in the *New York Times* by John Vernon: "Among the many triumphs of *The Known World*, not the least is Jones's transformation of a little-known footnote in history into a story that goes right to the heart of slavery." This demonstrates that one of the functions of historical fiction is to bring knowledge of the past into the broader public sphere, authorizing the novelist to speak about history. In an interview for the BookBrowse website, Jones states: "The county and town of Manchester, Virginia, and every human being in those places are products of my imagination." He goes on to explain that references to other counties and towns, and historical figures "were employed merely to give some heft and believability to the creation of Manchester and its people." This sort of artistic license does not undermine the credibility of the novel's exploration of history. The most important aspect of the narrator's authority is the status of the census data, for this underpins the authenticity of the author's treatment of slavery. Jones freely admits that he also fabricated census records for the purposes of verisimilitude, affording "a hard background of numbers and dates that makes the foreground of the characters and what they go through more real." That the census figures, the publications and state acts and the historians referred to are fictional, only demonstrates further an attempt to assert the cultural authority of the novelist to "know" the past, even as this must be framed as an encounter with the archive in order to claim the power of the novelist to demonstrate the real lesson of history.

Despite Jones's protestations that he did not research his book, the historian Thomas J. Pressley has shown, in an article for *The Journal of African American History,* how the information in *The Known World* largely correlates with that of available data from the 1830 U.S. Census, transcribed by Carter G. Woodson, the "Father of Black History." Pressley demonstrates that "in several Virginia counties, free black slaveowners reached 25 percent or more of the free black heads of families. Thus Jones's Manchester County is well within the general range" (86). His conclusion is that "Edward P. Jones's historical novel successfully meets major tests of statistical plausibility for its historical period—whatever may be its degree of success or failure in satisfying the various other literary or aesthetic criteria by which readers may evaluate it" (86). Pressley's article was occasioned by the fact that Jones's book brought this aspect of history to light in the public sphere. He then uses this attention to test the fictional statistics in the novel against that provided by Carter Woodson's scholarship, and to argue for more scholarly use of Woodson's statistical information.

For Katherine Clay Bassard, in "Imagining Other Worlds," the ongoing conflict between Augustus Townsend who bought himself and his family out of slavery, and his son, Henry, who became a slave owner, dramatizes scholarly debate about the extent of benevolent and commercial black slave owning, with Augustus epitomizing the "Woodson thesis" (that most black slave owners bought only their family members) and Henry its refutation (412). Despite his claims to have eschewed research, and particularly the sort of historical detail which Michel Faber claimed as crucial to the authority of his reconstruction of Victorian England, Jones nonetheless speaks with authority in the public sphere about this debate. In response to an interviewer's question about how common it was for free blacks to own slaves, Jones asserted:

> I don't have any hard data but I'm quite certain that the numbers of black slaveowners was quite small in relation to white slaveowners. The fact that many people—even many black people—didn't know such people existed is perhaps proof of how few there were. In addition, as I note in the novel, husbands purchased wives and parents purchased children, and so their neighbors may have come to know the people purchased not as slaves, as property, but as family members. Finally, owning a slave was not a cheap proposition, and the economic status of most blacks back then didn't lend itself to owning a human being. ("An Interview")

The phrase, "as I note in the novel" is significant for the way Jones wants to use the authority of his omniscient narrator to undergird his right to speak in public about the history of slavery. This narrative voice, with its rhetorical deployment of the discourse of history to supplement his impossible knowledge of the past, becomes an occasion to establish the cultural authority of the novelist in the public sphere.

The intrusive presence of the omniscient narrator, engaged in an ongoing critique of historical evidence, even as he reveals impossible knowledge of the fictional world and its characters, is crucial to the rhetorical effect of the novel. For Tim Ryan, the effect is to indicate "that the notion of accurate history is a contradiction in terms. Representations of slavery are always necessarily imaginative narratives, and, the text implies, the creative omniscience of the novelist seems more compelling than the compromised empiricism of the historian" (195). Ryan argues that the novel "defamiliarizes slavery" not only through its subject matter, but its "formal strategies," by deploying the structure of the Victorian novel, describing it as "a sort of *Middlemarch* of American slavery" (204). According to Ryan: "On the one hand, this choice allows *The Known World* to pursue traditional social realism, but, on the other, the novel is also an ironic and parodic invocation of an earlier literary form" (205). Why the need to make this claim? Ryan suggests the novel is not "purely a faux-Victorian panorama" because it employs "postmodernist or magic realist elements" such as the persistent prolepses and references to historical documents: "*The Known World*'s commitment to traditional realism and its informed engagement with historiography is balanced by its skeptical attitude toward history as a discipline and its unsettling metafictional characteristics" (205). Ryan's analysis of the novel's uneasy relationship to historiography is compelling, but it seems unnecessary to say that a part of its strategy is a parody of nineteenth-century omniscience, rather than simply a deployment of conventions of omniscience in the service of the narrative. What makes it post-postmodernist for me is precisely the sense of faith in an actual if ultimately unknowable past, and the belief that the "creative omniscience" of the novelist is one method for trying to know this past, as opposed to undermining the project of historical scholarship. In other words it posits fiction as a mode of historiography and sets up the novelist as a kind of literary historian. This strategic use of omniscient narration, rather than the "invocation" of an earlier form, is a means of establishing the cultural authority of the novelist in the discursive treatment of the past.

CHAPTER 4

Style and the Pyrotechnic Storyteller

THE PYROTECHNIC STORYTELLER is typically humorous or satirical, employing a flourishing and expansive narrative voice, a garrulous conversational tone, to assert control over the events being narrated, eschewing the impersonality of analytic omniscience to the extent that the narrative voice often overshadows the characters being described or analyzed. This third mode of narrative authority in contemporary omniscience includes Zadie Smith's *White Teeth,* Rick Moody's *The Diviners,* Nicola Barker's *Darkmans,* and much of the work of David Foster Wallace. While the novels discussed in this chapter display zero focalization and, in the case of Smith, overt commentary, the intrusive presence of their authorial narrators is produced most strikingly by expressive features of style which characterize the "voice" of the storyteller. Take, for example, this passage from *Darkmans:* "The house (which'd looked fairly bleak *prior* to this new development—with its sagging sills, mouldy fascia, and muddy garden) now peeked out, disconsolately, from beneath its perilous-seeming exo-skeleton like a sadly neglected poodle in an ill-fitting muzzle" (182). Of course, this authorial style is not a "quality" of omniscience, but in this instance it establishes an idiosyncratic expressive presence tied to the narrative voice itself.

Style in the literary-critical sense usually refers to elements of language—such as idiom, diction, tone, syntactic rhythm—which would be lost in a paraphrase of the story; the linguistic choices which distinguish the writing of one author from another. As a result of the foundational distinction between author and narrator, narrative theory has traditionally been less concerned with prose style—how a narrative is *written*—than with storytelling methods—how a story is narrated. Hence, in *Story and Discourse,* Seymour Chatman defines discourse as the "structure of narrative transmission," with style as the "texture of the properties of the medium" (10–11), pertinent only to the extent that it facilitates the presentation of discourse. In a more specific sense, style in narrative theory has generally referred to linguistic features which enable readers to distinguish a character's "voice" from a narrator's, particularly in the form of free indirect discourse. This narratological linking of stylistic elements to the evocation of subjectivity in narrative discourse echoes the literary-critical understanding of individual authorial style. In the study of free indirect discourse a narrator's formal diction is conventionally taken as the neutral voice against which to measure the stylistic deviation of characterial language. With the pyrotechnic storyteller, by contrast, colloquial language, informal tone, idiosyncratic syntax, and metaphorical excess all contribute to the evocation and characterization of a dramatized narrator, whose intrusive presence is established stylistically.

Dan Shen has argued for a need to include stylistic analysis of the language choices of writers alongside narratological analysis of the structural organization of a narrative in order for a fuller understanding of these two levels of presentation. She does not, however, relate this broad approach to narrative discourse as the "how" of narrative to the more specific question of discourse as the utterance of a narrator. Richard Aczel takes up the question of style in his essay "Hearing Voices in Narrative Texts," which criticizes the narratological definition of voice as the generating instance of a narrative. He claims that Genette's functional concept of voice as the agent responsible for telling a story, understood as the spatio-temporal location of the narrator in relation to the story, is limited because it does not establish *how* a narrator speaks and is thus "inherently deaf to qualitative factors such as tone and idiom" (468). Hence voice, for Aczel, must primarily be understood as a question of style. He argues for a distinction between the function of the narrator (the instance of enunciation) and the effect of the narrator, which he calls voice. This distinction, for Aczel, allows for a qualitative, as opposed to merely functional, concept of voice, and emphasizes the centrality of stylistic expressivity—features of style which evoke a deictic center or subjectivity—in the identification of voice effects and their agents. Positing voice as a textual effect rather than an originary anima, it insists on a radical separation between textual signs of stylistic agency and projected (metatextual) principles of narrative organization and unity. (467)

In dismissing the claims by Ann Banfield and Monika Fludernik for narratorless third-person fiction, he challenges accepted approaches to the presence of a narrator. Rather than first-person pronouns, addresses to a reader, reflexive statements and overt commentary, which he assigns to the function of narration, Aczel locates the presence of a narrator in lexical, syntactic, and rhetorical elements of style, claiming that only these features can be considered elements of voice:

This is not to say that style necessarily evokes a subjective center (there are, for example, impersonal, collective, and period styles), but where style does have an expressive function it will produce a voice effect. Not only, therefore, does stylistic expressivity—style anchored in subjectivity—have an important role to play in the *identification* of narratorial audibility, but it must play the central role in the *characterization* of a narrator's voice. Narratorial self-mention posits a speaker function, and comment names a subject position, but it is only stylistic expressivity which endows this speaking subject with a recognizable *voice*. (472)

Aczel's evidence is the fiction of Henry James. Despite the restricted focalization of *The Ambassadors* or *What Maisie Knew*, Aczel claims that James's narratorial presence is clearly audible in the style of narration, and this is far more important to the voice effect of the narrator than the occasional intrusive comment which can be found in James's work. It is easy to accept that James's ornate circumlocutive sentences can be seen as stylistic evidence of the subjective presence of a narrator despite the rigorous reflectorization of his narratives. However, Aczel's "qualitative" approach seems to leave a lot of interpretive leeway in identifying the voice "effect" of stylistic expressivity. Would we deny narratorial characterization to the objective narration of a Hemingway story because of its minimalist style? And doesn't stylistic expressivity—a deictic center of subjectivity—indicate a "trace" of the narrating instance in the narrative discourse?

While I would still retain the importance of the narrating instance as the subjective center which generates the stylistic effects of voice, and the importance of intrusive commentary as the most overt performance of omniscient authority, Aczel's approach is nonetheless particularly salient for understanding how the mode of the pyrotechnic storyteller asserts a pervasive narratorial presence. Drawing upon Bakhtin, Aczel argues that the voices of narrators and characters emerge in a quotational context, audible only in their stylistic difference from each other, and becoming functional via a dialogue between readers and a projected narrating instance. The narrator, then, is not a "uniform teller persona" but a "composite configuration of voices, whose identity lies in the rhetorical organization of their constituent elements" (495). By contrast, I will approach style in this chapter as an extranarrative function of the narrator. That is, style is part of the act of narration, employed not only in the service of telling a story, but of asserting the omniscient narrator's linguistic presence at the level of discourse.

Narratological attention to style further complicates the author-narrator distinction because the stylistic features which Aczel claims evoke the voice effect of a narrator—"tone, idiom, diction, speech-style" (469)—also enable us to identify the prose style of individual authors. In character narration, I would argue, an author's style is metadiscursive. That is, when Humbert Humbert writes, in the opening to his confession, "You can always count on a murderer for a fancy prose style" (9), we are invited to attribute the stylistic choices to Humbert's narrative voice, even though we know that they are a product of Nabokov's authorial craft in writing *Lolita*. In third-person narration, there seems little purchase in separating an author's stylistic choices discernible in the text from those which establish the narrator's voice at the level of discourse. If homodiegetic narrators are characterized as much by their manner of telling as their diegetic experience, then heterodiegetic narrators must be characterized as much by their stylistic choices as they are by their commentary. The pyrotechnic storytellers of contemporary omniscience invoke the highest degree of personalized narration by virtue of these stylistic choices.

There are two writers whose maximalist prose has had the greatest influence on the syntactic rhythms of contemporary fiction, and has provided a stylistic model for the narrative voice of the pyrotechnic storyteller: Salman Rushdie and David Foster Wallace. Here is a passage from the opening page of Rushdie's *The Satanic Verses*:

Gibreel, the tuneless soloist, had been cavorting in moonlight as he sang his impromptu gazal, swimming in air, butterfly-stroke, breast-stroke, bunching himself into a ball, spread-eagling himself against the almost-infinity of the almost-dawn, adopting heraldic postures, rampant, couchant, pitting levity against gravity. (3)

This hectic overdescription is accompanied by metaphorical excess: "The aircraft cracked in half, a seed-pod giving up its spores, an egg yielding its mystery. Two actors, prancing Gibreel, and buttony, pursed Mr Saladin Chamcha, fell like titbits of tobacco from a broken old cigar" (4). In two lines the narrator employs images of a seed-pod, an egg and a cigar, hurling language at us, and this prolixity seems almost to license in stylistic terms narratorial commentary, in the following case relating to the influence of aviation on modern thought and subjectivity:

Yessir, but not random. Up there in air-space, in that soft, imperceptible field which had been made possible by the century, and which, thereafter, made the century possible, becoming one of its defining locations, the place of movement and of war, the planet-shrinker and power-vacuum, most insecure and transitory of zones, illusory, discontinuous, metamorphic,—because when you throw everything up in the air anything becomes possible—wayupthere, at any rate, changes took place in delirious actors that would have gladdened the heart of old Mr Lamarck: under extreme environmental pressure, characteristics were acquired. (5)

For David Foster Wallace, stylistic pyrotechnics, in the form of extended sentences replete with qualifications and parentheticals, function as a way to elaborate the convolutions of individual character thought, while retaining a deliberately bland "style" in terms of lexical choice and figurative range. Here is a representative passage from "Luckily the Account Representative Knew CPR":

Particularly the divorced Account Representative, who remarked, silently, alone, as his elevator dropped toward the Executive Garage, that, at a certain unnoticed but never unheeded point in every corporate evening he worked, it became Time to Leave; that this point in the overtime night was a fulcrum on which things basic and unseen tilted, very slightly—a pivot in hours unaware—and that, in the period between this point and the fresh-suited working dawn, the very issue of the Building's ownership would become, quietly, in their absence, truly an issue, hung in air, unsettled. (46)

In this passage, the narrator tells us that the unnamed Account Representative "remarked silently, alone" that it was "Time to Leave," but the sentence is elongated by a paratactic clause following the semi-colon, shifting into a narratorial elaboration of the thought, overwhelming the character's subjective presence with its drawn out explanatory comment. These feature of style—overdescription, metaphorical excess, and narratorial elaboration of character thought—are all ways in which the omniscient pyrotechnic storyteller rhetorically performs the controlling presence of the authorial narrator.

Nicola Barker, *Darkmans* (2007)

Nicola Barker's *Darkmans* is the most striking example of the pyrotechnic storyteller. Set in the town of Ashford in contemporary England, the novel focuses on how the progress of modernity is haunted by the sedimentary layers of the city's medieval past. As one of the characters says, Ashford is "like history in paradigm. At its center beats this tiny, perfect, medieval heart, but that heart is surrounded—obfuscated—by all these conflicting layers, a chaos of buildings and roads from every conceivable time-frame. It's pure, architectural mayhem" (398). At the beginning of the novel we are introduced to sixty-one-year-old Daniel Beede, now a broken man working in a hospital laundry after spending much of his earlier life fighting the effects of the Channel Tunnel on his town. In particular, he had been devoted to restoring an historic water mill threatened by an arterial rerouting, a project during which he "had gripped the liver of history and had felt it squelching in his hand" (10), but which amounted to nothing once the mill was bulldozed. He remains galled by the disappearance of invaluable ancient tiles which had been salvaged from the building, and his desire to discover what happened provides the impetus of the plot. As the narrator says: "Beede was the vengeful tsunami of history" (13), and his actions appear to have unleashed the ghostly figure of the darkmans, spirit of John Scogin, the infamous court jester to Edward IV, whose life Beede is researching.

Throughout the novel, both Beede and his drug-dealing son, Kane, appear to be haunted by this figure, in dreams and in waking life, and sometimes possessed by him. Both father and son are besotted with chiropodist Elen whose disturbed husband, Isidore, is the most affected by Scogin, prone to amnesiac lapses of mind during which he unconsciously re-enacts the jester's tricks, and seeming to hear his voice in his head. Elen and Isidore's six-year-old son, Fleet, is monomaniacally obsessed with constructing a perfect matchstick replica of the Cathedral Basilica of Sainte-Cécile and its surrounding buildings, without actually having seen it, and which he does not finish because it had not been completed in Scogin's lifetime. Fleet also talks of a mysterious friend, "John," relaying information about Scogin's biography he could not possibly know. At one point, paternity tests based on DNA samples reveal Fleet genetically to be Isidore's ancestor rather than his son.

Most significantly, these hauntings take the form of a linguistic inhabitation, with the characters involuntarily thinking and speaking in archaic words and words from other languages of which they are unfamiliar. For instance, in one scene between Kane and Elen, Kane is trying to control both his feelings of sexual arousal and his jealousy of her relationship with his father. He looks down at a coin Elen is holding and thinks: "*Coin*— / *Cuneus*— / *Kunte*— / *Cunt*" (773). Cuneus is Latin for wedge, also an architectural element of medieval theatres, suggesting the jester's hand at play. In this context, Elen is the wedge between himself and Beede, leading associatively and phonetically to "cunt," which can be seen as an expression of both desire for and anger toward Elen. Kane is overwhelmed by his experience: "—he saw words clashing and merging and collapsing and rotating. He saw chaos—an infinity of teeth, tongues, mouths, breath. He saw a storm of confusion" (775).

This linguistic chaos is replicated in the act of narration. Barker's novel has a manic prose style, full of multiple overblown metaphors, colloquial language, parenthetical embellishments and, most strikingly, regular interpolations of characters' thoughts (typographically represented by italics and separated by line breaks) into the narrator's discourse. There are some overt narratorial assessments, such as this: "In bald truth, Beede's studious attempts to present himself as unfailingly approachable to his son were all just so much baloney" (73). However, the omniscient authority and intrusive presence of this pyrotechnic narration is largely stylistic, emerging from summary, descriptive pause and the representation of consciousness. The voice "effect" of stylistic expressivity which characterizes the narrator is clear in the excessive elaboration of metaphors which occur throughout the book. Here is an example of character summary: "To boil it all down (which might take a while—there was plenty of old meat, hard lessons and human frailty in this particular broth), Beede was wildly cynical about the functions of paternity" (73). Commenting on a conversation between Beede and his son Kane, the narrator writes: "The unmentionable hung between them like a dank canal (overrun by weed and scattered with litter—the used condoms, the bent tricycle, the old pram)" (340). In these passages the parentheses contain the excessive elaboration of metaphors which are extranarrative in their function.

Another example of stylistic presence is the extended introduction to one of the characters. "Mrs Dina Broad had a wonderful facility for getting total strangers to do exactly as she wanted" (104). This introductory statement is straightforward enough, but over the next page of character summary the narrator's presence is keenly asserted in the hyperactive prose with its regular parenthetical qualifications and extended metaphors. "If Dina's life was a carousel (which it was anything but), then there was only enough room on the rotating podium (midst the high-painted roses, the mirror-tiles, the lovely organ) for a single pony; and Dina's was it" (104). The metaphor of the single-pony carousel is exhausted before it segues into one of the character's life as a theatrical show: "The Dina Broad show (like Celine Dion in Las Vegas) was a show that never ended (it just went on and on and *on*); but this low-budget extravaganza (in perfect Technicolor) by no means ran itself" (104). "*Nuh-uh,*" the narrator says, before pursuing the metaphor for another two paragraphs.

In this following extract we have what appears to be a passage of free indirect discourse concerning Fleet's antisocial behavior at school and the response of his parents. The passage is not linked to any single character perspective, but its sentiments seem most attributable to the general opinion of the mothers of other children in the school, a summary of their assessment of Fleet and his parents:

Fleet on the other hand . . .

Hmmn

Fleet had . . .

What did Fleet have? Whatever it was, the parents wouldn't deal with it (were uncooperative, wouldn't face facts), which automatically rendered them a part of the problem. To care too much was a weakness all parents could quite reasonably be found guilty of, but to actively obstruct? To smother? To deny? Not only was it unhealthy, but in the voluminous wardrobe of parental misdemeanours, this was that fine-seeming, well-laundered garment hanging neatly alongside the foul and mouldering suit of abuse (contamination was always a possibility when two items were hung so close). (151)

This passage gives the appearance of the narrator reporting the collective opinion of the mothers emerging out of a discussion about Fleet and his parents, rendering this opinion in a form of free indirect discourse, complete with interrogatives. But as it continues it becomes less of a mediated report than a narratorial performance which linguistically overwhelms the characters and asserts the narrator's stylistic authority through the hyperbolic wardrobe metaphor. The last parenthetical line, "contamination was always a possibility when two items were hung so close," can, in the context of the narrator's overriding presence, also be read as a reflexive metaphor for the operation of stylistic contagion, showing the contamination of narratorial and character language.

Darkmans was shortlisted for the Booker Prize in 2007, the year in which Anne Enright won for *The Gathering*. In an article in *The Guardian*, one of the judges, Giles Foden, explains that, while the novel was an early favorite of the judges, "the general impression was that not enough thought had been given to the reader. It seemed a book written for the author whose evident zeal for language could only take one so far," and which "with much more disciplined handling, could have been a *Middlemarch* for our times." Enright's novel, on the other hand, was praised for its "controlled" and "carefully modulated" prose. Stylistic excess, then, may have cost Barker the chance at a Booker prize. In particular, Foden notes that a "number of judges had difficulty with italic interjections, broken out of the main text, as a way of presenting a character's thoughts." This style can be seen as idiosyncratic to Barker's writing, but it also matches the novel's preoccupation with the power of language, performing at the level of the discourse the chaotic inhabitation of characters' thoughts which the darkmans performs in the story.

The key stylistic technique is a kind of reflexive experimentation with stylistic contagion. Throughout the novel, the narration is fragmented by separate paragraphs of italicized words and phrases which must be attributed to a character. Often these appear as snatches of direct discourse supplementing an internally focalized passage such as in the following:

Elen had a sudden sense of how it might feel to be a student who wasn't excelling in Mrs Santa's class (that atmosphere of "tolerant" disappointment; of "accepting" disquiet). She didn't like it. The angry knuckle tensed itself up inside her stomach again—

Cow

—then the second, gentler knuckle—the pacifier—

She's his teacher—She just wants to help . . .

—predictably balanced it out. (141)

Sometimes these italicized passages of interpolated direct discourse appear to operate as a character's response to the narrator's comments. One section elaborates, in free indirect discourse, Kane's frustration with his father's uptight stoicism. This is interrupted by a narratorial evaluation of Kane's attempt to distinguish himself from Beede:

Of course, by comparison—and by sheer coincidence—Kane's entire life mission—

Oh how lovely to hone in on me again

—was to be mirthful. To be fluffy. To endow mere trifles with an exquisitely inappropriate gravitas. Kane found depth an abomination. (20)

The following passage is our first introduction to Kane's ex-girlfriend:

Kelly Broad was sitting on a high wall, chewing ferociously on a piece of celery. She was passingly pretty and alarmingly thin with artificially tinted burgundy hair. . . . She had bad circulation, weak bones . . . a penchant for laxatives and an Eating Disorder—

Might as well bring that straight up, eh?

Un,
Deux,
Trois . . .

Bleeeaa-urghhh! (39)

In the following example, the narrator—who is describing Beede's efforts, along with a group of volunteers, to restore the Old Mill—seems to respond to the character's interjection:

> It wasn't all plain sailing. At some point (and who could remember when, exactly?), it became distressingly apparent that recent "improvements" to the newer parts of Mill House had seriously endangered the older structure's integrity—
>
> *Now hang on—*
> *Just . . . just back up a second—*
> *What are you saying here, exactly?*
>
> The worst-case scenario? That the old mill might never be able to function independently in its eighteenth century guise; like a conjoined twin, it might only really be able to exist as a small part of its former whole. (10)

Here the narrator is articulating what Beede does not want to hear: that his attempts to restore the mill contributed to its destruction. If stylistic contagion is understood as an assimilation into the narrative voice of language a character might use to describe themselves (such as the famous "Uncle Charles repaired to the outhouse"), these moments seem to be the narrator's hypothetical interpolations of the response a character might have to being described by someone else. In other words, we have less the sharing of the narratorial function with the character's voice, than the narrator supplying the character's thoughts for them, linguistically penetrating the psyche of the characters. One of the characters, the historian Winifred, is researching the life of Scogin on Beede's behalf. At one point, Winifred tells Kane: "Words are his allies. It's like he's at his most powerful, his most mischievous, when experimenting with the variables of language" (646). In this way, the narrator's stylistic excess matches the Jester, for the characters' thoughts also suffer from linguistic intrusion at the diegetic level.

In one scene, Beede's cat scratches Elen's hand, and he takes her hand in his to inspect it: "'He's drawn *blut*,' Beede murmured thickly, his chest tightening as he inhaled the roses on her, then he frowned. 'Blood,' he repeated" (656). Later, in a scene where he appears to be completely possessed, prancing around, somersaulting, farting, and eventually hanging his cat, Beede notices blood on his arm and this list of words appears in his thoughts: *"Reudh? Ruber? Rood? Rud? Red? Red? Blut-red? Eh? Blut?"* (677). This might be explained by Beede's interest in the origins of languages, but the other characters have no such interest or knowledge. Indeed it is the resurfacing of archaic words across characters which links them together.

Toward the end of the novel, Dory explains to Beede that the darkmans, whom they know but cannot name, has been a constant voice in his head: "He keeps telling me that you made your own key. He keeps repeating it. He keeps going on and on and on and *on*. . . . I mean at first I didn't *understand*—he speaks differently to us. He kept repeating the word *kay* and I just couldn't . . . but then he said *luk* . . . then *loch* . . . and I knew he meant lock. Like a lock and a key. A *key* . . . " (713). The next chapter, focalized through Kane who is driving to meet an art forger called Peta Borough, opens this way:

Tenterden. He'd planned to head for Tenterden—

Peta—
Peta Borough—
The f-forger . . .
The f-fabricare . . .
She's definitely the k-k-kay, here

—but when he drew up at the roundabout—

Eh?

—the Rover was just one car ahead of him—

Kay?

—so he calmly proceeded to follow—

F-f-fabric-what?! (716)

Here we see Kane confused by this linguistic invasion of his own internal thoughts. Peta Borough in fact turns out to be the key to the plot, revealing to Kane in the denouement the fate of the missing tiles, as well as her and Beede's involvement in it. Later, Kane is discussing ash trees with a gardener who tells him they can be recognized by their seeds, known as keys.

> "Keys?" Kane repeated. "Why do they call them that?"
> "Because in the very old days they used to resemble the actual keys that people used for their locks."
> "Key," Kane mused, dreamily, "kay . . . " (785)

The word is now uttered in his speech. Later we have this line to introduce a chapter in which the word has found its way into the narration:

> Kane took out his kays—
>
> KEYS, Goddammit!
>
> (He shook his head—
>
> STOP this now!
> ENOUGH!!)
>
> —inserted them into the lock, then paused for a second and stared down, frowning, at his outstretched hands. (796)

This passage follows the pattern of reporting characters' thoughts that seem to be responses to the narration. In this instance, the narrator's use of "kays," as an instance of stylistic contagion, is an echo of the Jester's lexical infection of the characters' thoughts. If Kane cannot get the word out of his head, it is because neither the darkmans nor the omniscient narrator will let him. And if Scogin is "at his most powerful, his most mischievous, when experimenting with the variables of language" (646), then so is the narrator in her experiment with represented thought. At one point in the novel Kane reflects upon the strange words in his mind: "Almost as if his thoughts were a war drum (or a tom-tom or a bongo) being deftly played by a mysterious hand on the other side of a very distant, very stark and yet beautiful snow-capped mountain" (485). This mysterious hand of the darkmans, who embodies the return of a repressed history, infiltrating the characters' minds and intruding into their idiom, is also a kind of spectral figure of the omniscient narrator. Given the history of novelistic form as an attempt to repress the intrusive presence of the omniscient narrator by developments in impersonal narration, this presence can be seen erupting in the stylistic excess of the pyrotechnic storyteller exemplified by Barker's novel.

Zadie Smith, *White Teeth* (2000)

The pyrotechnic narrator is also the mediating voice for much of the fiction which the prominent British critic James Wood denounces as "hysterical realism." For Wood, much contemporary fiction is beset with an "excess of storytelling" (*Irresponsible* 171), neglecting the development of characters with genuine humanity. He describes hysterical realism in this way: "The big contemporary novel is a perpetual motion machine that appears to have been embarrassed into velocity. It seems to want to abolish stillness, as if ashamed of silence. Stories and sub-stories sprout on every page, and these novels continually flourish their glamorous congestion. Inseparable from this culture of permanent storytelling is the pursuit of vitality at all costs" (*Irresponsible* 167). Wood argues that this mode of fiction has absorbed the textual qualities of magic realism into the realist novel. The manic flourishes of verisimilar improbability do not tip into the surreal, but simply exhaust the conventions of realism. Wood coined the term "hysterical realism" in a review of Zadie Smith's *White Teeth,* and listed Smith's novel as the latest in a "hardening" genre including Rushdie's *The Ground Beneath Her Feet,* Pynchon's *Mason & Dixon,* DeLillo's *Underworld* and Wallace's *Infinite Jest.*

The publication of *White Teeth* at the turn of the millennium was a genuine media event: a debut novel about contemporary multicultural England by a young, attractive female writer, easily situated in a tradition of postcolonial fiction which explores the hybrid nature of migrant identities, with a direct line of descent from Rushdie's *The Satanic Verses.* "This has been the century of strangers," utters the omniscient narrator, "brown, yellow and white. This has been the century of the late immigrant experiment. It is only this late in the day that you can walk into a playground and find Isaac Leung by the fishpond, Danny Rahman in the football cage, Quang O'Rourke bouncing a basketball, and Irie Jones humming a tune" (326). If *The Satanic Verses* experiments with an omniscient narrator who asserts his noninterventionist stance while hinting he may also be Satan, *White Teeth* can be read as a postsecular novel in which the omniscient narrator refuses to organize the plot around the traditional concept of providence. Here, *White Teeth*'s narrative voice bears comparison with that in Henry Fielding's *Tom Jones,* the prototype of omniscient narration in the English novel. In *God's Plot and Man's Stories,* Leopold Damrosch argues that in Fielding's novel "[a]n omniscient and affectionate narrator acts as the disposing deity of the fictional universe, instructing the reader, by means of a plot whose coherence is only gradually revealed, to understand the operations of a Providence that subsumes all of the apparent accidents of chance or Fortune" (263). In the final book of *Tom Jones,* the narrator writes:

> Here an Accident happened of a very extraordinary Kind; one indeed of those strange Chances whence very good and grave Men have concluded that Providence often interposes in the Discovery of the most secret Villainy, in order to caution Men from quitting the Paths of Honesty, however warily they tread in those of Vice. (818)

If, as Wayne Booth argues in *The Rhetoric of Fiction,* Fielding's narrator establishes an intimacy with readers that "produces a kind of comic analogue of the true believer's reliance on a benign providence in real life" (217), the omniscient narrator of *White Teeth,* by contrast, engages readers by satirizing this reliance.

The novel opens with a scene in which the protagonist, Archie Jones, is attempting to commit suicide by gassing himself in his car. After the scene is established the narrator asserts her colloquial stylistic presence and intrusive authority in this passage of zero focalization:

> For, though he did not know it, and despite the Hoover tube that lay on the passenger seat pumping from the exhaust pipe into his lungs, luck was with him that morning. The thinnest covering of luck was on him like fresh dew. Whilst he slipped in and out of consciousness, the position of the planets, the music of the spheres, the flap of a tiger-moth's diaphanous wings in Central Africa, and a whole bunch of other stuff that Makes Shit Happen had decided it was second-chance time for Archie. Somewhere, somehow, by somebody, it had been decided that he would live. (4)

This passage seems deliberately designed to prevent us from reading Archie's escape from suicide as some sort of profound statement about the fragility of human existence. Its satirical references to various popular theories of universal cause and effect seem to terminate in the suggestion that the somebody who "makes shit happen" is either a divine entity about which the narrator can only speculate (she knows what happened, but not why), or simply the narrator herself, the storytelling author's proxy, who playfully acknowledges her analogous relation to God. Smith's narrator, in fact, regularly employs intrusive commentary to satirize the desire of characters to assign events to providence:

> The principles of Christianity and Sod's Law (also known as Murphy's Law) are the same: *Everything happens to me, for me*. So if a man drops a piece of toast and it lands butter-side down, this unlucky event is interpreted as being proof of an essential truth about bad luck: that the toast fell as it did just to prove to *you*, Mr Unlucky, that there is a defining force in the universe and it is bad luck. It's not random. It could never have fallen on the right side, so the argument goes, because that's Sod's Law. In short, Sod's Law happens to you to prove to you that there is Sod's Law. Yet, unlike gravity, it is a law that does not exist whatever happens: when the toast lands on the *right* side, Sod's Law mysteriously disappears. (44)

This passage occurs in the middle of narrating the involvement of two characters in a motorbike accident. The narrator goes on to point out the character Ryan's belief that he had escaped injury while his companion Clara had her teeth knocked out because God had chosen to save him: "Not because one was wearing a helmet and the other wasn't" (44). Most damningly, the narrator comments that if the opposite had occurred "you can bet your life that God, in Ryan's mind, would have done a vanishing act" (44).

Here we see the narrator extrapolating from the report of a character's experience to general commentary on "human nature." "Authorial narrative," according to Monika Fludernik,

> is most familiar to us in the form of a reliable guide to human affairs. There is a consoling ability to know, to see into characters' minds, to grasp the why, how and wherefore of life, and to uncover life's rules and regularities *sub specie aeternitatis et mundi*. (*Natural* 165)

This is a conventional understanding of the eighteenth- and nineteenth-century omniscient narrator established by critical consensus. Rather than offering consoling explanation, the narrative voice of *White Teeth* offers a world of random uncertainty, relativizing the authority of her commentary.

In an essay on the relationship between postcolonial fiction and postsecular thought, Graham Huggan argues that *White Teeth* is a contemporary postsecular text which performs in fiction the aims of postsecularism, defined as "a strategy for the deconstructive reading of established religious texts" (757). Like *The Satanic Verses,* he points out, Smith's novel is a celebration of hybridity and an attack on cultural purism:

> However, if the promises and illusions of Islam remain very much at the center of Rushdie's novel, their space in Smith's has largely been usurped by the secular history of the genome. . . . *White Teeth,* in this sense, is *The Satanic Verses* for the age of the Human Genome Project. (761)

A key character in *White Teeth* is the geneticist Marcus Chalfen, who publicly champions the potential for all humans arising from his attempts to produce a genetically engineered mouse. A press release announcing the launch of his "FutureMouse©" experiment states that this research "holds out the tantalizing promise of a new phase in human history where we are not victims of the random but instead directors and arbitrators of our own fate" (433). As Huggan points out, the novel undercuts this promise as events unfold "through a succession of biological accidents and historical contingencies" (762).

The final chapter of *White Teeth* brings all the strands of the plot together in a set piece centered on the launch of the FutureMouse©. If the denouement of *Tom Jones* resolves the plot to reveal the hand of Providence, here there is structural unification, but no real resolution. "*But first the endgames,*" the narrator writes, acknowledging the desire of readers to know what happens to the characters and projecting several possibilities. "But surely to tell these tall tales and others like them would be to speed the myth, the wicked lie, that the past is always tense and the future, perfect. And as Archie knows, it's not like that. It's never been like that" (541). Instead she concludes by following the mouse who has escaped. "He watched it dash along the table, and through the hands of those who wished to pin it down. He watched it leap off the end and disappear through an air vent. *Go on my son!* thought Archie" (542). So while Smith's narrator may reject providence, she also rejects secular belief in the promise of science to eliminate the random.

"The humanism that Smith's novel endorses," Huggan argues, "is neither intrinsically secular nor fundamentally religious; rather, it occupies a postsecular sphere of radical indeterminacy in which fundamentalist certainties are rejected and salvationist promises of all kinds are unmasked for the self-serving—and sometimes brutally destructive—ideologies they are" (763). Huggan makes no reference to the formal properties of narration in Smith's novel, but certainly the humanism that the novel "endorses" is facilitated by the narrative voice itself in overt commentary. There are substantial passages of digressive and garrulous commentary throughout the novel which directly address the reader. In each of the following examples, the narrator employs the editorial "we" to rhetorically invoke a general consciousness. On each occasion, the digression concludes with the narrator distancing herself from this "we" by taking issue with conventional wisdom.

After describing Irie's rationalization that Millat doesn't love her because he cannot, because he is damaged, the narrator digresses—"It's a funny thing about the modern world" (462)—wondering how this sort of thinking came to pass in this century:

> We are so convinced of the goodness of ourselves, and the goodness of our love, we cannot bear to believe that there might be something more worthy of love than us, more worthy of worship. Greetings cards routinely tell us everybody deserves love. No. Everybody deserves clean water. Not everybody deserves love all the time. (462)

In the following passage, the intrusive commentary invokes a narratee and hence implied reader who is culturally different from the characters under consideration, that is, not an immigrant. "Because we often imagine that immigrants are constantly on the move, footloose, able to change course at any moment, able to employ their legendary resourcefulness at every turn" (465). The narrator proceeds to discuss this belief in relation to Zeno's Paradox of pluralism, before concluding that "multiplicity is no illusion" despite the allure of the One: "Because this is the other thing about immigrants (fugees, émigrés, travellers): they cannot escape their history any more than you yourself can lose your shadow" (466). If it is true that omniscient narration invokes a conventional link between narrative voice and the social identity of the author, then the narrative authority of this voice invokes the cultural authority of Smith—as the child of an immigrant Jamaican mother and English father—beginning the section with an editorial "we" that establishes complicity with the implied reader's difference from the characters, and concluding with a direct address that speaks on behalf of the characters' experience.

As many critics have argued, Smith's public persona has been vital to the reception of her novel, with debate revolving around the extent to which *White Teeth* participates in a contrived multicultural exotica. Paying attention to the different styles of author photo in the hardback and paperback editions of the novel, Dominic Head writes: "For the author of a book that purports to speak authoritatively to a wide range of ethnic experience—including Caribbean British and Asian British experience—the ability to adopt different guises suggests a substantive hybridized identity that goes beyond the more cynical marketing objectives" (107). Head links this paratextual framing to Smith's celebration of contemporary multiculturalism by focusing on her satirical critique of genetic engineering. "From the point of view of ethnicity," he claims, "this signals Smith's conviction: that we are all hybrid post-colonials, biologically as well as culturally, and the pursuit of pure ethnic origins is a pointless objective. And in celebrating this hybridity, Smith embraces its contradictory and haphazard nature" (114).

The following passage of commentary indicates again how the narrator addresses assumptions about different cultural beliefs before showing how they are not so different from those of the narratee invoked by an editorial "we":

> And it may be absurd to us that one Iqbal can believe the breadcrumbs laid down by another Iqbal, generations before him, have not yet blown away in the breeze. But it really doesn't matter what we believe. It seems it won't stop the man who thinks this life is guided by the life he thinks he had before, or the gypsy who swears by the queens in her tarot pack. And it's hard to change the mind of the high-strung woman who lays responsibility for all her actions at the feet of her mother, or the lonely guy who sits in a fold-up chair on a hill in the dead of night waiting for the little green men. Amidst the strange landscapes that have replaced our belief in the efficacy of the stars, Millat's is not such odd terrain. He believes the decisions that are made, come back. He believes we live in circles. His is a simple, neat fatalism. What goes around comes around. (506–7)

In this last comment the narrator assumes our complicity in the absurdity of Iqbal's belief, before going on both to make light of this belief and normalize it by parodying other more quotidian attempts at fatalism. Matthew Paproth describes what he considers a "disconnect between postmodernist tale and modernist telling" (11) in Smith's novels which, despite their postmodern content, employ a stable narrative structure and authoritative omniscient narrator. It seems odd to describe these features of "telling" as modernist, given the radical experimentation with form and voice which characterizes modernist fiction. Nonetheless, Paproth's point is that "while the novels demonstrate the failure of various characters to assert their authority and autonomy in a postmodern world, the narrators are confident, in total control of their narratives, rarely demonstrating the uncertainty or fracturedness that is common in postmodernist fiction" (11). The assumption here is that "a confident omniscient narrator" must be conservative or at odds with postmodern thought. Referring to the neat conclusion of *White Teeth*, Paproth writes: "It is a typically modernist move, one intended to guide readers toward knowledge—paradoxically, we are being led toward the message that randomness and chaos prevail over resolution and closure. The point here is that the modernist structure problematizes the postmodernist message that the final scene reveals to readers" (22). I'm not sure what this problematization entails. That the "message" is obfuscated or diminished by the form? That Smith doesn't practice what she preaches? At any rate, the use of omniscient narration in *White Teeth* indicates that its form is not necessarily at odds with an exploration of postmodern culture, that it operates to establish the cultural authority of novelists in the wake of postmodernism, and that in doing so it projects a figure of authorship different from that of classic omniscience.

Rick Moody, *The Diviners* (2005)

In a 2001 interview for *Paris Review*, Rick Moody was asked about the literary traditions informing his writing. His response was: "The modernist notion that anything is possible, the postmodernist notion that everything is exhausted, the post-postmodernist notion that since everything is exhausted, everything is permitted" (David Ryan). The prologue, entitled "Opening Credits and Theme Music," which opens *The Diviners* is a highly flamboyant performance of the spatial freedom of omniscience, with clear echoes of the famous opening to Dickens's *Bleak House,* a canonical example of zero focalization. The second paragraph of *Bleak House* begins: "Fog everywhere. Fog up the river, where it flows among green aits and meadows; fog down the river, where it rolls defiled among the tiers of shipping and the waterside pollutions of a great (and dirty) city" (13). In Moody's novel, the fog over Victorian London becomes the light which spreads from Hollywood to the rest of the world in the year 2000 on the morning after the election of George Bush. And whereas Dickens's opening passage takes a handful of paragraphs, Moody's extends over twelve pages. Here is the opening:

The light that illuminates the world begins in Los Angeles. Begins in darkness, begins in the mountains, begins in empty landscapes, in doubt and remorse. San Antonio Peak throws shadows upon a city of shadows. There are hints of human insignificance; there are nightmares. But just at the moment of intolerability there's an eruption of spectra. It's morning! Morning is hopeful, uncomplicated, and it scales mountaintops, as it scales all things. The light comes from nowhere fathomable, from an apparently eternal reservoir of emanations, radioactivities. Light edging over the mountaintop and across the lakes of the highlands, light across the Angeles National Forest, light rushing across skeins of smog in the California skies. Light on Redlands, light on the planned communities, light on the guy tossing the morning newspaper from a Toyota with a hundred and ninety-three thousand miles on it. Light on the Santa Ana river, on a drunk sleeping tenderly beside its dregs, light on the Santa Ana mountains, the San Bernadino mountains, light on the Prado Basin, where a stabbing victim welters in her wounds. (3)

The title to the prologue suggests the narration is mimicking the neutral eye of the cinematic camera, as if voicing the implied message of the camera movements and theme music ("It's morning!" suggesting a swell of music). At the same time the stylistic reference to *Bleak House* demonstrates that the filmic opening wide shot derives its logic from the panoramic perspective of zero focalization. This sets up Moody's novelistic satire of the film and television industry which is said to be responsible for the decline of readership for print fiction. Here the omniscient narration is operating parodically, but it is not a parodic critique of a nineteenth-century fictional technique, or the fantasy of omniscience: it is a deployment of this technique to parody twenty-first-century American cultural imperialism, flagged from the opening line with its ironic assertion that the sun rises in Los Angeles to illuminate the rest of the world. This opening line also echoes the statement in Genesis about the omnipotent creative power of divinity—"And God said: Let there be light"—although the analogy with God is offset by the statement that the light "comes from nowhere fathomable" (3).

The zero focalization proceeds to range across the world, tracking the light over the Pacific Ocean—"Light upon the invisible phytoplankton and all organic material" (4)—but the narrative voice is not anonymous or impersonal: it draws attention to the many metaphorical applications of light as it offers commentary on geopolitical issues around the globe. The narrator's light shines from Japan—"now dawn upon Nagasaki, where the second of the explosions was detonated, light of dawn reflective of that other light" (6)—to China—"light upon the glass boxes of Chinese capitalism" (6)—to the Middle East—"light upon the troops belonging to a military dictator bent upon keeping as many Afghan refugees on the other side of the pass as is possible" (8)—where "[a]s far as the eye can see, the prophet and his vision, the dawn is his metaphor. . . . Dawn is for all the people's of Mohammed's country" (8). It moves to Europe—"light upon Western Europe and a history founded on light as a mythological tool" (10)—where "light is now visible, beginning to shine upon the Pantheon, that massive structure of such permanence that even a McDonald's just across the square from it cannot spoil its perfection" (10). Then across the North Atlantic before returning to the United States where people "have stuff on their mind" and "International concerns are not pressing" (12). The spatio-temporal freedom of omniscience is thus used to establish the broader international context in which a parody of the western media industry is played out, demonstrating the insularity of the American perspective before settling in New York—"Light upon all the insomniacs, across this city, metropolis of insomniacs" (13)—where the novel is set.

The narrative centers on a group of people who work in a small independent film company called Means of Production. The chief executive, Vanessa Meandro, has decided that the company needs to stabilize its revenue and branch out from art-house films to include television. The complication of the plot arises when one of Vanessa's assistants, Amanda Duffy, misplaces a script which had yet to be assessed. To help Amanda avoid the wrath of her boss, Thaddeus Griffin, a coworker and washed-up action movie star, concocts a treatment for a miniseries called *The Diviners*, supposedly based on a novel by a best-selling author. The satirical plot revolves around attempts by several companies to secure the script development rights to this nonexistent universally appealing historical drama about water diviners.

After the prologue the rest of the novel proceeds to orient the narrative perspective of each chapter around an individual character in a large cast with a minimum of intrusive commentary. This is a typical pattern, setting the scene with panoramic external focalization before "zooming" into variable internal focalization. However, the opening establishes a frame in which the *stylistic* presence of the narrator's voice remains palpable throughout the novel. Despite each focalized chapter relying heavily on free indirect discourse, there is very much the sense of the narrative voice moving from one character to another, performing their thoughts in pyrotechnic fashion, in much the same way that the light is traced in the prologue, rather than this narratorial consciousness yielding linguistically to shifting deictic centers.

This link between the prologue and the tracing of character thought is made to resonant linguistically in a scene describing the addiction of the corpulent Vanessa, nicknamed "Minivan" by her employees, to Krispy Kreme doughnuts. In this scene Vanessa escapes a meeting for compulsive overeaters and is compelled to seek out doughnuts as solace. As she approaches the store we have this passage, inviting readers to share the experience:

> Just stand a little, here, beside the Rite Aid pharmacy, to which Vanessa trots with such purpose that the commuters coming up the PATH train escalators veer out of her way. Doesn't matter that the Krispy Kreme at concourse level is neither flashy nor fashionable. She will not be diverted from the mission, which is the mission of doughnuts. Is the sign illuminated? Do you need to ask? The sign that indicates that the doughnuts are fresh. Yes, there is a *light* at Krispy Kreme, which indicates that the original glazed doughnuts of Krispy Kreme are just off the assembly line. She looks for the indicator lamp; she looks for a sympathetic light in the eyes in her fellow men and women. Yes, the light is still illuminated! . . . She is destined to have a doughnut that melts in her mouth, a doughnut that tastes like the happy ending of a romantic comedy as purveyed by a vertically integrated multinational entertainment provider under German ownership. (53)

Here we see embedded in the free indirect rendering of Vanessa's consciousness—"Yes, the light is still illuminated!"—the same narratorial language which rendered the opening scene of zero focalization: "The light that illuminates the world begins in Los Angeles." The passage then shifts into commentary which overtly satirizes Vanessa's gustatory desire. After Vanessa has purchased her doughnuts and begun to consume them, we have this passage of commentary:

> She doesn't even wait to be in the open space of the concourse before she has one in her mouth. And here's the lesson. The great spiritual benefit of the Krispy Kreme original glazed doughnut is the sensation of nothingness. The satori that is the Krispy Kreme is the obliteration of self, the silencing of the voices that are attached to the oppressions of life. As

soon as she has the original glazed doughnut in her mouth, relief floods in. (54)

Descriptions of light and its metaphorical applications abound throughout the narrative. The first chapter is centered on Vanessa's alcoholic mother, Rosa, who suffers from migraines: "These headaches begin with visitations, with rainbows, celestial light" (15). Annabel hopes her boss will one day display tenderness to those around her, and wants to be there "when the world of light opens in Minivan like a flower" (64). Annabel's adoptive father, the Reverend Duffy, opens his door to find his son, Tyrone, returned: "the prodigal son is now in the light on the front step, here he is, and the prodigal son is loved!" (380). In another scene, Tyrone is sitting on a train peering out the window: "Lighting effects are consistent with the light of late afternoon in Connecticut, which is the flickering light of things passing away, the light of things coming to an end" (210).

The taxi driver, Ranjeet Singh, who meets Vanessa when she orders him to ferry her around New York City to feed her doughnut addiction, somehow convinces her to hire him as an expert on television in order to help her company infiltrate the television market and, as she says to her employees, "rocket toward the light" (136). In one of his rants Ranjeet argues that television has replaced literature in its pseudo-religious influence. The "tale of written words, words on the page in alphabets. This tale is a sickness . . . This is not the true way because these tales of the alphabet have no light in them. . . . No, as you can now see, the true way must be the way of bringing light to all the people, and there is but one way to do that" (131). Here Ranjeet's surging monologue to the employees at Means of Production sounds exactly like the omniscient opening with its pomposity, its use of anaphora ("the light") and syntactic rhythm:

> That way is the way of television, which is the one light, the light in the house, the light in the darkness, the light of the satellite dish, the light of the dishwallahs of India, the light of the rural places coming out of the darkness, the light of television that brings together all men and women in red bathing suits on a shore, the light of a talking horse, the light of a red-haired woman and her bandleader husband when they argue and she crosses her eyes, the light of an army hospital and its surgeons during the war, the light of a special team of policemen from a city in Florida, the light of a family of oil barons, the light of four women who sleep with many men and talk about it in cafes, the light of all persons who wish to be millionaires. (132)

Throughout the novel the narrator acts as a sort of ventriloquist, taking on and parodying the characters' linguistic habitus, but with the same syntactic rhythm. For instance, in a chapter in which Thaddeus Griffin is having sex with a yoga instructor we have this focalized passage:

> She is allowing herself to be kissed by Thaddeus Griffin, movie star and practitioner of yoga, and she is kissing back a little bit, and this is the pose called the Adulterous Union, wherein two practitioners, who are elsewhere participants in love's vast covenant, conjoin their mouths on the Oriental carpet in the ashram. (283)

Similar to Barker's *Darkmans,* the psychonarratorial summary of a character's opinion is often elaborated in such hyperbolic fashion that we have to see it as neither a narratorial report nor a mediated indirect quotation, but a kind of linguistic overwriting of the character's own metaphor:

> If Annabel's mother, the psychologist, has a view on sexuality as depicted on television, it's that the excessive saccharine of this sexuality is bound to create expectations, and not just among young people, who are almost honor bound to expect that when they finally get naked with their friends the earth will tremble or there will be the sounds of rockets going off in their ears or they will feel an overwhelming and intoxicating love, more addictive than heroin, and this love feeling, called forth by the commingling of bodily fluids, will never take leave of them, until death comes for them. (459)

So the stylistic excess established in the opening display of zero focalization, and which clearly characterizes the narrator's voice, is employed to retain overt narratorial presence even in passages of internal focalization and free indirect rendering of character thought, spilling over into narratorial commentary.

CHAPTER 5

Polymathic Knowledge, the Immersion Journalist, and the Social Commentator

THE FOURTH MODE of contemporary omniscience contains both the *immersion journalist* and the *social commentator*. The narrator as immersion journalist is a fictional counterpart of the narrators of documentary nonfiction novels, such as Truman Capote's *In Cold Blood*, and is exemplified by the work of Tom Wolfe, who shifted from the New Journalism to the social novel with the publication of his first novel, *The Bonfire of the Vanities*. The desire to diagnose and report a social problem through the techniques of omniscience links Wolfe's immersion journalist with the social commentator, under which I would include Don DeLillo's *Underworld*, Jonathan Franzen's *The Corrections*, and Richard Powers's *Generosity*. The narrative authority here operates by deploying the capacious knowledge of the narrator to analyze postmodern culture. If omniscient authority must be granted by the reading public, rather than unselfconsciously assumed by the narrator, "all-knowing," in this case, has come to mean less a divine or telepathic knowledge of the human interior, than a polymathic knowledge of how the world works. "Time and again," James Wood complained in a post-9/11 assertion that hysterical realism and the social novel must be abandoned, "novelists are praised for their wealth of obscure and far-flung social knowledge. Richard Powers is the best exam-

ple, but Tom Wolfe also gets an easy ride simply for 'knowing things')"
("Tell Me"). In other words, contemporary narrators "know" more than
any character not simply because of their omniscient privilege, but because
of their intellectual scope. In a 2003 article, Judith Shulevitz refers to the
work of DeLillo and Franzen, among others, when she claims, somewhat
ruefully, that "novelists, in short, have become our public intellectuals—
our polymaths, our geographers, our scholars of the material world. And
yet, oddly, you will find very few intellectuals in the modern novel" (B31).
The intellectuals in the novels under scrutiny here are the narrators themselves, extradiegetic characters who function as proxies for the author.
And the polymathic knowledge which the immersion journalist and social
commentator deploy to underpin their narrative authority manifests itself
in intellectual encounters with competing nonliterary paradigms of knowledge, from evolutionary science to the forces of history.

Tom Wolfe, *I Am Charlotte Simmons* (2004)

> This is why God invented journalists. A journalist is as good as an omniscient narrator any day. Good at piecing the story together from the raw data, at hearing the many voices. You can't miss him. He's the guy in the white suit.
>
> —Susan Reynolds, "Down from the Mountains"

In this section I will discuss Tom Wolfe's third novel, *I Am Charlotte Simmons*, in terms of its contribution to the contemporary mode of the omniscient narrator as immersion journalist. Wolfe's position in relation to the development of twentieth-century fiction is staked out in two manifestos: his introduction to *The New Journalism* and his article "Stalking the Billion-Footed Beast." The central premise binding these two manifestos is Wolfe's claim that serious writers in the 1960s turned to avant-garde experimentation with fabulism, absurdism, surrealism, metafiction, the novel of ideas, etc., in the belief that realist fiction was a redundant genre incapable of capturing the fragmentation and absurdity of twentieth-century existence. Yet, for Wolfe, this was precisely the period in which realist fiction should have been flourishing, for the cultural revolution of the sixties and the global juggernaut of American society offered an abundance of material about how we live. There is an evolution across these manifestos, however, in terms of what the solution may be to this abandonment of American society by writers. In 1973, Wolfe argued that journalists were taking up the slack from fiction writers and producing nonfiction novels, employing the techniques of fictional realism—which he identifies as dialogue, scenic narration, status detail, and point of view—to report on actual events. By 1989, Wolfe was no longer championing the emergence of the New Journalism at the expense of the novel, but exhorting the revival of the social realist novel precisely in order to reclaim the territory lost to journalism.

In his introduction to *The New Journalism* Wolfe describes how this form of writing emerged out of dissatisfaction with the style of traditional objective reportage. The point of his introduction to this anthology, however, is not to recount the impact on journalism of this new hybrid style of nonfiction; it is to situate the New Journalism in relation to the American novel after World War II, and indeed to the history of literary fiction itself. He claims that the journalistic experimentations of the sixties introduced a new literary genre. Within a decade or so, the extended form of this literary journalism, the nonfiction or documentary novel, had the effect of "dethroning the novel as the number one literary genre, starting the first new direction in American literature in half a century" (15).

The success of the New Journalism, for Wolfe, can be attributed to its commitment to social realism. The nonfiction novels of writers such as Truman Capote, Norman Mailer, and Hunter S. Thompson are placed as the heirs to a form abandoned by postmodern fiction (although he doesn't use this word). What gives the nonfiction novel credibility as a social document, for Wolfe, is the fact that it records real events. He points out that major novelists such as Dickens or Balzac have always employed reportage, only this element has been seen biographically rather than as a generic feature of the novel itself. "It took the New Journalism to bring this strange matter of reporting into the foreground" (28). For the nonfiction novel makes reportage an explicit feature of the novel itself.

The irony of Wolfe's declamations is that he has since abandoned New Journalism and the nonfiction novel to become a writer of fiction himself. He announced this change with his 1989 manifesto, "The Billion Footed Beast." David Lodge had claimed that the nonfiction novel was itself a postmodern genre emerging out of the rejection of realism, but Wolfe's essay, subtitled "A literary manifesto for the new social novel," suggests that it was simply a means of reintroducing social realism to novelistic form. By this stage Wolfe himself had recently published *The Bonfire of the Vanities*. Despite his bold claims for nonfiction as a literary genre in previous decades, Wolfe writes that he always feared a realist novel would come along and render irrelevant his nonfiction about American cultural life. It never did, he claims, and his essay is both a call to arms to fiction writers and a justification of his own turn to fiction. This was partly motivated, he candidly admits by

> the question that rebuked every writer who had made a point of experimenting with nonfiction over the preceding ten or fifteen years: Are you merely ducking the big challenge—The Novel. Consciously, I wanted to prove a point. I wanted to fulfill a prediction I had made in the introduction to *The New Journalism* in 1973: namely, that the future of the fictional novel would be in a highly detailed realism based on reporting, a realism more thorough than any currently being attempted, a realism that would portray the individual in intimate and inextricable relation to the society around him. (50)

The new social novel would still make a feature of its commitment to reportage and to charting contemporary American life, but it would no longer have the imprimatur of fact. My argument here is that Wolfe's new social novel is another means of reviving the omniscient narrator in contemporary fiction, a narrator whose authority invokes the authorial figure of the novelist as a type of immersion journalist.

Central to Wolfe's construction of narrative authority for *I Am Charlotte Simmons,* and to his operation as a public intellectual, is the "extrafictional" voice of this novel emerging out of its prefatorial material and linking it to his 1973 account of the New Journalism, his 1989 manifesto for the social realist novel, and his 2001 essay collection *Hooking Up*. Wolfe might argue that the style he developed in his nonfiction has now become a style for the writing of fiction, but he is compelled still to point out that his work is the product of journalistic immersion. The preface to this book, in which he acknowledges the help of staff and students at a range of universities, and the input of his two daughters, firmly establishes the authenticity of the book by demonstrating the depth of research behind it. Advance publicity also let it be known that Wolfe spent several years visiting universities, attending undergraduate parties and observing student life. This is an appeal not just to verisimilitude (the nonfiction credo "this actually happened" becomes in fiction "this actually happens") but to the authority of the narrator. Wolfe's narrator is omniscient in every sense, even to the extent of knowing what the characters don't know about themselves, but the omniscience doesn't rely upon moral authority, it relies upon journalistic research.

The appeal to observational fieldwork established by this voice provides a kind of ethnographic distance from the characters as the source of omniscient knowledge, both grounding and relativizing the narrator's authority. Two key elements of narrative authority in this book are the generational/sociological distance of the narrator from the characters and the anthropological/ethnographic mode of character analysis. Throughout *I Am Charlotte Simmons*, the detailed scenic construction is supplemented by explanatory commentary. For instance, after an expletive-laden exchange of dialogue between two college basketball players we have this line: "Without even realising what it was, Jojo spoke in this year's prevailing college creole: Fuck Patois" (35). This observation is followed by a linguistic analysis of these subcultural speech habits, describing with examples the multiple grammatical uses the word fuck can be put to. Following this paragraph is a line of narration in which the narrator parodically adopts the patois himself: "The fucking freshman in question was standing about twenty fucking feet away" (36).

These supplementary explanations clearly establish a tone of bemusement and an irony which relies upon the appeal to an implied reader who is not familiar with the world being reported. In the following two quotes we have evidence of Wolfe's narrator "reporting" on youth culture through expositional commentary:

> "Aw-right!" said another huge black youth with a shaved head who was sitting next to the white giant, whereupon the two black giants bumped each other's fists together in a celebratory gesture called "pounding." (102)

> Charlotte recognized none of them, but pastel cashmere sweaters in the Reading Room at night screamed out . . . *sorority girls!* So did the little bags they held in their hands. The girls were back from what sorority boy-scouters called a "candy run." (560)

Another observation that seems to deliberately flaunt the generational distance of the narrator from his characters occurs when Charlotte meets her first friend at Dupont College. After introducing themselves to each other as Bettina and Charlotte, this line follows: "They were members of the first generation to go through life with no last names" (145).

As well as this pseudo-sociological generational distance, the narrator draws upon the framework of evolutionary science to chart the inevitability of Charlotte's absorption into the libidinal preoccupations of college students. A recurring phrase in the novel, and the title of one of the chapters, is: "the conscious little rock." This phrase comes from a lecture on neuroscience which Charlotte attends, sparking her interest in the field. According to this lecture, genetic coding controls our actions to such an extent that free will may be a myth: humans may be nothing more than conscious little rocks. Buoyed by her lecturer's praise for her work, Charlotte walks through campus thinking the students around her are "blithely ignorant of the fact that they were merely conscious little rocks, every one of them, whereas . . . *I am Charlotte Simmons*" (285). In a later chapter detailing Charlotte's crush on a handsome frat boy, we have the following line of narration embedded in a passage of narrated perception: "With that, the conscious little rock moved her head ever so slightly closer to his and ever so slightly parted her lips" (342). This line hammers home the irony of Charlotte's belief in her own capacity to stand above mating rituals hardwired by genetic coding. The chapter ends with an ironic rendering in free indirect discourse of her mantra of individuality: "In all of Dupont College, only *she* was Charlotte Simmons!" (342).

The mock anthropological distance of the narrator which provides the overarching approach of the novel is highlighted to the point of caricature in this comment during a scene where Charlotte hears shrieking in the campus hallway:

> A girl came running from the entry hall into the Common Room. She shrieked again. She was slim and blond and wore shorts that showed off her perfect legs, and the shrieks were ones that any girl on earth could have interpreted. They were the cries of the female of the species feigning physical fright at the antics, probably physical, of the male. (145)

The omniscient narrator's capacity to divine and articulate motivations which characters themselves are little aware of is based less on exploration of the character's individual psyche, than on the same anthropological observations offering biologically determined explanations of gendered behavior:

> She knew this was the moment to put a stop to it. The thought of his starting to "hit on" her again was unpleasant and even frightening . . . and yet she didn't *want* to put a stop to it. The present moment was much too early in her experience for her to have expressed it in a sentence, but she was enjoying the first stirrings, the first in her entire life, of the power that woman can hold over that creature who is as monomaniacally hormonocentric as the beasts of the field, Man. (181, original ellipsis)

The presence of the narrator is felt not only through overt commentary or evaluation, but almost as a silent observer, a peripheral character. Generally a character, especially Charlotte, is used as a deictic anchor but the presence of the author as an immersion journalist tends to be signified by the explanatory references employing the second-person pronoun:

> Soon all three cashmeres were standing around the skank, and the whisper party had begun. In these Reading Room whisper parties, girls whispered entire conversations, they whispered chuckles, they popped consonants and sighed vowels until everyone within earshot wanted to cry out "Shut the fuck up!" Nothing could be any worse than these whispered conversations, which got under your hide like an unreachable itch. Charlotte put her hand up to her eyes like a blinker, to make sure *they* didn't recognize *her*. (560)

Here we have the scenic narration of an event in the library largely through Charlotte's perspective. The first line linguistically orients us to Charlotte's perspective with its absorption of her metonym (cashmeres) and slang noun (skank) into the narrational idiom. There is then a shift into iterative narration to explain to the narratee what a whisper party is. The use of the second-person pronoun ("which got under your hide") in this context gives the effect of a narrator who knows from observation what a whisper party is like and is now looking over Charlotte's shoulder to assimilate the expositional report into her perspective. This is how the figure of the immersion journalist as an "immanent" presence is built up throughout the book, beginning from the opening paragraph:

> Every time the men's-room door opened, the amped-up onslaught of Swarm, the band banging out the concert in the theater overhead, came crashing in, ricocheting off all the mirrors and ceramic surfaces until it seemed twice as loud. But then an air hinge would close the door, and Swarm would vanish, and *you* could once again hear students drunk on youth and beer being funny or at least loud as they stood before the urinals. (3, emphasis added)

This immanent narratorial presence, the fictional equivalent of Wolfe's immersion research, lends a kind of eye-witness authority to the evaluative comments through the novel, such as this description of a frat house party: "Gales of laughter, clapping, whistling, unintelligible shouts. By this stage of the evening, the brothers were drunk enough to believe that Vance's verbose buffoonery actually gave the brotherhood an aura of elegance" (466).

The historical importance of Wolfe's faith in fictional realism is that, for Wolfe, postmodern fiction, as a result of its penchant for formal experimentation, has retreated from any obligation to deal with contemporary culture. What establishes his work as an example of post-postmodernism, is the appeal of its omniscient narrative authority not to the convention of the Victorian novel but to the figure of the journalist. Or rather, in his attempt to remake the Victorian novelist as a journalist and revive this figure in the form of a contemporary omniscient narrator.

Don DeLillo, *Underworld* (1997)

> Only all-seeing God, some might say, could highlight the sidetracks and U-turns, the back-doubles and sudden veerings-off. Only a god or a novelist.
> And Don DeLillo duly starts this, his eleventh novel, in a mode of thrilling bravura, of rip-roaring godlike omniscience.
> —William Boyd, "'The Course of True Life'"

While *Underworld* is a multi-voiced novel, shifting between first- and third-person narration, its narrative authority is established by the celebrated prologue, originally published as a stand- alone piece, "Pafko at the Wall", in *Harper's* magazine in 1992, providing a frame which subsequent sections are assimilated into. The prologue takes the classic form of zero focalization, sweeping through the consciousness of multiple characters as it ranges across a panoramic description of the 3 October 1951 National League playoff between the Dodgers and the Giants, won by the Giants with a Bobby Thompson home run, subsequently glorified in sporting history as "the shot heard 'round the world." The description both "reconstructs" the famous baseball game, or, more specifically, the feeling of being at the game, through its attention to scenic detail and its showy use of a periodizing argot, and separates it from the narrating instance by a narratorial awareness of the game as a spectacle embedded in American cultural memory and associatively connected with Cold War history. The simultaneous immediacy and nostalgic distance is facilitated by the conjunction of present-tense narration with prolepsis, by the use of direct address, and the reporting of a coincidence which has resonance only after the event: the simultaneity of the "shot heard 'round the world" with the testing of an atomic bomb in the Soviet Union, connected by the fact that J. Edgar Hoover was at this match when he received notice of the testing.

This prologue is concerned with an historical moment, and thus could be classified under the mode of the literary historian. John N. Duvall has described "Pafko at the Wall" as an example of postmodern historiographic metafiction, and Kathleen Fitzpatrick, in "The Unmaking of History," follows his lead in applying this label to *Underworld*. However, she also argues that the novel

> acts to dismantle the genre of historiographic metafiction and its preconceptions, working not to create the past out of its narratives but instead to excavate and deconstruct the traces a reified history has left in the present. In so doing, the novel undermines all narrative processes, both the realist and the metafictional. (151)

The book as a whole, then, projects a figure of its author as social commentator as the novel sets out to trace the effects of this historical moment on the present, with one key strand of the plot following the fate of the home run ball over the ensuing decades. At the same time, it is narrated backwards after the prologue, from 1992 to 1952.

The narrator's omniscient authority is established on the first page with this aphoristic statement: "Longing on a large scale is what makes history. This is just a kid with a local yearning, but he's part of an assembling crowd" (3). This sense of history in the making animates the reconstruction of the game as the narrator charts the swelling of the crowd. The key feature of this effect of nostalgic immediacy, of the forces of history at play, is the pervasive presence of the second-person pronoun which performs several different grammatical functions in the service of establishing narrator-narratee relations.

The first function is that of the direct address. In this case, the narrator seeks to invoke a general consciousness in relation to a very specific cultural memory. The opening line is: "He speaks in your voice, American, and there's a shine in his eye that's halfway hopeful" (3). The "he" in question is a black youth, the kid with a local yearning, who has skipped school to try and gain entry to the game, which he does by vaulting the turnstiles and evading security guards before disappearing into the crowd. DeLillo's "engaging" narrator, then, invites narratees to participate in the unfolding of the game, and thus readers to perceive this game as something enshrined in their own cultural memory which becomes internationally significant in geopolitical terms. The direct address also operates at the level of description: "He has wiry reddish hair and a college jacket—you know those athletic jackets where the sleeves are one color and leathery looking and the body is a darker color and probably wool and these are the college colors of the team" (45).

Building upon this direct address is the use of "you" as an informal variant of "one." Directly following a passage focalized through the kid, Cotter, as he laments the state of the game, we have this line, inviting readers to share Cotter's experience as a sports fan: "You know that thing that happens when you give up before the end and then your team comes back to perform acts of valor and you feel a queasy shame stealing over you like pond slick" (30). Again, at the level of description: "Branca who is twenty-five but makes you think he exemplifies ancient toil" (38). This version of "one" also operates as a form of hypothetical focalization, postulating what readers would perceive were they present at the scene:

> He stands at the curbstone with the others. He is the youngest, at fourteen, and you know he's flatbroke by the edgy leaning look he hangs on his body. (4)

> You can see it in his face, chin thrust out, a glower working under his brow. (30)

The persistent recurrence of this strategy serves to deictically orient readers to the scene by enacting a pseudo-metaleptic move toward the autotelic second person in which the narratee is addressed as a protagonist. The deictic center shifts, however, to follow the variable focalization of the narrator. Here are some examples. In reference to Cotter evading security guards, as if the narratee is an onlooker: "Then you lose him in the crowd" (14). In the middle of a section focalized through Russell Hodges, the commentator in the broadcasting box (but separated by paragraph breaks which invite attributive hesitation):

> Look at Mays meanwhile strolling to the plate dragging the barrel of his bat on the ground. (16)

> Look at Durocher on the dugout steps, manager of the Giants . . . (17)

In the middle of dialogue between Cotter and Bill, a spectator who befriends the kid, as they sit in the stands: "Look at Robinson at the edge of the outfield grass watching the hitter step in and thinking idly, Another one of Leo's country-boy krauts" (22). After a section focalized through J. Edgar Hoover, sitting in another part of the crowd:

> Look at the man in the bleachers who's pacing the aisles, a neighborhood crazy. (28)

> Look at the man in the upper deck. He is tearing pages out of his copy of *Life* and dropping them uncrumpled over the rail, letting them fall in a seesaw drift on the bawling fans below. He is moved to do this by . . . (38)

In each of these instances, the focalizing imperative is directed toward readers as if they were sharing the perception of a character, but supplemented by narratorial knowledge.

Fourth, the second-person pronoun functions as a feature of free indirect discourse in the performance of characters' internal dialogue. In relation to Cotter: "he's located near the tail of the rush, running and shouting with the others. You shout because it makes you brave or you want to announce your recklessness" (4). In relation to Russ Hodges, the broadcaster: "Somebody hands you a piece of paper filled with letters and numbers and you have to make a ballgame out of it" (25). In relation to Bill, who chases Cotter in an attempt to wrest away the home run ball as a souvenir: "Bill stops completely but is too smart to look around. Best to limit your purview to straight ahead. Because you don't know who might be looking back at you. And the more enlightened he becomes, the more open grows the space for Cotter's anger" (57).

All four uses of the second-person pronoun bleed into each other, creating the effect of a narrator both addressing an extradiegetic narratee and positioning this narratee as an intradiegetic participant in the action, linked sometimes to a character, sometimes to a hypothetical onlooker, sometimes to the zero focalization of the narrator. These types are combined in this section: "Dodgers go down in the top of the ninth and this is when you sense a helpless scattering, it is tastable in the air, audible in the lone-wolf class from high in the stands. Nothing you've put into this is recoverable and you don't know whether you want to leave at once or stay forever, living under a blanket in the wind" (34). Here the "you" could refer to the specific thoughts of Cotter, but by virtue of employing the second rather than third person, the passage encompasses the collective consciousness of the crowd as well as functioning as a version of "one."

In the following passages the internal focalization operates as the narrator's psychonarration invoking the collective "one":

> Thompson's not sure he sees things clearly. . . . He is frankly a little fuddled is Bobby. It's like the first waking moment of the day and you don't know whose house you're in. (40)

> He takes a guess, he anticipates, it's the way you feel something will happen and then you watch it uncannily come to pass, occurring almost in measured stages so you can see the wheel-work of your idea fitting into place. (45)

In another section the focalization is with Russell and a colleague, but it doubles as another second-person pseudo-metalepsis: "They leave by way of the Dodger clubhouse and there's Branca all right, the first thing you see, stretched facedown on a flight of six steps, feet touching the floor" (59). In other sections, the focalization doubles as the occasion for narratorial comment: "Russ keeps pausing at the mike to let the sound collect. This is a rumble of a magnitude he has never heard before. You can't call it cheering or rooting. It's a territorial roar, the claim of the ego that separates the crowd from other entities, from political rallies or prison riots—everything outside the walls" (37). In this passage the first two sentences establish the perspective of Russell. The anaphoric reference of the third sentence ("it") may invite us to attribute its account of the "territorial roar" of the crowd to Russ, but the combination of the second-person pronoun with the analysis of the sound lends the last two sentences the authority of narratorial comment employing the informal variant of "one."

Further conflations occur in the following, where the subject of address is both character and narratee:

> And Cotter's hand around the rival's arm, twisting in opposite directions, burning the skin—it's called an Indian burn, remember? (48)

> He holds the ball chest high and turns it in his fingers, which isn't easy when you're running—he rotates the ball on its axis, spins it slowly over and around, showing the two hundred and sixteen raised red cotton stitches.
> Don't tell me you don't love this move. (57)

And here a character momentarily becomes the subject of the address: "Edgar loves this stuff. Edgar, Jedgar. Admit it—you love it. It causes a bristling of his body hair" (50).

The prologue contains one key prolepsis which establishes the narrator's authority as a recorder of history, based on retrospective knowledge:

> There's a man on 12th Street in Brooklyn who has attached a tape machine to his radio so he can record the voice of Russ Hodges broadcasting the game. The man doesn't know why he's doing this. It is just an impulse, a fancy, it is like hearing the game twice, it is like being young and old, and this will turn out to be the only known recording of Russ' famous account of the final moments of the game. The game and its extensions. . . . The game doesn't change the way you sleep or wash your face or chew your food. It changes nothing but your life. (32)

To link back to the opening comment about the making of history, DeLillo's point is made clearly in the final pages of the prologue:

> Russ thinks this is another kind of history. He thinks they will carry something out of here that joins them all in a rare way, *that binds them to a memory* with protective power. People are climbing lampposts on Amsterdam Avenue, tooting car horns in Little Italy. Isn't it possible that *this midcentury moment* enters the skin more lastingly than the vast shaping strategies of eminent leaders, generals steely in their sunglasses—the mapped visions that pierce our dreams? Russ wants to believe a thing like this keeps us safe in some undetermined way. This is the thing that *will pulse in his brain come old age* and double vision and dizzy spells—the surge sensation, the leap of people already standing, that bolt of noise and joy when the ball went in. This is *the people's history* and it has flesh and breath that quickens to the force of this old safe game of ours. (59, emphasis added)

Here is the notion of cultural memory, which perhaps the second person facilitates. While the passage contains Russell's focalized thoughts about the significance of the game as a form of local, communal history, the phrase "midcentury moment" evokes the sense of history established by temporal distance, and the line "the thing that will pulse in his brain come old age" performs the function of a prolepsis as much as a character thought.

The range of grammatical uses of the second person which I have identified continue throughout the novel—"She was fifty-four now, let that number rumble in your head" (372)—along with the use of second-person narration. According to David Pike, DeLillo echoes the trope of the Asmodean devil with his metaphorical explorations of the word underworld, and "by sustaining a rooftop vantage point throughout the novel that clearly echoes his own authorial position typing away on his Olympus" (86). By this Pike means that throughout the novel perspective is often oriented to characters looking down from on high, from Russell Hodges in the broadcaster's booth to Klara Sax on her rooftop to Nick Shay in a hot air balloon. He goes on to claim that "for all his omniscience, DeLillo's narrator resolves nothing. . . . The halting devil has enough chthonic power to unroof the secrets of the urban world to us but not enough either to gloss them or to make them cohere" (89).

To coincide with the publication of *Underworld,* DeLillo wrote an article for the *New York Times* titled "The Power of History." In this article he presents the novel as under threat from the consumptive speed of contemporary culture: "Maybe it is the evanescent spectacle of contemporary life that makes the novel so nervous" (2–3). DeLillo argues that the collapse of time in our contemporary experience is evident in the way that celebrity becomes instantaneous, pervasive, and then evanescent. "The fast-forward nature of the decade is an apt subject for a novelist. But the novel itself, the old, slow water-torture business of invention and doubt and self-correction, may seem to be wearing an expiration date that takes effect tomorrow" (3). He goes on to suggest that fiction can find significance in the evocation of history as a counterpoint to the spectacle of contemporary life: "In a period of empty millennial frenzy, we may begin to see a precious integrity in the documents of an earlier decade or century" (3).

The essay's argument hinges upon DeLillo's account of the genesis of *Underworld,* the accidental discovery in the archives of a newspaper with two items on its front page: the Giants' victory in the playoffs, and the Soviet atomic bomb test. This moment is presented as a discovery of the power of history, thus framing the prologue to *Underworld* as not only a fictional demonstration of this power, but a demonstration of the novelist's capacity to find connections in the past which are beyond the scope of historical discourse: "Against the force of history, so powerful, visible and real, the novelist poses the idiosyncratic self" (4) Here DeLillo replicates the standard claim for the capacity of fiction to imaginatively recuperate the private, unwritten experiences of history: "Fiction will always examine the small anonymous corners or human experience. But there is also the magnetic force of public events and people behind them" (4). And he romanticizes this capacity in terms of the language of fiction itself:

> There is pleasure to be found, the writer's, the reader's, in a version of the past that escapes the coils of established history and biography and that finds a language, scented, dripping, detailed, for such routine realities as sex, weather and food, for the ravel of a red thread on a woman's velvet sleeve. (8)

The essay argues for the capacity of fiction to harness the "power of history" in more effective ways than historical language can, but not in the service of recuperating the past from the archive. Instead, DeLillo mobilizes the claims of the novelist as literary historian to explicitly establish his authority to intervene in contemporary cultural life.

This article performs DeLillo's own critical interpretation of his novel. In the prologue to *Underworld,* the narrative voice draws its authority from a showy display of omniscience in which the presence is DeLillo's. The link between narrative and authorial voice encouraged by DeLillo's omniscient narrator enables his comments in "The Power of History" to provide the narratorial commentary at the level of public discourse, sitting alongside the novel, even as the novel performs in fictional form the point DeLillo wishes to make about the role of the novel. While individual readers may or not have knowledge of this article when reading *Underworld,* an approach to fiction as public discourse makes it clear that DeLillo is asserting his narrative authority through a conjunction of authorial and narrative voice, each one reinforcing his claims as a social commentator.

Jonathan Franzen, *The Corrections* (2001)

> Franzen's *Harper's* essay proposed, in effect, a softened DeLilloism. What is retained from DeLillo is the tentacular ambition, the effort to pin down an entire writhing culture. The DeLilloian idea of the novelist as a kind of Frankfurt School entertainer, fighting the culture with dialectical devilry, has been woefully influential, and will take some time to die.
>
> —James Wood, *The Irresponsible Self* 190

> Clearly Mr. Franzen's novel would have benefited enormously from a strict editing job. There are lengthy digressions about Lambert friends and acquaintances,

which serve no purpose but to provide the author with a wider array of social types to send up; and there are passages where the omniscient narrator's voice gratuitously intrudes to tell us exactly what we are witnessing.

—Michiko Kakutani, "A Family Portrait as Metaphor for the 90's"

Authorial presence in *The Corrections* is not manifested in overt intrusive commentary, despite Kakutani's complaint quoted above, at least not in the form of direct addresses to the reader. However, there are evaluations of character embedded in narratorial summary and passages of internal focalization describing aspects of the character's motivations of which they themselves are unaware or unwilling to admit, and which cumulatively establish a detached assessment of the flaws and interrelations of the Lambert family:

> Unfortunately Enid lacked the temperament to manage such a house, and Alfred lacked the neurological wherewithal. (6)

> None of this occurred to Denise then or after. She was still feeling responsible ten years later. (367)

> She was too proud to admit to herself, let alone to Don Armour, that he wasn't what she wanted. She was too inexperienced to know she simply could have said, "Sorry—big mistake." . . . She suffered for her reluctance. (375)

The omniscient or polymathic knowledge of the narrator, as well as his stylistic presence, is more specifically performed through the recurring metaphor of "corrections" which links the exploration of intergenerational family dynamics with a broader account of the corporate health industry and the global economy. This metaphor begins with the individual, charting how three siblings each view their lives in relation to the influence of their parents. The character Chip Lambert, we are told, had a lengthy, unsatisfying relationship with a woman whom he supported through college and beyond as a defiant response to his father's belief in maintaining rigid distinctions between "Men's Work and Women's Work": "in a spirit of correction, he stuck with Tori for nearly a decade" (33). Chip's brother, Gary, is burdened with acute depression, and the narrator reveals through internal analysis that "his entire life was set up as a correction of his father's life" (181). Later in the book, an analeptic scene shows their father, Alfred, contemplating his unborn child, Denise: "A last child was a last opportunity to learn from one's mistakes and make corrections, and he resolved to seize this opportunity" (281). By virtue of being isolated in its own paragraph, the following line could be attributed to Alfred or the narrator: "What made correction possible also doomed it" (281). The metaphor recurs with Denise, where, again through internal analysis, the gradual erosion of her lifelong antipathy toward her mother is described in these terms: "Not until she was at the pier and her mother kissed her . . . did the extent of the correction she was undergoing reveal itself" (425). And on the final page, when Enid reflects upon the death of her husband, Alfred, we have this line: "The one thing he never forgot was how to refuse. All of her correction had been for naught" (567).

Central to the plot is a breakthrough in neurobiological therapy extolled by a corporate representative as "Corecktall," for "disorders of the brain" such as Parkinson's and Alzheimer's, and the "social disease" of criminality, unchecked by traditional correctional institutions (208). A spokesperson for Axon Corporation describes prisons as having "zero corrective benefit, and, just to keep this in mind, *still the basic model for corrections in the United States today*" (209, original emphasis). The economic sense of the word, in which free markets return to equilibrium, is also used: "Bearish analysts, mindful of recent gutwrenching corrections in the biotech sector, were cautioning against investing in an untested medical technology that was at least six years from market" (189–90). The denouement of the final chapter opens: "The correction, when it finally came, was not an overnight bursting of a bubble, but a much more gentle letdown, a year-long leakage of value from key financial markets" (563). This correction to the global market occurs as the volatile family dynamics of the Lamberts settle down in the wake of the death of the patriarch, Alfred.

With this recurring word, across internal analysis, narratorial comment, and interior monologue, the narrator encourages us to see how the desire to correct neurological disorders and aberrant social behavior is facilitated by an intrusion of the market economy on all aspects of life. A central thread of the story is the attempt by Alfred's children to secure money from Axon Corporation for using Alfred's patented discovery to develop Corecktall. In one scene, Gary and Denise attend a promotional dinner at which Axon executives are extolling the benefits of Corecktall to potential investors. "Simply put," a company spokesperson says, "Corecktall offers for the first time the possibility of renewing and *improving* the hard wiring of the human brain" (189, original emphasis). Gary's motivation for attending is explained by the narrator as both entrepreneurial and as part of his desire to correct his father's mistakes in the conduct of his own life: "He saw an opportunity here to make some money and avenge Axon's screwing of his father and more generally, be *bold* where Alfred has been *timid*" (190, original emphasis). As the benefits of the drug are explained we have this interchange between Gary and Denise:

> "We've got to get Dad signed up for testing," Denise whispered.
> "What do you mean?" Gary said.
> "Well, this is for Parkinson's. It could help him."
> Gary sighed like a tire losing air. How could it be that such an incredibly obvious idea had never occurred to him? He felt ashamed of himself and, at the same time, obscurely resentful of Denise. (199)

The metaphorical connection between the market and mental health is then shown to penetrate into modes of thought, especially centered on Gary, a banker who cannot admit that he is depressed. In his constant state of self-assessment he believes in "the overall robustness of his mental economy. He was not the least bit clinically depressed" (140). Later we have this metaphor: "Ordinarily Gary wouldn't have let Aaron get away with this. Ordinarily he would have battled his son all evening if that was what it took to extract an apology from him. But his mental markets—glycemic, endocrine, over-the-synapse—were crashing" (161–62). The metaphor is then embedded in Gary's consciousness: "*What this stagnating economy needs,* thought Federal Reserve Board Chairman Gary R. Lambert, is a massive infusion of *Bombay Sapphire Gin*" (162, original emphasis).

The thematic connection between the personal and social afforded by the word "correction" extends to a connection between narrative and authorial voice in the title of the book itself. The recurring metaphor of Franzen's narrator—our desire to correct a perceived malaise in ourselves and in our culture—clearly underpins the argument of Franzen's famous *Harper's* essay. If we approach fiction as one mode of public discourse available to the writer alongside others (such as the journalistic, the essayistic, etc.), this continuum across the discourses of fiction and nonfiction is more important to an understanding of narrative authority than any generic or "ontological" distinction between narrator and author. The *Harper's* essay, titled "Perchance to Dream: In the Age of Images, a Reason to Write Novels," is a perfect example of the perceived crisis of the novelist I outlined in chapter 1, functioning as an agonistic bid for the cultural authority—defined in the essay as "an appeal beyond the academy, a presence in household conversations" (47)—required to assert the significance of *The Corrections* to public life. The essay anatomizes a crisis in American culture which Franzen attributes to "technological consumerism": the conditioning of social behavior by the logic of the economy and the pervasiveness of electronic media. One result of this conditioning, Franzen argues, is the decline of readership for serious literature, because electronic media has both usurped the role of fiction as social report and reduced the attention span required to read long novels, demonstrating "the incompatibility of the slow work of reading and the hyperkinesis of modern life" (39).[1] Furthermore, the gratifications of the self afforded by a consumer economy have diminished the desire for connection with other minds (both characters and the author) which the novel traditionally provided. In the course of this argument, Franzen harkens back to the authority of the nineteenth-century novel sustained by a culture of readership:

> A century ago, the novel was the preeminent medium of social instruction. A new book by William Dean Howells was anticipated with the kind of fever that today a new Pearl Jam release inspires. The big, obvious reason that the social novel has become so scarce is that modern technologies do a better job of social instruction. Television, radio, and photographs are vivid, instantaneous media. Print journalism, in the wake of *In Cold Blood,* has become a viable creative alternative to the novel. (41)

The crux of Franzen's essay is the challenge facing novelists today who are committed to the oppositional criticism of the social realist novel, embodied in his own "despair about the possibility of connecting the personal and the social" (36). Franzen's decision to frame this essay as a confessional account of his personal depression performs this very connection of the personal and the social in his nonfictional authorial voice: "does the distress I feel derive from some internal sickness of the soul, or is it imposed on me by the sickness of society?" (36). Anchoring his critique of the diminished "social currency" (38) of the novel, its inability to combat the problems of American society, is the story of how he grapples with his own sense of obsolescence and irrelevance (his words) as a novelist in contemporary culture.

In a consumer economy fuelled by the speed of information dissemination, Franzen argues, a novelist's desire to bring the news to society is doomed because this news will become out of date before the novel is even published. In the course of the essay he criticizes Tom Wolfe's 1989 manifesto, pointing out Wolfe's "failure to explain why his ideal New Social Novelist should not be writing scripts for Hollywood" (42). He also echoes David Foster Wallace's manifesto in his critique of television—"television has killed the novel of social reportage" (42)—and the lack of genuine relationships between people fostered by "our technological and economic systems" (44) designed to gratify our self-oriented needs. There is a further echo of Wallace's trope of the (white male) fiction writer as an exemplar of the disconnected self, performing this trope in confessional fashion: "But of course the more TV I watched the worse I felt about myself. If you're a novelist and even *you* don't feel like reading, how can you expect anyone else to read your books?" (40).

The narrative arc of this personal essay is Franzen's path out of depression throughout the 1990s, from the end of his second novel—the "culturally engaged" *The Twenty-Seventh City* which failed to engage with the culture—to the writing of his third novel, which would become *The Corrections*. Ultimately, the essay is a story about how he overcame writer's block by abandoning his ambition to write the all-encompassing social novel in favor of a novel of character, by realizing that "bringing 'meaningful news' is no longer so much a defining function of the novel as an accidental by-product" (48). This epiphany enables him to claim: "To write sentences of such authenticity that refuge can be taken in them: isn't this enough? Isn't it a lot?" (49). And to realize, personally, "that the despair I felt about the novel was less the result of my obsolescence than of my isolation" (50). This enables him to claim that the novel is crucial for establishing a community of writers and readers, like-minded, lonely people who take comfort in the solace of fiction. Finishing his third novel, then, became a path out of loneliness to reconnect with a diminishing community of writers and readers. His conclusion is that once he abandoned the desire to compete with contemporary media and attended to the unique qualities of fiction, its use of language, its construction of character, the connection of the social and the personal would be a natural outcome.

In terms of the interrelation between cultural and narrative authority, the *Harper's* essay enabled Franzen to offer, in advance of *The Corrections,* an authorial "direct address" to the culture which overtly provides the public context for his novel: a sweeping critique of American foreign policy, national debt, the solipsistic victimhood of multiculturalism, environmental degradation, the pursuit of money and self-gratification, the opiate of mass culture, the problems of academe, the economics of the book publishing industry, and so on. In his essay he criticizes "the ideology of the market economy" and its consumer products, listing all the technological changes he saw taking place as a result: "I saw leaf-blowers replacing rakes" (39). In the opening paragraph of *The Corrections*, we have a description of an eerie pre-storm suburban afternoon which includes a reference to "the nasal contention of a leaf blower" (3), establishing an oblique lexical continuum between the novel and the essay. The *Harper's* essay successfully established one of the most powerfully centripetal paratexts in contemporary fiction, exploiting the very genre of victimized confessionalism which Franzen critiques in fiction, and locating *The Corrections* in a larger extrafictional narrative of the novelist's search for cultural authority. In the essay's confessional nature we see a recognition of the genre required to connect with an audience in the marketplace of celebrity and personality, despite Franzen's critique of this marketplace: "To speak extranovelistically in an age of personalities seemed to be a betrayal; it implied a lack of faith in fiction's adequacy as communication and self-expression" (50).

When the *Harper's* essay was republished in 2002 in a collection of his nonfiction, Franzen claims in the preface that interviewers constantly asked whether he saw *The Corrections* as the fulfillment of his essay's promise that his third book would be a big social novel. His response, each time, Franzen writes, was that they had misread his intention, for *The Corrections* was written out of a desire to escape from that ambition. He then writes that the essay is in fact highly confused but should be preserved as a document of his feelings at the time, as "a stalled novelist's escape from the prison of his angry thoughts" (5). In this way, Franzen leaves open for continued speculation the link between the essay and the novel.

Some critics have enthusiastically taken up the narrative of Franzen as the savior of the social novel in the wake of postmodernism. For instance, in a cringe-inducing, self-important review of Franzen's latest novel, *Freedom*, in the *New York Times,* Sam Tanehaus claimed that, in the wake of September 11, 2001, *The Corrections* "towered out of the rubble, at once a monument to a world destroyed and a beacon lighting the way for a new kind of novel that might break the suffocating grip of postmodernism" (11). Tanehaus quotes James Woods's critique of hysterical realism to categorize the sort of postmodern writing prevalent at the time. Taking up Franzen's infectious metaphor, Tanehaus asserts that *The Corrections* "did not so much repudiate all this as surgically 'correct' it. Franzen cracked open the opaque shell of postmodernism, tweezed out its tangled circuitry and inserted in its place the warm, beating heart of an authentic humanism" (10).

Academic critics, on the other hand, have been anxious to preserve Franzen's postmodern credentials, established in his earlier novels. In his 2008 book, *Jonathan Franzen at the End of Postmodernism*, Stephen Burn writes:

> Jonathan Franzen occupies a revealing position amongst America's millennial novelists. While critics at century's end began to anatomize the end of postmodernism, . . . the conflict between postmodern innovation and more conventional narrative forms was internalized and played out in Franzen's novels and essays. (ix)

And Fitzpatrick positions Franzen, along with DeLillo, as the exemplar of the postmodern novelist's anxiety of obsolescence.

Richard Powers, *Generosity* (2009)

> Having seen a glimpse of the future, Powers has also become known as one of the twenty-first century's notable writers of big cosmic novels to make frequent use of that most nineteenth century of literary devices, the omniscient narrator.
>
> —Jan Alexander, "Happy People Need Love Too"

I conclude with Richard Powers's *Generosity*. Stephen Burn ("The End") classifies Powers as a post-postmodern novelist for the way he combines the techniques of realist fiction with experimental metafiction and deploys this combination to explore the tension between art and science as modes of explicating human behavior. In *Generosity*, Powers's intrusive omniscient narrator bleeds across both the social commentator in the way he displays comprehensive knowledge of genetic science in a commentary on the preoccupations of late capitalism, and the ironic moralist in his metafictional reflections on the possibilities of writing to establish human relations.

In *Generosity*, the conventional authority of the omniscient narrator is complicated by the events of the story itself, which concern current scientific research into the operation of the mind. If, by literary convention, the highest authority is granted to a narrator who has access to the minds of characters, and the novelist's traditional insight into human nature is predicated on this access, the omniscient narrator of *Generosity* is cognizant of the challenge to his authority presented by scientific knowledge of consciousness. This awareness is highlighted in the following passage of thought report: "She sits in the rocker for a moment, examining herself. It's not even an effort, really. Not even a decision. Just large molecules, passing their oldest signals back and forth across the infinite synapse gap" (179). In this scene, the host of a science television show, Tonia Schiff, is deciding whether to stay overnight with the scientist Thomas Kurtzon, with whom she has spent the day as part of her research for a documentary film. The first line is reminiscent of a novel by Ann Radcliffe or Jane Austen in which the heroine sits down to review the virtue of her conduct, or of the cue for an extended interior monologue such as Isabel Archer's in James's *Portrait of a Lady*. Instead, it is followed by three sentences eschewing internal analysis in favor of a comment on the workings of the brain, which is as much as to say, why try to represent a character's thoughts which can be reduced to a neurological process? A paragraph later, there is one line of direct discourse: "*I have no center*. The thought wastes her. Not even a thought: just a fact the exact size of her body. She's disappeared into playing herself. She has no clue what her bliss is, and trying to follow it would lead worse than nowhere" (179–80).

Generosity, like Powers's earlier novels, is thus an example of what Gary Johnson calls neuronarrative: a subgenre of narrative fiction in which novelists engage with new advances in cognitive studies to explore the problem of human consciousness. Johnson's two examples in his essay "Consciousness as Content: Neuronarratives and the Redemption of Fiction" are Powers's *Galatea 2.2* and David Lodge *Thinks*. He also includes Franzen's *The Corrections,* Ian McEwan's *Saturday,* and A. S. Byatt's *A Whistling Woman*. One could add Wolfe's *I Am Charlotte Simmons* to this list. The challenge for the fiction writer which these works explore, according to Johnson, is that working with consciousness in the wake of cognitive science involves "an epistemological dimension as well as a mimetic one" (171) for scientific research now offers knowledge of the human mind not available until recent decades. If the technical challenge for novelists has traditionally been how to represent consciousness, thus relating to the level of narrative discourse, developments in science now make it necessary for novelists to consider consciousness a problem at the level of story. In this context, Johnson argues that

> the encroachment of neuroscience on the field of literature results in a kind of revaluation of narrative fiction on the part of novelists who produce it. Even as neurologists, psychologists, medical doctors and others in the scientific community embrace narrative as a legitimate area of

inquiry, Lodge and Powers seem to need to convince themselves of the potential value of narrative fiction. (172)

Johnson talks about how Lodge and Powers seem to use their books as occasions to reevaluate the value of fiction in the light of cognitive studies, although he makes no conclusion about what the novels offer, beyond the continued mutual skepticism of art and science and the significance of human consciousness as an area of fictional "content." Instead, Johnson dwells on what he considers one "of the most fascinating characteristics of neuronarratives . . . the novelist's perceived need to inform his or her audience about the current state of neuroscience. To put this in narratological terms, the authors seem compelled to facilitate the readers' entry into the 'authorial audience'" (174). I don't find this "perceived need" as fascinating as Johnson: it is simply a demand of the craft of writing. What is fascinating is how Johnson describes the writer's craft of dramatic exposition in terms of the social function of the public intellectual, defined by Russell Jacoby as "writers and thinkers who address a general and educated audience" (5). According to Johnson: "Lodge's and Powers's neuronarratives serve two important epistemological functions: they implicitly validate the notion that science produces a kind of useful and true knowledge and they artfully disseminate that knowledge to the lay public" (180).

The omniscient narrator's authority in *Generosity,* then, relies upon its function as an authorial proxy for the figure of the novelist as public intellectual: a translator of specialized knowledge through the genre of fiction, and a social commentator on the current cultural state. The specialized knowledge which informs the book is genomics. The plot revolves around the fate of Thassadit Amzar, a young Algerian refugee whose beatific, almost unsettling, optimism belies the trauma of her past. She becomes the object of study for Thomas Kurtzon, an entrepreneurial scientist who believes she may possess what he has identified as the "happiness gene." Research into genetic dispositions for happiness is ongoing and was reported in newspapers and popular science magazines in the two years preceding Powers's novel. While much of this scientific knowledge is dispensed through the dialogue and thoughts of Kurtzon, it also informs the commentary of the intrusive narrator. The universal here is couched in the authority of science, for the characters' motivations are examined not from the perspective of the Thackerayan "observer of human nature" but from that of a scientifically knowledgeable narrator who can explain characters in terms of genetic coding and evolutionary science. Commenting on an awkward scene of budding courtship between the protagonist, Russell Stone, who is Thassa's writing teacher, and Candace Weld, a psychologist, the narrator writes: "They stand there awkwardly, two more victims of natural selection, caught between negativity bias and the eternal belief that the future will be slightly better than the present" (96).

The narrator does not assume a posture of specialized knowledge so much as one of general commentary. "According to many of the two thousand new self-help titles that appear every year . . . nothing short of pharmaceuticals can help sustain contentment as much as a satisfying job" (38). Musing on the level of job satisfaction that Russell might experience, the narrator comments: "What pleasure does he get from his selfless editing? Stone strikes me as the kind of guy who might not know what his pleasures *are*. He's not alone. No one does: the happiness books are adamant on this. We're shaped to think the things we want will make us happy. But shaped to take only the briefest thrill in getting. *Wanting* is what *having* wants to recover" (38). This narratorial comment reveals the thematic crux of the novel, shifting from a supposition about the character to a comment on human nature, complete with the aphoristic final sentence, but its authority is couched less in the universal wisdom of the narrator, than in a report on the science of happiness.

The paradigm of evolutionary genetics underpins narratorial commentary throughout the novel: "From where I sit, the whole human race did something stupid when young—pulled some playful stunt that damaged someone. The secret of survival is forgetting" (19). This model of narrative authority also extends to reflections on the role of the novel itself. "In my country," the narrator points out in an intrusive interlude, "a new work of fiction is published every thirty minutes. . . . I try to calculate how many of those million-and-growing volumes are saddled with a romance—bright or doomed, healthy or diseased. I can't do the math. Surely it must be most of them" (94–95). The narrator goes on to offer a reason for this proliferation:

> Sexual selection, the surest and most venerable form of eugenics, has molded us into the fiction-needing readers we are today. Part of me would love to belong to a species free, now and then, to read about something other than its own imprisonment. The rest of me knows that the novel will always be a kind of Stockholm syndrome—love letters to the urge that has abducted us. (94–95)

The hesitation about the novelist's role in explaining human nature seems to underpin the metafictional anxiety which animates the intrusive presence of the narrator. The determinism of evolutionary science which provides the model for "universalizing" commentary about human nature finds its parallel in self-reflexive addresses to the reader about the fatalism of generic plot structures: "So you know this story: *Lord Jim,* or a plot to that effect" (15); "He knows this story. *You* know this story: Thassa will be taken away from him" (87); "Of course they had to arrive here, eventually. What self-respecting author would let them escape alive?" (262). These comments function less to assert the authorial narrator's creative control over the fictional world, or to satirize the artificiality of plot, than to demonstrate his own "imprisonment" by narrative structures. I engage further with the novel's metafictionality in chapter 7.

From Minimalism to Maximalism

Richard Powers has long been considered one of the most knowledgeable and intelligent contemporary novelists for his capacity to draw upon a range of disciplines to explain how the world works. In a 1998 article, "Ecologies of Knowledge: The Encyclopedic Narratives of Richard Powers and His Contemporaries," Trey Strecker claims that, following the lead of Pynchon, a number of contemporary novelists, including Powers, David Foster Wallace and William Volkman, are producing encyclopedic narratives distinguished by the disparate range of information systems they organize in their novels. "One notable feature of these encyclopedists' books is the diversity of specialized knowledge—from biology, chemistry, economics, entomology, linguistics, music, mythology, painting, physics, psychology, and other fields—that they process" (68). What prevents these novels from being mere compendiums of knowledge, argues Strecker, is the "imposition of narrative. For when narrative enters a static encyclopedic system, a living, evolving textual ecology unfolds" (68).

Obviously the figure which holds this knowledge together, organizing and directing it through narrative, is the author who becomes a kind of public intellectual synthesizing specialized knowledge for readers. The polymathic narrator is a clear proxy for this authorial figure, drawing upon and reinforcing the authority of the novelist. The narrator's authority is less a product of reliable knowledge of the fictional world than of a capacity to mobilize a range of extraliterary discourses to make sense of this world. "The new encyclopedists," according to Strecker, "do not capitulate to the overwhelming amount of information in postmodern culture" (69). The narrator of *Generosity* is clearly concerned with the problem of this excess of information, as he points out in an intrusive comment: "The price of information is falling to zero. You can now have almost all of it, anytime, anywhere, for next to nothing. The great majority of data can't even be given away. But meaning is like land: no one is making any more of it" (110).

All four modes of narrative authority employed by contemporary omniscient narrators, but in particular the last two, indicate a general shift in fiction from minimalism to maximalism. Throughout the 1980s minimalism of the kind exemplified in the tradition from Hemingway to Carver was considered dominant in American fiction and slated home to the problem of writing workshops. John W. Aldridge's *Talents and Technicians: Literary Chic and the New Assembly-line Fiction* (1992) is a good example of this type of criticism. As James Wood's critique suggests, minimalism is not so much a problem now as its opposite. In a 2004 article titled "The War for the Soul of Literature," Laura Miller argues that what Wood denounces as "hysterical realism," and what Dale Peck calls "recherche postmodernism," can be understood in terms of this shift. For Miller, maximalism, in the form of the big ambitious social novel, has become the new focus of complaint about the direction of contemporary fiction, replacing Carveresque minimalism which had prevailed for the previous two decades as a symptom of literary decline.

The return of omniscience in contemporary fiction has been facilitated by the emergence of encyclopedic fictional narratives as an assertion of novelistic authority in the postmodern knowledge economy. Maximalist fiction need not necessarily be omniscient in narration, but the scope and narrative freedom of omniscience certainly lends itself to an expansive exploration of social relations, and the garrulousness of narrative voice which maximalism encourages is a means of competing with the dynamism of other discourses in the marketplace of opinion and entertainment.

What James Wood lamented in his "Hysterical Realism" essay as the hardening genre of the "big ambitious novel" is now being located in history by scholars as the contemporary manifestation of the impulse traced in Franco Moretti's *Modern Epic: The World System from Goethe to García Márquez*. For instance, in a 2009 essay, "'The Death of the Novel' and Its Afterlives: Toward a History of the 'Big Ambitious Novel,'" Mark Greif writes: "One knows that Thomas Pynchon's *Gravity's Rainbow,* William Gaddis's *J R,* David Foster Wallace's *Infinite Jest,* and William T.

Vollmann's *Europe Central* help draw a circle around a particular form of the novel, if not quite a genre" (11). As his title suggests, Greif argues that the "'big ambitious novel' as it emerged in the postwar period first appeared in response to, then came to depend upon, the maintenance of a conceit of the 'death of the novel'" (12). First gaining traction with Lionel Trilling and other literary critics in the 1950s—who saw the novel's decline resulting from genre exhaustion, changed social conditions, and the speed of contemporary life—this conceit was perpetuated by writers as a literary challenge, articulated in essays from Philip Roth's "Writing American Fiction" (1961) to the essays by Wallace and Franzen which I have discussed here. "Vitality," Greif suggests, "becomes its own pursuit in an age when 'the death of the novel' is a presumption that never can be laid to rest" (27). Significantly, he points out that these meganovels

> rejected the first-person narration of Ellison and Bellow for a kaleidoscopic 'third-person close,' in which all knowing is accomplished through countless limited and idiosyncratic characters who together prove a kind of encyclopedic or superhuman range that must belong to the author but is never acknowledged as an authorial possession. (28)

Here we see that what is vital to these novels is the projection of a figure of the author as polymath, as omniscient in the hyperbolic rather than divine sense of the word. The narrative voices of these novels, then, in combination with their authorial statements, seek to carve out a space for the cultural importance of the novel and the status of the author in the public sphere.

In his 2012 essay, "The Maximalist Novel," Stefano Ercolino sets out to define the contemporary maximalist novel as a genre and place it in relation to postmodernism. Ercolino argues that this genre emerged in the United States in the last quarter of the twentieth century with Pynchon's *Gravity's Rainbow* before emigrating to Europe in the new millennium with novels such as Roberto Bolaño's *2666*. His examples include the usual suspects of Wallace's *Infinite Jest,* Smith's *White Teeth,* DeLillo's *Underworld,* and Franzen's *The Corrections,* and he names novels by William T. Vollmann and Richard Powers. According to Ercolino, "there are ten elements that define and structure" the maximalist novel "as a genre of the contemporary novel: length, encyclopaedic mode, dissonant chorality, diegetic exuberance, completeness, narratorial omniscience, paranoid imagination, inter-semioticity, ethical commitment, and hybrid realism" (242). For Ercolino, certain of these elements, such as encyclopedic mode and diegetic exuberance, are centrifugal in their function while others, such as narratorial omniscience and paranoia, operate as a centripetal countermeasure.

Ercolino understands omniscience purely in terms of focalization, as a "narrative regime" which operates on both the micro-structural level of the fragment and the macro-structural level of the narrative as a whole. By this he means that despite the range of shifts in focalization and substantial sections of internal focalization, the sum of the parts in each novel constitutes a freedom of perspective best understood as omniscience. He claims that omniscience

> is the consequence of the particularly pressing demand to lend order to the novelistic representation; as a result, there is a fundamental need to construct a narratorial gaze capable of perceiving from above, and thus of dominating the entire narrative flow. This does not mean, of course, that in every maximalist novel the narrator must necessarily be omniscient; however omniscience is a narrative mood that adapts itself more efficiently than others to the control of the narrative material. (249)

In keeping with my argument in this book, focalization is best understood as a rhetorical strategy of the narrator, as the product of the "generating instance" of narrative voice. Hence, to talk of a "narratorial gaze" we must link this gaze to a narrator. Ercolino also sees omniscience as crucially linked to paranoia, which "remains the engine of maximalist literary imagination" (250). The idea that everything is linked is

> the indestructible conviction of the paranoid, a conviction that finds its formal correspondence in the interconnection (direct or indirect) of all the stories, all the characters, and all the events with which maximalist novels are filled. . . . Such an interconnection could have no more effective support than an omniscient narratorial regime in which the hyper-vigilant gaze of the narrator controls the narrative material as a whole. (250)

Here Ercolino seems to be suggesting that the narrative voice supports and facilitates the paranoid imagination, indicating that the controlling presence of Providence in classic omniscience has become the paranoia of contemporary omniscience.

We could characterize contemporary omniscience as a verbose narrative voice nostalgically invoking the friend and guide of classic omniscience, or desperately filling the silence left by the postmodern absence of character. But we could more productively approach this narrative voice as a kind of heuristic technique, where form is generated by the architectonic function of the sentence as a line of flight. The idiosyncrasy of Wolfe's prose stems from his claim in *The New Journalism,* that journalists who deploy the techniques of fiction in the service of nonfiction writing are free from the constraints of aesthetic convention governing point of view and other narrative elements. "For the gluttonous Goths," Wolf wrote, "there is still only the outlaw's rule regarding technique: take, use, improvise" (48).

Narrative form here is not determined by any sense of formal unity, by the categories of narrative theory, but by the writer's authority as a reporter of contemporary culture. For the social commentator, the tentacular reach of omniscience is underpinned by a creative freedom at the syntactic level. As Don DeLillo explained in an interview about the writing of *Underworld:*

> The prologue is written with a sort of super-omniscience. There are sentences that may begin in one part of the ballpark and end in another. I wanted to open up the sentence. They become sort of travel-happy; they travel from one person's mind to another. I did it largely because it was pleasurable. It was baseball itself that provided a kind of freedom that perhaps I hadn't quite experienced before. It was the game. (DePetrio 136)

CHAPTER 6

Voice and Free Indirect Discourse in Contemporary Omniscient Narration

> To read a sentence as free indirect discourse, we must indeed use our ingenuity. We must infer who is quoted and which words of the sentence are quotation.
>
> —Ann Waldron Neumann,
> "Characterization and Comment in *Pride and Prejudice*" 390

IN CHAPTERS 2–5, I focused on the ways in which contemporary omniscient narrators draw attention to the narrating instance to rhetorically perform their narrative authority: mobilizing the function of narration via overt commentary and direct addresses to the reader; displaying the proleptic knowledge of history enabled by the spatio-temporal distance of the narrator from the storyworld; asserting their stylistic presence through metaphorical excess and linguistic control over characters' thoughts; and offering synoptic wisdom through the display of polymathic knowledge in which nonliterary paradigms of knowledge (history, journalism, science) compete with the narrator's conventional insight into the psychological interior of characters to explain "human nature." As discussed in previous chapters, reliable knowledge of characters' interior lives has typically been seen as the basis of narrative authority. In this chapter I investigate how contemporary omniscient narrators perform their "privileged" access to the consciousness of characters and the concept of the self that emerges from the formal techniques employed. If we accept that a general sensibility of fiction after postmodernism is its attempt to explore the problem of character as a knowable human self, distinct from a postmodern critique of subjectivity embedded in the realist concept of character, then the representation of characters' psychological interior, of their consciousness, becomes a key area of investigation. Contemporary omniscient narrators explore this problem of character, I will argue, through a self-reflexive manipulation of existing conventions of thought representation.

I will begin by quoting a lengthy passage from chapter 22 of Walter Scott's 1822 novel, *The Fortunes of Nigel*:

> At length his meditations arranged themselves in the following soliloquy—by which expression I beg leave to observe once for all, that I do not mean that Nigel literally said aloud with his bodily organs, the words which follow in inverted commas, (while pacing the room by himself,) but that I myself choose to present to my dearest reader the picture of my hero's mind, his reflections and resolutions, in the form of a speech, rather than in that of a narrative. In other words, I have put his thoughts into language; and this I conceive to be the purpose of the soliloquy upon the stage as well as in the closet, being at once the most natural, and perhaps the only way of communicating to the spectator what is supposed to be passing in the bosom of the scenic personage. . . . In narrative, no doubt, the writer has the alternative of telling that his personages thought so and so, inferred thus and thus, and arrived at such and such a conclusion; but the soliloquy is a more concise and spirited mode of communicating the same information; and therefore thus communed, or thus might have communed, the Lord of Glenvarloch with his own mind. (295–96)

In this passage Walter Scott's omniscient narrator shares with readers the choice between two modes of representing consciousness: reporting a character's thoughts through narratorial summary or quoting them in the form of a soliloquy. What this self-reflexive comment highlights is the artificial and hypothetical nature of translating thoughts into speech: "thus communed, or thus might have communed, the Lord of Glenvarloch with his own mind." Histories of the novel tell us that authors from Jane Austen onwards pioneered ways of combining the quotation of inner thoughts with the voice of the narrator in the grammatical form of free indirect discourse (FID), and trace the development of this technique from ironic narratorial distance in the nineteenth century to empathetic figural closeness in the twentieth. As Casey Finch and Peter Bowen claim, "the development in Austen's hands of free indirect style marks a crucial moment in the history of novelistic technique in which narrative authority is seemingly elided, ostensibly giving way to what Flaubert called a transparent style in which the author is 'everywhere felt, but never seen'" (3). In describing this elision of narrative authority as a key feature of the move away from the intrusive presence of the omniscient narrator in Victorian fiction to the effaced presence of the narrator in modernist fiction, these histories tend to present FID as a means of liberating character consciousness from that of their creator. "Imagine FID," writes Kathy Mezei, "as an expression of the character's bid for freedom from the controlling narrator" (68).

In *The Dual Voice*, one of the earliest comprehensive studies of FID in the novel, Roy Pascal takes up where Percy Lubbock left off, providing an historical account of the progression from indirect to direct means of representing consciousness, clearly echoing Lubbock in his account of Flaubert's *Madam Bovary* as the historical touchstone. According to Pascal:

> Flaubert wanted to hide the very function of story-telling, as it were, to allow the story to tell and interpret itself, as far as this was possible; hence the narrator should, as he put it, "transport himself into his characters." Thus free indirect speech is not an occasional device, nor something employed for a specific situation or person; it is a major instrument for achieving the Flaubertian type of novel. (98)

Pascal is thus extending Lubbock's preoccupation with point of view and the dramatization of consciousness to demonstrate, in greater analytic detail, how the aesthetic doctrine of impersonality is achieved by authors. For Pascal, what he calls free indirect speech "belongs essentially to the third-person novel in which the narrator, depersonalised and impossible to name, has the right to enter into every mind and every closet" (100). From Pascal's "dual voice" to Bakhtin's "double-voiced" language to Ann Banfield's "unspeakable sentences," the historical development of FID has been posited as a challenge to the singular voice of omniscient narration. Here the paradox of presence and absence in theories of literary omniscience is dramatized as a kind of struggle between narrator and character. On the one hand, the effacement of narratorial presence is figured as a rejection of authorial omniscience; on the other hand, the more an author's presence is given over to the perspective and consciousness of characters, and the urge to comment is resisted, the more the key feature of access to consciousness comes to the fore. In this chapter I will address how the critical reception of contemporary omniscience is framed by this scholarship on FID. In pointing out the limitations of this critical reception, I want to suggest the need to reconsider some of the ways in which we theorize the relation between narratorial report and character thought.

Grammatical Transformation and the Method of Attribution

FID is generally understood as a phenomenon of speech and thought representation which appears to merge the perspective of both narrator and character. Much of the scholarly debate over FID has been generated by different methodological approaches derived from narrative theory, stylistics and linguistics, governed by a taxonomic impulse which focuses on how this phenomenon is to be identified and defined. Debate centers on the range of possible indices, from the purely grammatical to the more interpretive semantic and contextual, with difficulties arising from attempts to reconcile two methods of study: the linguistic identification of individual sentences which are grammatically discrete from indirect and direct discourse; and the literary-critical analysis of techniques of thought representation along a continuum from diegesis to mimesis. Moreover, FID gains its dynamism as a literary technique and as an object of study by virtue of being placed within a tripartite model of representing consciousness: as a mediating technique between a narrator's report of mental activity on the one hand, and a direct quotation of a character's thought on the other.

FID is traditionally defined as a syntactic unit in which a character's "original" utterance or thought has undergone a pronominal and tense shift to the grammar of the narrative discourse, typically from first to third person, and present to past tense, and is marked by an absence of tag clauses or reporting verbs. The central method of analyzing FID is one of linguistic attribution, which functions by parsing sentences of thought representation and assigning a range of stylistic features to the subjectivity of the narrator or the character. Anne Waldron Neumann highlights the methodological difficulties that emerge from the hesitancy of attribution that the ambiguity of FID fosters: "Because free indirect discourse lacks attribution, how do we recognize it as possibly reported discourse? That is, how does a novelist foreground the subjective language and viewpoint of a particular character against the usually more objective narratorial background?" (367). The more salient problem arises, I suggest, when scholarship on FID is put in the service of interpretive criticism, where aesthetic and ethical prejudices latent in novelistic theory are operationalized via the method of attribution.

This method is founded on the traditional idea of FID as the transformation of a character's utterance into the grammar of its narrative report. In her classic study, *Transparent Minds,* Dorrit Cohn describes FID, or what she calls "narrated monologue" as a "transformation of figural thought-language into the narrative language of third-person fiction" and suggests that "a simple transposition of grammatical person and tense will 'translate' a narrated into an interior monologue" (100). For Cohn, this translation is a grammatical "litmus test" for confirming the attribution of "a narrative sentence to a character's, rather than to a narrator's, mental domain" (101). Many scholars have rejected the derivational properties of FID which underlie this theory because in fiction there is no "original" utterance which can be recovered as a measure of reportorial fidelity: we have only the narrator's representation of a fictional act, in the same way that the fictional storyworld is constructed from the narrative discourse.

Despite this criticism, it is recognized that the hypothetical postulation of a character's direct thought derived from its narrative report is a useful analytic tool, precisely because such a possibility is an essential element of the mimetic illusion of fiction, and an intuitive cognitive process of readers. So those who reject what is called the "representational fallacy" or "direct discourse fallacy" often recuperate the transformational properties of FID via the notion of naturalization (McHale, "Free Indirect Discourse"; Sternberg, *Expositional Modes*; Fludernik, *Fictions of Language*). The argument here is that expressive elements may not be directly attributable to an original utterance, but we can *surmise* that a character would have used such language were they called upon to articulate their thoughts. Alan Palmer describes this as the hypothetical argument:

> Although the discourse may appear to present the "actual" words of inner speech, it is in fact presenting a reconstruction by the narrator that is hypothetically based on what characters would have said that they were thinking, had they been asked; and although the discourse may appear to present an "actual" episode of inner speech, it is really presenting a summary of several possible such episodes. (71)

The phrasing of this passage implies the narrator hypothetically reconstructs a character's thought, although scholarship has emphasized the interpretive role of readers in identifying FID. Monika Fludernik's monumental study of FID in *The Fictions of Language and the Languages of*

Fiction provides a good example of this approach, offering a linguistically founded "anti-mimetic model of speech and thought representation in language" (398), and providing an exhaustive list of potential indices, before invoking cognitive theory to lend theoretical weight to the naturalizing tendencies of readers.

In other words, the rejection of a derivational approach to defining FID has had little effect on the analytic practice of attribution. Now, the method of attribution is essential to the study of FID—in the sense that a method constructs its own object of study. The problem resides in what signals of subjectivity are privileged by this method. Besides pronominal and temporal shifts, as well as deictic adverbials which establish the "here" and "now" of a character's subjective center of perception, the most prominently analyzed indices of FID tend to be expressive features, especially idiomatic markers of a character's "voice" in the narration. Identifying examples of FID, then, often relies as much upon psychologizing assumptions about the lexical range and intellectual capacities of characters (would a character use this word, or think this way?), and upon stylistic assumptions about narratorial diction (would a narrator, or author, use such language?) as it does upon linguistic evidence. For instance, in analyzing a passage from Flannery O'Connor's "Good Country People," Lucy Ferriss writes:

> The hint is slight, but unmistakable. *Though she was thirty-two years old and highly educated.* Mrs. Hopewell would never use this expression, nor would Mrs. Freeman. Nor is the description neutral; it passes a judgment on Mrs. Hopewell for which the story has provided scant evidence. Such judgment comes—and has to come—from Joy herself. (182)

Here, the narratological analysis of FID is inseparable from character evaluation. FID is not just recognized by its context, but by the reader's subjective attribution. I myself can easily imagine both Mrs. Hopewell and Mrs. Freeman, or the author, using such an expression.

FID, Voice, and Focalization

"By leaving the relationship between words and thoughts latent," Dorrit Cohn argues, "the narrated monologue casts a peculiarly penumbral light on the figural consciousness, suspending it on the threshold of verbalization in a manner that cannot be achieved by direct quotation"

(*Transparent Minds* 103). Cohn thus recognizes FID as the evocation of an unverbalized consciousness. Two pages later, however, she says that narrated monologue imitates "the language a character uses when he talks to himself" and thus superimposes the two "voices" of narrator and character (105). This "voice" is thus largely identified by idiomatic attribution, backed up by Cohn's claim that narrated monologue "may be most succinctly defined as the technique for rendering a character's thought in his own idiom while maintaining the third-person reference and the basic tense of narration" (100). The emphasis on the presence of a character's idiom as a key textual marker of FID, even in its hypothetical formulation, can be found in this well-known definition by Anne Waldron Neumann: "that mode of indirectly reported speech or thought which quotes what we feel could be at least some of the *words* of a character's actual utterances or thought, but which offers those words interwoven with the narrator's language" (366, my emphasis).

The privileged method of lexical attribution means that FID is often taken to be an instance of, or even synonymous with, the broader phenomenon of stylistic contagion, or what Hugh Kenner, in *Joyce's Voices,* dubbed the Uncle Charles Principle, where any word in the narrative discourse which seems to "belong" to a character's lexicon can be taken as an example of a character's voice "infecting" the more formal or sophisticated language of the narrator. For instance, in a recent study of narrative authority in Jane Austen's *Emma,* Daniel Gunn argues: "But why, in a narrative situation such as Austen's, should such 'coloured' or 'infected' passages be seen as a phenomenon distinct from FID. I would propose that, in Austen at least, what happens in 'stylistic contagion' is the same thing that happens in FID" (37). The conflation of FID and stylistic contagion makes sense in literary critical analysis which is less concerned with identifying discrete syntactic units of FID than with analyzing overall passages of thought representation in terms of their relative closeness to a character's consciousness. However, this is part of the problem. There is a difference between a narrator imitating figural subjectivity by deploying language associated with a character, and a narrator yielding deictically to a character's perspective through a range of strategies for which characterological idiom is but one indice.[1] It is a difference recognized by the distinction between voice and focalization.

The method of attribution in the study of FID, as I pointed out earlier, is typically a means of answering questions such as: Whose language is this? Whose voice is this? and Who's speaking here? In the phraseological formulation of these questions we can see that the difficulties of theorizing FID are apparent precisely in its capacity to manifest the analytic interdependence of voice and focalization. However, there is also a tendency to collapse the distinction between the two categories and thus return to the "regrettable confusion" between who sees and who speaks which Genette set out to remedy. This confusion can be found in Pascal's book, which is a study of point of view in the Anglo-American tradition, of the relative presence of narratorial subjectivity in the representation of a character's perspective. According to Pascal, FID can operate in passages of description which record a scene entirely through a character's impression and subjective response to her environment. "Perhaps it is stretching the concept of free indirect speech too far to apply it to such writing?" he asks, before concluding that the "essence of the free indirect form" is the "reproduction of the inner processes of the character, expressed in the same syntactical form as objective narrative and embedded firmly in the narratorial account, but evoking the vivacity, the tone and gesture, of the character" (108). On this basis he describes the technique of FID as the "dual voice" of narrator and character, even though the character cannot be said to be "speaking" in any meaningful way.

When employed to represent thought, I suggest, FID is primarily a question of focalization, what Genette calls the regulation of narrative information, dictated by degrees of restriction on a narrator's reporting of character's thoughts. Genette's brief discussion of FID (what he calls transposed narration) is included in his chapter on mood, thus establishing its relationship to focalization. The presence of idiom or other expressive features attributable to a character may indicate a "deictic shift" which is a feature of focalization, but it does not alter the narrating instance, the generating instance of the narrative. The relationship of FID to other modes of thought representation is more properly a question of distance. However, most scholarship on the phenomenon of FID departs from Genette in categorizing this phenomenon as a feature of voice.

Part of the confusion in the study of FID, then, stems from the combination of several different concepts of voice, all designed to demonstrate the structural dispersal of the narrating instance and the stylistic fragmentation of authorial voice. In these approaches, narratives become populated with a variety of voices, from the stylistic infections of characterological idiom to the polyphonic clashing of living social languages in a dialogic novel. Or, in its ultimate manifestation, FID effects the modernist ideal of impersonality in the negation of any narrator, as in Ann Banfield's notorious formulation of the unspeakable sentence: "Es with a third person SELF cannot also contain a SPEAKER" (111). Banfield's work is the extreme version of scholarship on the empathic or neutral relation of narrator to characters, while accounts of stylistic contagion and dialogism emphasize the ironic relation between narratorial and other "voices."

Whether FID is understood as the grammatical transformation of a direct thought, or the hypothetical postulation of what a character might have said were they called upon to articulate their thoughts, it rests conceptually upon the potential of a character to take on the act of narration and speak for him or herself. As a result the study of FID often tends to elide the terminological difference between "language" and "voice." So when the method of linguistic attribution is described in terms of voice we see a tendency to equate the presence of *language* which is indicative of a character's subjectivity with a *speaking position* for that character within the narrative.

As an example of how this works in interpretations of contemporary fiction, I refer again to Timothy Aubry's article on the "politics of interiority" in contemporary American middlebrow fiction, which claims that "most third-person narrators, at least within American mainstream literary fiction, report the action of the novel almost entirely from the standpoint of the character or characters through free indirect discourse" (85). Aubry's analysis is thus predicated on a standard assumption about the natural relationship between FID and focalization. His case study is Anita Shreve's Oprah Book Club selected novel, *The Pilot's Wife*. This novel, Aubry writes,

> is written entirely in free indirect discourse, exclusively from Kathryn's perspective, without a single statement of authorial wisdom or entry into another character's consciousness. And it is all written in Kathryn's voice. Moreover, in certain moments, Kathryn actively assumes the narrator's function. (90)

Here is the passage which Aubry provides as evidence:

> The camera slid back to the old man and moved in close to his face. He looked shocky around the eyes, and his mouth was hanging open, as though it was hard for him to breathe. Kathryn watched him on the television, and she thought: That is what I look like now. Gray in the face. The eyes staring out at something that isn't even there. The mouth loose like that of a hooked fish. (11)

This quotation only demonstrates the hyperbole of Aubry's claim that the novel is written "entirely" in FID. It may be a passage of internally focalized narration, and perhaps the second sentence could be described as narrated perception, but, beyond the word "shocky" potentially indicating stylistic contagion, there is no evidence of FID. "Kathryn watched him on the television" is obviously narratorial report. Furthermore, the last four sentences, supposedly evidence that the character Kathryn has assumed the narrator's function, are clearly lines of direct discourse or quoted monologue. Aubry's assertion is that the "style Kathryn deploys in her self-description is identical to the overall style of the book" (90). Here we have the idea of stylistic contagion, described by Hugh Kenner as "the normally neutral narrative vocabulary pervaded by little clouds of idioms which a character might use if he were managing the narrative" (17) extended so far as to be meaningless, because if the novel is all written in Kathryn's voice there is no narrative voice to infect.

The equation of language with voice has led many critics to champion stylistic contagion or the dual voice or double-voiced language as a liberation of the character from the governing ideology of authorial discourse. Or if not a liberation, a site of conflict between textual agents, as if characters had some kind of cognizance and control over their modes of representation. In a book chapter titled "Who is Speaking Here? Free Indirect Discourse, Gender, and Authority in *Emma, Howard's End,* and *Mrs. Dalloway*," Kathy Mezei claims that in these three novels "a struggle is being waged between narrators and character-focalizers for control of the word, the text, and the reader's sympathy" (66) and "[t]he site for this textual battle between author, narrator, and character-focalizer and between fixed and fluctuating gender roles is the narrative device 'free indirect discourse'" (67).

Hence the practice of linguistic attribution is used not just to identify the perspectival orientation of the narrative, but to reconstruct a character's voice from the narrative discourse, and this voice becomes both mimetically and politically representative of the character's autonomy. FID is thus one of the key elements in what Dorothy J. Hale calls the "aesthetics of alterity" which informs and unites novelistic theory from James to Bakhtin. Hale describes this strain of theory as social formalism, a belief in the capacity of novelistic form to instantiate social relations which generate a sympathy for otherness.[2] Hale points out that "Pascal's brief overview of the discovery and early theorization of FID shows how, from the outset, this syntactical form was associated with an all-consuming appreciation of alterity" (92), before demonstrating that "Pascal's own account of 'dual voice' is primarily interested in a single question: has an author been able to represent a character in his own terms?" (93). This sort of ethical investment in recuperating the representative voice of a character's alterity is at the heart of theoretical discussions of FID.

Free Indirect Discourse and the Interpretive Frame of "Alterity"

From a pragmatic and cognitive perspective, Monika Fludernik writes: "What makes speech and thought representation recognizable as such, then, is its interpretability as an evocation of linguistic or mental alterity within the current discourse" ("Linguistic Illusion" 108). From a Bakhtinian perspective, Richard Aczel claims "in the narrative representation of speech and thought, voice is best identified contextually as an alterity effect" (494). Although differing in their methods, and their stance on the dual voice thesis, both Fludernik and Aczel define alterity as the projection of a subjective textual presence different from that animating the narrating instance. This embeds in formal terms the philosophical concept of alterity as a self defined in relation to its other, providing the methodological basis for ethical evaluation in terms of the aesthetics of alterity. Furthermore, the emphasis on context, particularly in Fludernik's formulation, shows how FID is as much a heuristic strategy as it is an analytic category, an interpretive frame which informs the search for alterity and the method of attribution as an evaluative practice: the extent to which a character is given a "voice" by the narrator.

In his discussion of some of the "theoretical problems arising from free indirect speech," Pascal writes:

> The first difficulty arises from the interweaving of FIS and narratorial description. Once FIS has become of frequent incidence in a novel, once we have become used to descriptions that are projections from the viewpoint of a character, we tend to expect it everywhere, and may find it confusing if the objective, narratorial mode is used instead. This is especially likely when few and unobtrusive indicators accompany FIS passages. (103)

Here Pascal is claiming that the use of FID establishes a cognitive frame of reception—an invitation to identify a passage of writing as generated by the perspective of a character—which is ruptured if the passage displays a narratorial style too sophisticated for the character or for that character's mental state at a particular moment. Pascal describes this as a kind of "usurpation" of a character's language and perspective (110). This usurpation is not simply narratorial presence, he is careful to explain, for the constant presence of the narrator in passages of FID is necessary to the "dual voice" effect of irony or empathy. Usurpation occurs when an author's concern with style, rather than the perspective of the character, dictates the language of narration. And although he discusses narratorial usurpation as a theoretical problem, he displays an evaluative bias in also describing it as a "stylistic flaw" (108) because "the lure of fine writing . . . may infect the passages in FIS themselves" (119). Here we see stylistic contagion is lauded when a narrator's style is infected by the idiom of the character, but when a focalized passage of FID is infected by narratorial language it becomes inartistic, intrusive, and dictatorial. My point is that scholarship on FID retains this evaluative bias by establishing the cognitive frame of alterity as a default effect and the motive for the practice of attribution, and by mobilizing the historical narrative of novelistic development in support of this frame.

Here we see the metatheoretical explanatory value of Fludernik's pragmatic account of FID as an interpretative strategy of readers made possible by a set of syntactic conditions. Fludernik writes:

> According to my own model, FID can be defined by means of the conjunction of an interpretative intervention on the part of the textual recipient, who posits a discourse alterity (that is, a notional discourse SELF different from that of the reportative SELF of the current narrator-speaker), with a minimal set of syntactic features, which constitute a sort of necessary condition, a mold that has to be fitted. ("Linguistic Illusion" 95)

The two minimal syntactic conditions, as I understand them, are the capacity for a sentence to be contextualized by anaphoric reference to a previous instance of character perspective (which could include the back shifting of tense), and the traditional absence of tag clauses or reporting verbs.

If we accept the claim that FID is an interpretive act, a decision on the part of the reader to attribute a statement to a character, then we can see FID not simply as a choice which individual readers make, but a kind of overarching critical paradigm fostered by the modernist aesthetic with its emphasis on impersonality and the erasure of narratorial presence, a paradigm in which our default position is to assume the existence of FID whenever Fludernik's minimal syntactic conditions occur. "If a passage contextually signifies discourse alterity," Fludernik argues, "and if it fits the minimal requirements for a prototypical FID form, then—in a flexible account of forms of speech and thought representation—one can categorize it as FID" (111). The question is: why would one want to? My argument is that when omniscient narrators in contemporary fiction provide access to the consciousness of a character through internal focalization, critics look for indices of FID, not necessarily because it is a feature of the work, but because they are deploying the interpretive frame of alterity. In other words, since the "discovery" of FID by scholars such as Charles Bally in the early twentieth century, and the linking of this discovery to theories of point of view, we now search for FID *instead* of other modes of thought representation. As Alan Palmer claims, in a critique of the verbal bias of the speech category approach which leads to a privileging of consciousness as inner speech: "I would also dispute the weighting given to free indirect thought and would suggest that it can only be arrived at by classifying a good deal of coloured thought report as free indirect thought" (62). And when FID is invoked in textual analysis, it is with the aim of constructing alterity as an aesthetic and ethical ideal, thus condemning writing which complicates this interpretative intervention.

I now turn to ways in which the interpretive frame of FID as an alterity effect operationalizes the historical, aesthetic, and ethical prejudices of modernist criticism in the reception of contemporary fiction, specifically via the method of linguistic attribution. A good example can be found in a 2004 article by Brian Phillips, called "Character in Contemporary Fiction." In this essay Phillips argues that contemporary prose style has inherited from Hemingway an impulse for plainness and efficiency which has become stale, not so much at the level of syntax, but in terms of the capacity to create character. He goes on to claim that Zadie Smith's *White Teeth,* Jonathan Franzen's *The Corrections,* and Don DeLillo's *Underworld* are all examples of books where characters have been buried by the style of contemporary fiction. Phillips claims that the characters in *The Corrections,* for instance, often "speak and think like Franzen, whose management of indirect discourse is compromised by his enthusiasm for narratorial incursion, and who places too much faith in the comedic and analytical properties of his crude interruptions" (640). As evidence, he cites this passage of thought representation in the novel:

> With a pounding heart Enid made her way to the bow of the "B" Deck. After the nightmare of the previous day and nights she again had a con-

crete thing to look forward to; and how sweet the optimism of the person carrying a newly scored drug that she believed would change her head; how universal the craving to escape the givens of the self. No exertion more strenuous than raising hand to mouth, no act more violent than swallowing, no religious feeling, no faith in anything more mystical than cause and effect was required to experience a pill's transformative blessings. *She couldn't wait to take it.* (324)

Phillips then employs the analytic method of attribution to ask: "Whose thoughts are these? They are certainly not Enid's" (640). And by virtue of asking these questions, he must conclude that Franzen's style is incapable of fully rendering Enid's character. He "adjourns to analysis and the ease of his own vocabulary. And so Enid disappears. . . . Her words are the wrong words, because they are not hers" (640). Hence the governing method of FID analysis—the attribution of language to either narrator or character according to the psychological measure of plausibility, the mimetic measure of verisimilitude, and the aesthetic measure of authorial style—underpins an interpretive frame animated by ethical evaluation of the relative "alterity" of the character. Phillips isolates the phrase "givens of the self" for censure on the grounds that it is incompatible with language we might expect from Enid. Yet it is clear that the passage quoted is not FID, besides the last italicized line; it is psychonarration or thought report. Indeed, the phrase resonates with one used earlier to describe the mental state of her husband, Alfred: "The dream of radical transformation: of one day waking up and finding himself a wholly different (more confident, more serene) kind of person, of escaping that prison of the given, of feeling divinely capable" (272).

One of the most significant features of contemporary fiction in the wake of postmodern experimentation, as I have pointed out, is the trend away from the impersonality of limited third-person narration, and toward an aesthetic of maximalism in which the presence of the narrator is constantly foregrounded. I turn again to the work of James Wood, who has relentlessly excoriated contemporary fiction for its stylistic excesses. Wood codified his critical principles in his 2008 book, *How Fiction Works,* which is significant for being the modern successor to Percy Lubbock's *The Craft of Fiction.* Wood follows Lubbock in his commitment to modernist psychological realism, the importance of "point of view" as the means to show rather than tell, and in his reliance on Henry James as his aesthetic touchstone. However, whereas Lubbock and others such as Joseph Warren Beach historicized modernist fiction as a move toward dramatization which eradicated the intrusive authorial presence of earlier omniscient narration, Wood rails against postmodern fiction as the debasement of these achievements. His critique of authorial presence as a rupturing of verisimilitude rests less on overt evaluative commentary than on "annoyingly authorial" (23) style resulting from technical mishandling of FID.

What is important to note is that Wood draws upon many of the established principles of FID to underpin his evaluative denunciation of what he calls "the contemporary writing project" (27): an authorial style committed to evoking the "debased language" of today's media-saturated world found in writers such as DeLillo and Wallace. First, if Lubbock described the development of novelistic method as an ongoing refinement of point of view, Wood notes that "the history of the novel can be told as the development of free indirect style" (58). Modernist impersonality, achieved by the development of FID, thus becomes the aesthetic standard by which to judge subsequent experiments in writing. Secondly, Wood upholds the "transformational" theory of FID, such as when, in a discussion of Nabokov, he writes: "As usual, if we turn it into first-person speech, we can hear the way in which the word 'thing' belongs to Pnin and wants to be spoken" (22). This quote, which concerns a passage of narrated perception, also demonstrates the third principle: a willing conflation of thought with speech, and hence indicative of a "verbal bias" which allows the equation of character language with a character's "voice." Fourthly, Wood extends the category of FID beyond its grammatical limits and privileges lexical features of expressivity when he claims: "The Uncle Charles principle is just an edition of free indirect style" (17). Fifthly, all of these principles are brought into play by the key metholodgical tool of linguistic attribution. In fact, Wood's most common critical strategy is to scour passages of thought representation and weed out for condemnation any expressive elements that indicate intrusive authorial style. Often Wood is in fact criticizing novelists for employing psychonarration or thought report because they are unable to manage the empathetic subtleties necessitated by FID.

In condemning the intrusive features of authorial style, Wood is ultimately betraying an ethical judgment about how characters *should* be represented in fiction. In his review of Zadie Smith's *White Teeth,* he writes: "And what of that phrase, 'he was going to beat but he wasn't going to eat'? 'Beat' is not Samad's word; he would never use it. It is Smith's word, and in using it she not only speaks over her character, she reduces him, obliterates him" ("Human" 45). When it comes to the representation of speech this sort of naturalization might make sense, but when applied to the representation of consciousness we have what I think is an unproductive assumption that characters must think in the same linguistic register in which they would speak or write. What follows is that if a passage of thought representation contains language which does not seem to "belong" to a character it becomes marked as a sign of narratorial intrusion into their interior monologue. This leads to a collapsing of the distinction between authorial style and narratorial reportage, glossed as an instance of aesthetic failure on the part of the author, an inability to fully imagine characters in their own idiom, or an unwillingness to refrain from evaluative commentary, rather than a deliberate rhetorical strategy of the narrator.

In an interesting inversion of the idea of stylistic contagion as an idiomatic deviance from a formal style of narration, Wood here assigns the colloquialism "beat" in the passage from *White Teeth* to the narrator, indeed to the author, rather than the character. This is indicative of the linguistic register of much contemporary fiction, and here we find the challenge to many of the assumptions underlying theories of FID which inhere in the privileged method of lexical attribution. I would suggest that if we eschew the transformational presupposition of the "direct discourse fallacy," and see FID as a mode of represented thought without necessarily being a translation of the verbal form of that thought, then the emphasis on lexical attribution should become less important to analysis. We might then see FID not as an indirect report of a mental utterance, or even as a mediated representation, but as a performative statement, a narratorial performance of the kinetic flow of a character's thought, incorporating the rhythm of the thought process into the syntactic structure of narration.

Here we would foreground indices which evoke the activity of thinking rather than its verbal form, indices such as hesitations, ellipses, and intonations, alongside the more common exclamations and interrogatives. In which case, language which cannot be attributed to a character may be understood less as an intrusion in the character's interior monologue, than an element of the narratorial performance which highlights the speculative nature of verbalizing thoughts. That is, we can see the hypothetical approach to FID—this is what a character would have said were they asked—not only as a theoretical explanation of the cognitive reconstructions of readers, but as a rhetorical strategy of narrators, invoking doubt about the linguistic nature of a character's thought processes. The hypotheticality of FID might also then be construed as an example of what the narrator would say were he or she to adopt the character's perspective. Rather than presenting a transparent mind or knowable self, contemporary omniscience suggests we can only know the self through the otherness of the narrator.

We would then be in a better position to see how the use of FID in contemporary fiction displays a reflexive awareness of the technique itself, by overt reference to its artificiality or by deliberating stretching its boundaries: collapsing the linguistic borders between narrator and character which inform the principle of stylistic deviation, or parodically highlighting these borders, shading the already hazy distinction between authorial psychonarration and figural narrated monologue, and producing what might be described as a kind of immanent psychonarration: with commentary or analysis embedded in the stylistic evocation of character thought (this is what the character would have thought if they had the narrator's insight), or invoking a deictic center of consciousness but verbalizing the thought in narratorial language.

Narratorial Self-Reflexivity

In discussing a passage of FID in *Pride and Prejudice* which is included in quotation marks, Anne Waldron Neumann writes: "The quotation marks in this passage—Austen did not know that free indirect discourse is supposed to omit them—ensure that we are reading Mrs. Bennet's 'actual' reply to Mr. Collins (with the usual grammatical transformations)" (371). The first thing to remark about contemporary omniscience is that it manifests a high degree of authorial awareness regarding FID as a convention of writing: authors today know what FID is "supposed" to do. Here are some examples of narratorial self-reflexivity in contemporary omniscient narration which highlight the arbitrariness of grammatical and expressive features derived from modernist literature:

> Richard looked at his watch and thought: I can't tell him yet. Or rather: Can't tell him yet. For the interior monologue now waives the initial personal pronoun, in deference to Joyce. (Amis, *The Information* 11)

> But how can he *possibly* make his mark in any of these (William frets as he finds his favourite bench in St James's Park) when he's being virtually blackmailed into a life of tedious labour? How can he possibly be expected. . . . But let me rescue you from drowning in William Rackham's

stream of consciousness, that stagnant pond feebly agitated by self pity. (Faber, *The Crimson Petal and the White* 57–58, original ellipsis)

Here is an example of a narrator mocking the representation of thought in verbal form:

> You know what they are feeling. They are feeling enjoyably fucked. It is what they are thinking that is the problem. You already know what would be written inside Moshe's thought balloon. "Nana," he would be moaning in this sketch, "darling Nana." His thought balloon was soppy and romantic. Anjali's thought balloon was different. (Thirlwell, *Politics* 201)

I have already pointed out in my chapter on the pyrotechnic storyteller how authors such as Nicola Barker and Rick Moody play with the conventions of thought representation, asserting linguistic control over characters' own modes of self-description by staging hypothetical dialogues between narrator and character regarding lexical choices, and hyperbolically extending in the narrative discourse metaphors attributed to characters. I will focus here on two other features of FID in contemporary omniscience: shared linguistic habitus (the self-reflexive mixture of stylistic contagion and narratorial usurpation); and characterological cognitive self-awareness (the concept of self animating this deployment).

Shared Linguistic Habitus

Shared linguistic habitus operates when narratorial colloquialisms and syntactic rhythm disrupt the sense of a neutral or formal diction against which to measure stylistic deviation. It also operates in the sense of characters and narrator sharing a professional language (Charlotte Simmons studying neuroscience, Gary Lambert reading books on clinical depression, Russell Stone reading books on happiness and genetic science, Richard Tull being a writer of fiction) which complicates the projection of alterity.

To demonstrate the first case, I return to Nicola Barker's *Darkmans*. On the whole, this novel eschews interior monologues, but it has multiple instances of diegetic summary of a character's past which function as what Alan Palmer calls thought report of states of mind rather than a single mental event or series of events. A good example is this passage:

Progress, *modernity* (all now dirty words in Beede's vocabulary) had kicked him squarely in the balls. I mean he hadn't asked for much, had he? He'd sacrificed the Spider Orchid, hadn't he? A familiar geography? He'd only wanted, out of *respect,* to salvage . . . to salvage . . .

What?

A semblance of what had been? Or was it just a question of . . . was it just a matter of . . . of *form?* Something as silly and apparently significant as . . . as *good manners?* (12)

Employing the method of attribution, we could read the first sentence as an example of FID, particularly due to the presence of the colloquial expression, marking the parenthesis with its proper noun as narratorial intrusion. However, given the informal nature of the narrative voice, we could easily assign the colloquialism to the narrator and see the sentence as psychonarration. The hesitancy of attribution which arises from the ambiguous nature of FID itself leads me to see this simply as a narratorial performance of the character's mental state.

The second sentence is a very interesting example: "I mean he hadn't asked for much, had he?" What should be a clear instance of FID is complicated by the inconsistency of pronoun and tense. On one hand you could say the author had no choice but to retain this inconsistency because a full grammatical "transformation" into "He meant he hadn't asked for much" wouldn't make sense. However, the fact that the sentence is *not* rendered in direct discourse demonstrates to me a willingness to court confusion in order to retain the presence of the narrative voice. In fact because this passage is part of a much longer section of analeptic summary, and not a scenic report of Beede's reflection, we could easily assert that here the *narrator* is fumbling for the words to articulate Beede's mental state, highlighting the hypothetical nature of FID. "I mean" is in fact a recurring phrase in the thought representation of virtually all the characters, such that it becomes a stylistic device associated with the narrator, rather than something idiosyncratic to the characters. It is often used as a parenthetical supplement to dialogue in sentences of thought representation which effect a backshifting of tense while retaining the pronoun. Here are two examples: "'No *salad?!*' Kelly's jaw dropped (no salad?! I mean where'd he think this *was?* Fucking *Ethiopia?*)" (221); "'Okay.' Gaffar nodded (registering Kane's inner turmoil, but taking it all with a pinch of salt: I mean, how hard could life be for this spoiled, flabby,

Western pup?)" (85). In the following passage the narrator seems to summarize collective thought: "The whole party was quiet for a moment, as if jointly considering the most feasible solution to this perplexing dilemma (I mean what *could* Kelly do?)" (107). Here we have a sense of the narrator intruding to agree with the characters. The following passage occurs in an expositional summary of the character Gaffar, a Kurd who barely speaks English: "An epiphany. Or this was the mythology. The truth was much simpler. Things didn't actually change all that much in Turkey (I mean, the Kurds were persecuted everywhere, weren't they?). The fabric of his life remained virtually identical. He'd simply crossed over (or turned inside out, like a polythene bag)" (66–67). These passages all echo the narrator's device of parenthetical elaborations of descriptive metaphors, carrying the stylistic presence into the performance of FID.

The most reflexive example of linguistic intrusion or narratorial usurpation as a conscious stylistic technique is Tom Wolfe's *I Am Charlotte Simmons*. Here is a passage from a scene where the virginal eponymous heroine is making out with a frat boy called Hoyt and trying to stop him from going any further:

> Slither slither slither slither went the tongue, but the hand—that was what she tried to concentrate on, the hand, since it had the entire terrain of her torso to explore and not just the otorhynolaryngological caverns—oh God, it was not just at the border where the flesh of the breast joins the pectoral sheath of the chest—no, the hand was cupping her entire right—*Now!* she must say "No Hoyt" and talk to him like a dog—. (369)

This is clearly a passage of internal focalization, but how much of it is rendered in FID? In narratological terms, we might say that the passage opens with narrated perception, shifting to psychonarration after the dash, and perhaps into narratorial comment with the explanatory conjunction, "since." The ejaculation, "oh God" is a clear instance of FID, along with the anaphoric pronoun "it," but the deictics of the rest of the sentence (*the* breast, *the* chest) suggest a narratorial perspective. We could then say that the passage shifts into a line of narrated perception and concludes with a line of FID, marked by the ejaculation "Now!". Thus, a lexically oriented analysis of the micro-shifts between narrator and character might yield only the two exclamations as instances of FID in an overall passage of psychonarration or narrated perception rendered in the anatomical discourse of the narrator. However, the most important quality of the passage is the syntactic structure which is not indicative of an original mental utterance so much as it is expressive of the rhythm of Charlotte's hyperconscious mental activity. This, along with the third-person pronoun and back-shifted tense, is why the passage as a whole can be defined as free indirect thought.

Now if we employ the method of lexical attribution we are clearly going to see a term such as "otorhynolaryngological" as evidence of narratorial usurpation and claim that the mimetic effect of FID has been diluted because Charlotte would never use such a word, particularly at this time of heightened emotion. The whole passage can be condemned as an example of reverse stylistic contagion, the author writing over the character's thoughts. Yet this seems to be the wrong judgment to make, because it is based on an assumption of what FID *should* do.

The key line for me is the one which begins with the ejaculation, "oh God." There is an obvious irony in the juxtaposition of phrases such as "Oh God" and "pectoral sheath" in a single sentence, highlighting the anthropological distance from the characters which the narrator adopts throughout the book. But I don't see why irony, with its implication of narratorial distance, is any less *mimetic* than empathetic figural closeness. Do we not get a clear sense of Charlotte's thought processes? Rather than dramatizing this sentence as an uneven conflict between "voices," I see it as the clearest example of what I mean by describing FID as a self-conscious narratorial performance of the process of characterological thought, mimicking the character's own disembodied perspective on the action.

There are several passages throughout the book in which the omniscient narrator relays what characters don't know about themselves—which, for Dorrit Cohn, is the prime feature of psychonarration—but nonetheless employs the conventions of FID. Here is a passage concerning the nerdy Adam Gellin and his crush on Charlotte Simmons:

> He had no way of knowing it, but he was filled—suffused—with a love for a woman that only a virgin could feel. In his eyes she was more than flesh and blood and more than spirit. She was . . . an essence . . . an essence of *life* that remained tactile and *alive*—his loins certainly remained alive at this moment, welling up beneath his tighty-whiteys—and yet a . . . a . . . a *universal solvent* that penetrated his very hide and commandeered his entire nervous system from his brain to the tiniest nerve endings. If he could only embrace her—and find that she had been *dying* for him to do just that—she, her tactile *essence,* would come flooding into every cell, into all the billion miles of spooled DNA—he couldn't

imagine a unit of his body so minute that she would not *suffuse* it—and they would . . . *explode* their virginities in a single sublime ineffable yet neurological, all too neurological, moment! (379–80)

The first line in this passage could be described as what Cohn calls dissonant psychonarration, revealing an aspect of Adam's mind which he is not conscious of, and cannot express, establishing an ironic distance between narrator and character. Phrases which follow—such as "In his eyes," "If he could only embrace her" and "he couldn't imagine a unit of his body"—indicate internal focalization, but the passage offers a mocking neurobiological explanation of his supposed "love" for Charlotte embedded in the form of FID, with hesitations and emphases tracing the flow of Adam's thoughts, and pronouns and tense in the grammar of the narrative report: "She was . . . an essence . . . an essence of *life*." To read this passage as FID, however, we cannot hypothesize that this is how the character would narrate his thoughts. Instead it is a kind of immanent psychonarration, not simply representing his "thoughts" in narratorial language, but performing them from the basis of the narrator's omniscient insight.

Toward the end of the novel, after Charlotte has been in a prolonged state of depression, Adam becomes exasperated and yells at her in attempt to break her out of her funk. This is the turning point for her, leading her out of depression:

There was also, unbeknownst to either of them consciously, a woman's thrill!—and that's the word for it!—her delicious thrill!—when, as before, a man expands his chest and drapes it with the sash of righteousness and . . . *takes command!* . . . upon the Heights of Abraham. (608)

The word "thrill" in this passage cannot be attributed to Charlotte or Adam, as the narrator makes clear, for they are unconscious of the thrill itself. Yet the narrator's account of the underlying implacable biological forces at play here, unconsciously governing their behavior, is nonetheless rendered in the same form as other instances of FID, including exclamations and ellipses, where the "vivacity, the tone, and gesture," to use Pascal's phrase, evoke a narratorial rather than characterological subjectivity.

Throughout the novel there are different manifestations of a shared linguistic habitus: between narrator and character, from stylistic contagion to narratorial usurpation; and between characters and their social milieu. To take the latter phenomenon first:

> A small matter, very small, for Charlotte was now transported! ... not so much by the Olfactory Workers and their odors and music and dancing and singing as by the fact that this was something experimental, esoteric, cutting-edge (*she had picked up that term in the modern drama course*), one of the exciting, sophisticated things Miss Pennington had assured her awaited her on the other side of the mountain, the things that would open up her eyes to harness and achieve great triumphs with ... (364, original ellipsis; emphasis added)

Later in the novel, the narrator describes "a skanky girl facing front at the far end of the table. 'Skanky' had slipped into Charlotte's vocabulary by social osmosis; and this girl was skanky" (560). In both of these passages we have the narrator "borrowing" words from Charlotte's lexicon to render her perspective, while pointing out that these words do not in fact "belong" to her. This reflexive reference to stylistic contagion in the service of focalization serves to undermine the linguistic unity of Charlotte's consciousness itself.

> He paused. The ensuing silence, in a roomful of drunks in an advanced stage of wreckage, was a tribute to the periphrastic performance he was putting on. *Charlotte wondered if anybody in the room other than herself knew the adjective "periphrastic."* She doubted it. A smile of superiority stole over her face. And the coolest guy in all of Dupont, who has fallen in love with me, is massaging my back, and everyone in this room can see that. (466, emphasis added)

In this passage there is again a kind of reflexive use of stylistic contagion, in which the colloquial "advanced stage of wreckage" is juxtaposed with the more sophisticated "periphrastic performance," but the following sentence indicates that not only has the narrator borrowed the term periphrastic from Charlotte's linguistic field, she is consciously thinking it as she perceives the scene.

On the other hand, we have passages of textually identifiable narratorial usurpation. In a chapter titled "The Conscious Little Rock," Charlotte meets up with the Frat boy, Hoyt: "So moved was she by the dreadful wounds, the awful beating he had taken for her sake, that she barely noticed the incidental bit of Fuck Patois" (335). This recalls the narrator's elaboration of the grammatical forms of "Fuck Patois" in an earlier chapter focused on the basketball player, Jojo Johanssen. In the next chapter, Charlotte is waiting in line with other underage college students hoping to gain access to a nightclub: "As usual, their nervousness took the form of the Fuck Patois, which they thought gave them a front of cool and confident twenty-one-year-old moxie" (348). The phrase then surfaces a page later in Charlotte's interior monologue: "Momma. If Momma showed up right now and saw her, thought Charlotte, saw her in a line full of people talking Fuck Patios, about to sneak into a *bar* with a *fake ID* . . . Everybody does it, Momma . . . *Everybody?*" (349). Here, as if by another sort of osmosis, the narrator's term has slipped into Charlotte's vocabulary. She is the conscious little rock of his narratorial manipulation, and he is Charlotte Simmons.

Characterological Cognitive Self-Awareness

The broader argument I want to make is that the representation of consciousness in contemporary fiction is not just a device for rendering character's thoughts with greater or lesser degrees of mimesis, but a means for interrogating the relation of language and thought. Which is to say, the question of how a character would articulate their thoughts is foregrounded as a technical challenge because it is a preoccupation of the characters themselves. In contemporary fiction, the classic interior monologue in which characters subject themselves to a self-scrutiny of their behavior, motivations, and beliefs, is often accompanied by an extra level of self-conscious awareness, a detached reflection on the act of cognition itself, including of their own lexical choices, and this becomes a way of highlighting the importance of language as a shared medium which structures thought itself, rather than "belonging" to an individual as a marker of their alterity. Here is a passage from another interior monologue in Wolfe's novel, indicating Charlotte's self-conscious awareness of her own changing linguistic habitus: "You . . . bastard! Sharp intake of breath—she had never used that expletive before, not even in her thoughts. Hoyt had done this just to torment her! Comes over as if to see her and veers off to some little . . . slut! Never even thought that word before, either . . . or had she once, about Beverly" (387).

This characterological cognitive self-awareness is highlighted in much of the fiction of David Foster Wallace. Here is a quote from the story "Mr. Squishy":

> At various intervals throughout the pre-GRDS presentation the limbic portions of Schmidt's brain pursued this line of thinking—while in fact

a whole other part of his mind surveyed these memories and fantasies and was simultaneously fascinated and repelled at the way in which all these thoughts and feelings could be entertained in total subjective private while Schmidt ran the Focus Group through its brief and supposedly Full-Access description of Mister Squishy's place in the soft-confection industry. (31)[3]

Another example is David Lodge's "neuronarrative" *Thinks,* in which the protagonist attempts to dictate his own "stream of consciousness" to a tape recorder, and by necessity reflects upon his own cognitive processes: "Ah, a blank, a definite blank, for an instant, not more than a second or two, I didn't have a reportable thought or sense impression, my mind as they say went blank, I thought of nothing" (4). In this passage from Zadie Smith's *White Teeth,* the narrator reports a character's assumption that language can infiltrate his prelinguistic consciousness: "It was his most shameful secret that whenever he opened a door—a car door, a car boot, the door of KEVIN's meeting hall or the door of his own house just now—the opening of *Goodfellas* ran through his head and *he found this sentence rolling around in what he presumed was his subconscious:* As far back as I can remember, I always wanted to be a gangster" (446, emphasis added).

An example of how a character's cognitive self-awareness is self-reflexively performed by a narrator can be found in this passage from Jonathan Franzen's *The Corrections,* which must be quoted in full:

He turned to the doorway where she'd appeared. He began a sentence: "I am—" but when he was taken by surprise, every sentence became an adventure in the woods; as soon as he could no longer see the light of the clearing from which he'd entered, he would realize that the crumbs he'd dropped for bearings had been eaten by birds, silent deft darting things which he couldn't quite see in the darkness but which were so numerous and swarming in their hunger that it seemed as if *they* were the darkness, as if the darkness weren't uniform, weren't an absence of light but a teeming and corpuscular thing, and indeed when as a studious teenager he'd encountered the word "crepuscular" in *McKay's Treasury of English Verse,* the corpuscles of biology had bled into his understanding of the word, so that for his entire adult life he'd seen in twilight a corpuscularity, as of the graininess of the high-speed film necessary for photography under conditions of low ambient life, as of a kind of sinister decay; and hence the panic of a man betrayed deep in the woods whose darkness was the darkness of starlings blotting out the sunset or black ants storming a dead opossum, a darkness that didn't just exist but actively *consumed* the bearings that he'd sensibly established for himself, lest he be lost; but in the instant of realizing he was lost, time became marvelously slow and he discovered hitherto unguessed eternities in the space between one word and the next, or rather he became trapped in that space between words and could only stand and watch as time sped on without him, the thoughtless boyish part of him crashing on out of sight blindly through the woods while he, trapped, the grownup Al, watched in oddly impersonal suspense to see if the panic-stricken little boy might, despite no longer knowing where he was or at what point he'd entered the woods of this sentence, still manage to blunder into the clearing where Enid was waiting for him, unaware of any woods—"packing my suitcase," he heard himself say. This sounded right. Verb, possessive, noun. (11)

In this scene we find the faltering patriarch Alfred standing in front of his dressing table, in a haze of dementia. Alfred is interrupted by his wife, who asks what he is doing. His response—"I'm packing my suitcase"—is punctuated by a long paragraph of ostensibly iterative summary, employing the psycho-analogy of being lost in the woods to explain the intricacies of Alfred's thought processes when he is confronted with such neurological failures. When the elaboration of this psychoanalogy describes the darkness of the woods as "a teeming and corpuscular thing" we have a tangential comment about how from his teenage years, Alfred confused the words corpuscular and crepuscular. Here we have what seems to be a narratorial acknowledgement of stylistic contagion, of having borrowed the character's word. As the passage continues, however, it describes the self-conscious detachment that Alfred has in these moments, with the narrator inhabiting the cognitive space between one word and the next, and performing Alfred's own reflection as he "watched in oddly impersonal suspense." So the passage hovers between psychonarration and FID as a self-conscious narratorial performance of Al's own self-conscious reflection on his cognitive process, as if seeing himself as a character.

According to Dorrit Cohn, psycho-analogies are found in modern novels "most frequently in works where the narrated monologue is the prevailing method for rendering consciousness, but at moments when an author is for some reason unwilling to entrust the presentation of the inner life to the character's own verbal competence" (*Transparent Minds* 45). In this passage from *The Corrections,* the psychoanalogy performs this function because the character has momentarily lost his verbal competence, but it also appears to be the case that the psychoanalogy is Alfred's. In this case, it is a mimetic rendering of Alfred's thoughts.

The Hypotheticality of Free Indirect Discourse

I don't want to suggest that any of these examples necessarily indicate new types of FID, because one can always find similar examples in earlier work. For instance, Dorrit Cohn draws attention to this passage in *The Magic Mountain*: "But for him and his relationship with Madame Chauchat—the word 'relationship' must be charged to his account, we refuse to take the responsibility for it" (qtd in Cohn, *Transparent Minds* 121). I make two claims, however. First, that there is a high degree of self-reflexivity in the use of FID in contemporary fiction, particularly in relation to idiomatic indices, highlighting a skepticism about linguistic difference as a marker of alterity; and secondly, that this self-reflexivity facilitates the representation of characters who themselves reflect on their own cognitive processes and the role of language in producing rather than expressing thought. I am also arguing that these features of thought representation require different ways of talking about the function and effect of FID than those offered by a method of linguistic attribution underpinned by the interpretive frame of alterity. In particular, that an interpretive frame which mobilizes the aesthetic and ethical prejudices of modernist criticism and its attendant history of novelistic progression is not suitable for the analysis of FID in contemporary omniscience.

Consider a passage from Richard Powers's *Generosity* which I quoted in a previous chapter: "She sits in the rocker for a moment, examining herself. It's not even an effort, really. Not even a decision. Just large molecules, passing their oldest signals back and forth across the infinite synapse gap" (179). This passage presents the syntactic conditions of FID and invites an alterity effect, before undermining it. One would normally read the last two sentences as narratorial commentary. Given the fact that this character, Tonia Schiff, is a television science journalist immersed in the world of genetic science, one might at least consider attributing the sentences and even their idiom to her thoughts. If we do, they then indicate characterological self-awareness of thought processes.

FID, then, is one of the major strategies which contemporary omniscient narrators employ to perform their narrative authority. My argument is similar to that of Daniel Gunn who demonstrates how, in Jane Austen's novels, passages of FID do not give voice to the autonomous subjectivity of characters because they are always framed by the controlling presence of the narrator and hence must be understood as a "narrative mimicry of figural thought" (40). I use the term "narratorial performance" rather than "mimicry" to highlight the self-reflexive use of conventions of thought representation; the sense of acting a role, of performing a character's lines rather than imitating them; and the connotation of pretense, in the sense that FID is a hypothetical projection of character thought. The hypothetical approach is best able to engage with the hesitancy of attribution that arises from the characteristic ambiguity of FID. The logic of this approach is not only that the verbal representation of character thought is a speculative adoption of the character's mode of articulation, but that the represented thought itself may sometimes be a hypothetical postulation of a possible thought.

This conception of FID can be found in Michel Faber's *The Crimson Petal and the White*. The global narrative frame of this novel has an intrusive omniscient narrator who persistently addresses readers via a form of autotelic second person, "introducing" them to characters and guiding them through the fictional world. In the following passage the narrator performs, as a direct address to readers, the thoughts of Sugar regarding how she might respond to the narratee's presence as she eavesdrops on Agnes, the wife of Henry Rackham (a response which she may or may not be rehearsing to herself):

> Don't be judgemental: this is not the way Sugar usually occupies her Tuesday afternoons; in fact, it's her first time. No, really! William Rackham is in Cardiff, you see, until Thursday, and Agnes Rackham is indisposed. So, rather than being idle, what's the harm in following Clara, Agne's lady's-maid, on her afternoon off, and seeing what comes of it?" (354)

Given the potential counterfactuality of FID, I would conclude by suggesting we can profitably think about the relationship between FID and what David Herman calls hypothetical focalization. I will discuss this concept in more detail in the following chapter. For now I will quote Herman's general explanation of hypothetical focalization as "the use of hypotheses, framed by the narrator or a character, about what might be or have been seen or perceived—if only there were someone who could have adopted the requisite perspective on the situations and events at issue" ("Hypothetical Focalization" 231). If we substitute here the phrase "what might have been thought in this way" we can see that omniscience provides the "requisite perspective" for seeing into a character's mind and that FID is the form the narrator employs to perform this character's thoughts had they been able to adopt this perspective. This means that FID does not need to be an account of how the character may have articulated their thoughts, hence requiring a kind of lexical fidelity to the character's linguistic habitus, but a kind of translation of these thoughts which is not "telling" as opposed to "showing" them but a performative inhabitation of a fictional mind.

CHAPTER 7

Paralepsis and Omniscient Character Narration

> But what the hero cannot say, the author cannot tell.
> —Anna Laetitia Barbauld, "Life of Samuel Richardson" xxv

> How to dispense with Padma? How give up her ignorance and superstition, necessary counterweights to my miracle laden omniscience?
> —Salman Rushdie, *Midnight's Children* 170

> No individual owns any story. The community is the owner of the story, and it can tell it the way it deems it fit. We would not be needing to justify the communal voice that tells this story if you had not wondered how we became so omniscient in the affairs of Toloki and Noria.
> —Zakes Mda, *Ways of Dying* 12

IN THE INTRODUCTION to *Transparent Minds,* Dorrit Cohn draws attention to the paradox of realist fiction: that its realism is heightened by the fantasy of complete access to a person's inner life: "narrative fiction attains its greatest 'air of reality' in the representation of a lone figure thinking thoughts she will never communicate to anyone" (7). Hence the conventional authority of omniscience is founded upon what Cohn calls "the unnatural presentation of the inner life found in third-person fiction" (*Distinction* 16). In this chapter, I discuss a different paradox: when the unnatural knowledge of omniscience is mobilized by the narrative voice of first-person character narrators.

There is a long history of character narrators saying more than the conventions of realism dictate they should know, in novels from *Tristram Shandy* to *Moby Dick* to *The Great Gatsby*, sometimes on isolated occasions throughout the narrative, sometimes persistently, with lesser and greater degrees of explanation for this excess of knowledge. My focus here is on novels over the past few decades which collectively have developed "first-person omniscience" as virtually another category of narrative voice. Some well-known examples include best-selling and prizewinning novels such as Salman Rushdie's *Midnight's Children* (1981), Peter Carey's *Oscar and Lucinda* (1988), Toni Morrison's *Jazz* (1992), Rick Moody's *The Ice Storm* (1994), Carol Shield's *The Stone Diaries* (1995), Jeffrey Eugenides's *The Virgin Suicides* (1993) and *Middlesex* (2002), Ian McEwan's *Atonement* (2001), Alice Sebold's *The Lovely Bones* (2002), and Junot Diaz's *The Brief Wondrous Life of Oscar Wao* (2007). It is no coincidence, I think, that these works have appeared at the same time that new modes of heterodiegetic omniscience have been developed, together firmly establishing omniscient narration as a key feature of experimentation in contemporary fiction.

When first-person narrators adopt the privilege of omniscience typically associated with authorial narration, and narrate with authority the thoughts of other characters or events at which they were not present, our default response seems to be: how do they know? I want to suggest that the ways in which narrative theory has engaged with this question demonstrate the extent to which it is in thrall to an "epistemological fallacy," where questions regarding practices of storytelling are framed as a problematics of knowledge. The debates which result from this approach point to a narratological preoccupation with attribution: to whom do we assign vision, voice, consciousness, intentionality, etc., resulting in a multiplication of possible agents: author, implied author, narrator, focalizer, character, and reader. In this case, the "problem" has been: to which agent do we assign responsibility for impossible knowledge?

Paralepsis and Focalization

The most common approach to the "problem" of first-person omniscience has been through an extension of Genette's concept of paralepsis. In his chapter on mood in *Narrative Discourse*, Genette claims that "a change in focalization, especially if it is isolated within a coherent context, can also be analyzed as a momentary infraction of the code which governs that context without thereby calling into question the existence of the code" (195). Genette gives the name alterations to these "isolated infractions" (195), and christens as paralepsis any alteration of focalization which involves "giving more [information] than is authorized in principle in the code of focalization governing the whole" (195). This "excess of information" is not an "epistemological" problem in third-person narration, where it is assumed the narrator knows more than the focal character, but it is framed as such in first-person narration.

Some apparent paralepses in first-person narration can be understood as speculations or reconstructions of events based on subsequent knowledge. "The real difficulty arises," Genette says, "when the narrative reports to us, on the spot and with no perceptible detour, the thoughts of another character in the course of a scene where the hero himself is not present" (207). In particular, for Genette, when Proust's narrator provides us with "access to the last thoughts of Bergotte on his deathbed" (207–8), this is "one paralepsis to end all paralepses; it is irreducible by any hypothesis to the narrator's information, and one we must indeed attribute to the 'omniscient' novelist" (208). Some critics argue that instances of Marcel's impossible knowledge highlight the fictionality of his autobiographical writing, the tension between his novelistic desires and his memoiristic project. For Morton P. Levitt there is no "omniscient inconsistency" in the novel if we separate narrator from character and attend to the fact that the novel we are reading is the work Marcel devotes himself to writing: "The presumed autobiography turns inevitably—for Marcel is above all an artist, and he has an agenda of his own—into a fiction" (82). It is possible, then, that in this paraleptic moment Marcel could be *assuming* the omniscience of the novelist in the act of narration. Genette does not countenance this hypothesis because Marcel does not admit speculation, unlike other instances where modal locutions become indices of a focal restriction. This is consistent with Genette's project to apply grammatical categories to narrative theory, in which he claims the function of narrative is to tell a story by reporting facts and therefore "its one mood, or at least its characteristic mood, strictly speaking can only be the indicative" (161).

In *Narrative Discourse Revisited* Genette reiterates that focalization is to be understood as "a selection of narrative information with respect to what was traditionally called omniscience." He goes on to write: "In pure fiction that term is, literally, absurd (the author has nothing to 'know,' since he invents everything), and we would be better off replacing it with completeness of information—which, when supplied to a reader, makes him 'omniscient'" (74). For Genette, then, the *author* selects what information about the story to convey in the narrative, with the various modes of focalization offering choices of restriction or regulation of this information. The function of the narrator in Genette's model is really only to be the instrument of this focalization, what he calls "a sort of information conveying pipe," to report the story which the author has invented (74). This allows Genette to claim, in *Narrative Discourse,* that Balzac's narrator is never Balzac, "even if here and there he expresses Balzac's opinion, for this author-narrator is someone who 'knows'" the events being narrated "whereas all Balzac himself does is imagine them" (214). A key methodological claim which results from this separation of author and narrator is that "the narrating situation of a fictional account is *never* reduced to its situation of writing" (214). This is fair enough, but when Genette attributes a paralepsis to the novelist's omniscience, I think he is effectively reducing the instance of narrating to the instance of writing, and this is because his theory cedes responsibility for the regulation of narrative information to the author rather than the narrator.

Genette's solution to Marcel's moments of impossible knowledge is to explain them as elements of what he calls Proust's transgressive polymodality. However, I think it is worth looking again at his theory of focalization. In his revision of earlier theories of point of view, Genette argued that what was traditionally understood as omniscient narration can be termed "*nonfocalized* narrative, or narrative with *zero* focalization" (189). Following Todorov, he provides this definition: "where the narrator knows more than the character, or more exactly *says* more than any of the characters knows" (189). I want to dwell for a moment on this relationship between knowing and speaking.

In the introduction to *Narrative Discourse,* Genette is clear in stating that "[s]tory and narrating thus exist for me only by means of the intermediary of the narrative" (29). This is a statement of method. Its premise is that we reconstruct the temporal order of events, receive information about the story, and identify traces of the narrating instance solely from the narrative discourse itself. If we approach a narrative with this method, rather than the presuppositions of convention, Genette's formulation of omniscience suggests to me that we know a narrator possesses more knowledge than the characters *only* because the narrator *says* more than they know. Hence my claim that the authority of omniscience is constituted by a narratorial performance which invokes the conventional assumption of competence.

It could therefore also be the case that a narrator does not necessarily possess more diegetic knowledge than the characters, but, in *saying* more, possesses a narrative authority predicated on the assumption of superior knowledge. In other words, omniscience is the performative effect of a text's narrative voice, rather than a product of its focalization. The idea that knowledge about the story world is called into being by the act of narration should make sense when we consider Genette's definition of *narrating* as "the generating instance of narrative discourse" (213). But in separating voice from focalization, Genette methodologically prioritizes knowing over saying. This is the basis of the epistemological fallacy in narrative theory.

Genette's extra-textual recourse to the omniscient novelist to explain paraleptic instances is more coherent, I think, in James Phelan's rhetorical narratology, which takes a more explicitly pragmatic approach to paralepsis. For Phelan, these "deviations from the dominant narrative technique" (*Living* 83) are cases of the implied author providing necessary information to the authorial audience while still trying to retain the mimetic effect of the overall narrative. Phelan calls this the disclosure function, describing it as an authorial strategy which trumps the narrator function. Again, there is no room to attribute the paralepsis to the *narrator's* invention for the sake of the story. We can see here that the theory of paralepsis functions as an interpretive vacuum, in which critics feel compelled to furnish an explanation for a character narrator's impossible or illicit knowledge.

Unnatural Narratology

As examples of first-person omniscience have increased in volume and prominence over the past three decades, they have demanded attention from narrative theorists, and have continued to be understood in the epistemological terms determined by the theory of paralepsis. In *Narrative Discourse Revisited,* Genette describes the "correlations between mood and voice" in terms of a contract where "the heterodiegetic narrator is not accountable for his information," but a homodiegetic narrator "is obliged to justify" any illicit knowledge (77). For Genette, any breach of this trust is a paralepsis, and, "as a consequence of its 'vocal' selection," homodiegetic narrative "submits *a priori* to a modal restriction" which he calls "prefocalization" (78).

When he goes on to add homodiegetic narration with zero focalization to his typology of possible combinations of voice and focalization, offering *Moby Dick* as an example, Genette has completed the transition of paralepsis from a focal alteration which could apply to heterodiegetic narration with external or internal focalization, to a synonym for first-person omniscience. Paralepsis is no longer an isolated infraction of a governing code, but a governing code itself which is *by definition* an infraction. The foundations laid by Genette's structuralist narratology have since been reworked by cognitive narratology concerned with readers' naturalizing practices, enabling paralepsis to become a key object of study for the emergent research field of unnatural narratology.[1]

In their 2010 manifesto, "Unnatural Narratives, Unnatural Narratology: Beyond Mimetic Models," Alber, Iversen, Nielsen, and Richardson argue that paralepsis should be understood as the product of an unnatural mind. In keeping with their critique of the "mimetic bias" of narrative theory, which they claim rests upon "the idea that narratives are modeled on the actual world" (114), they emphasize that many forms or techniques which may have become "conventionalized over time" are nonetheless inherently unnatural, in the sense that they do not occur in real-world acts of communication. The capacity of fictional minds to know the thoughts of characters is a chief example. "The differences between the rather diverse forms of unnatural minds," they argue, "may be sketched out as a continuum ranging from well-known and thus conventionalized cases" such as omniscient narrators, "to the most bizarre and opaque cases found in experimental fiction" (120). Toward this end of the continuum are "the unnatural minds of 'omniscient' (or telepathic) first-person narrators" (120).

So here is the claim that we cannot rely on the idea of human consciousness to explain narratorial models. "In some first-person narratives," it is pointed out, "the narrator knows significantly more than he could if he or she were a real person" (124). This is a theory of paralepsis which highlights how the code of prefocalization which first-person omniscient narrators defy is founded on real-world possibilities, making the obligation for homodiegetic narrators to justify their knowledge a product of the mimetic bias. The difference in approach between classical narratology and unnatural narratology then lies in how this "deviation" is explained, how the interpretive vacuum is filled. In challenging the mimetic bias, unnatural narratology also seeks to resist the impulse of much cognitive narratology to explain strange narratives by adapting them to real-world scripts, such as the Theory of Mind, arguing instead that "one can simply accept the fact that many narratives go well beyond imaginable real-world situations" (129).[2]

I'm not sure, however, whether the category of the unnatural mind really challenges the mimetic bias, or that it leads to more insightful interpretations. The problem with unnatural narratology for me is that in wanting to preserve the "unnatural" qualities of first-person omniscience from the conventionalization undergone by third-person omniscience it is obliged to keep the mimetic bias always present as a default model to be challenged. If the theory of a paraleptic infraction is based on a mimetic bias, why continue to label it paralepsis? All that it is accomplished is a displacement of the infraction from a textual convention to a cognitive framework. Furthermore, the desire to resist conventionalization leads to an oversimplification of what counts as real-world cognitive parameters. If the *authors* of unnatural narratives are able to imagine impossible storyworlds, antinomic temporalities, mind reading and unnatural narrative voices, presumably these imaginative acts are real-world cognitive activities. To put it bluntly, writing fiction is a natural act of communication, and this is the model first-person narrators invoke when performing omniscience in the act of narration.

Paralepsis and Naturalization

To demonstrate some of the interpretive problems and typological limitations generated by the "unnatural" approach to first-person omniscience, I turn to Ruediger Heinze's 2008 essay "Violations of Mimetic Epistemology in First-Person Narrative Fiction." Heinze presents the existence of first-person omniscience as a research problem to be addressed by narrative theory: "How, then, can one conceptualize first-person narrators in fictional narratives whose quantitative and qualitative knowledge about events, other characters, etc., clearly exceeds what one could expect of a human consciousness and would thus make them prone to being labeled 'omniscient'?" (280).

His first move is to claim that these narrators can't be "naturalized" or "narrativized" as unreliable, because, despite their unusual knowledge, there are no indicators of insincerity or inconsistency in the narrative report. He also dismisses the possibility of satisfactorily explaining these narratives as narratorless or voiced by nonhuman narrators because of the clear presence of human consciousness in the act of telling. And he dismisses recourse to possible worlds theory on the same grounds: "With the slight but significant exception of unusual knowledge, the narrators belong to a 'natural' world very much like the actual one" (285).

Heinze's approach is to follow Culler's lead and reject the concept of "omniscience," instead using "the term 'paralepsis' whenever referring to the phenomenon of a first-person narrator knowing and/or sensing something to which he/she should not have access by all that we as readers know about human cognition and perception" (282). One can see by this definition that Heinze is not using the term "paralepsis" in the classical structuralist sense that Genette employed it, where the infraction is defined in relation to the dominant mood of the text. Instead, rather than an "alteration" of focalization, paralepsis is defined as the infraction of real-world frames of reference which readers bring to a text. "As a purely text-immanent phenomenon," Heinze argues, "paralepsis cannot be adequately explained. . . . Without knowledge of some basic cognitive and phenomenological aspects of the actual world (for example our inability to mind-read)," statements requiring unusual knowledge would not "qualitatively differ" from mere report of action (283).

The result is to limit his account of first-person omniscience to what he calls a violation of mimetic epistemology. With this method in place, Heinze presents five types of "first-person paraleptic narrators" before "discarding" or "disqualifying" three of them because their impossible knowledge can be naturalized. The case of *illusory* paralepsis can be explained by the delayed disclosure of a plausible reconstruction from available evidence; *humorous* paralepsis can be seen as parody or unreliable narration; and *mnemonic* paralepsis can be seen as an extension of accepted narrative conventions. This last category refers to the "impossibly comprehensive and infallible memory" of some narrators, but is dismissed because readers are habituated to the fact that "all first-person narrators remember pages and pages of dialogue verbatim" (286).

So after discarding the majority of examples of first-person omniscience for being "natural" paralepses and thus not paraleptic enough, we are left with two "real" cases of paralepsis which, Heinze says, "can be called 'non-natural' because their paralepsis cannot be rationalized within a natural world. They are true *violations of mimetic epistemology*. The explanation is either beyond the known physical laws or simply not given" (286). These two paralepses are the global and the local. *Global* paralepsis "is situated within a non-natural impossible frame" such as the narrator of Alice Sebold's *The Lovely Bones* narrating the story of her murder from heaven (286). *Local* paralepsis is "situated within a natural world but, nevertheless, is assumed by a first-person narrator in a style that suggests epistemological sincerity" (286). The example here is Rick Moody's *The Ice Storm,* in which a character, Paul, assumes the role of authorial third-person narrator to look back upon his adolescence and tell the story of the *annus horriblis* of his family.

The problem I have here is that if, as Heinze indicates, his typology is determined by the degree to which each paralepsis can be naturalized, and local paralepsis "is perhaps more difficult to naturalize because it is situated in a basically natural and realistic world with the physical laws of the real world intact" (286), then positing *The Ice Storm* as his exemplar makes his case difficult to sustain. *The Ice Storm* opens with the line: "So let me dish you this story about a family I knew when I was growing up. There's a part for me in this story, like there always is for a gossip, but more on that later" (3). This opening leads us to believe the narrator is a homodiegetic witness, but the novel quickly moves into an authorial voice employing variable internal focalization to shift perspectives between the father, mother, daughter, and son, while also containing many nonfocalized "authorial" comments about the 1970s. The last paragraph of the novel, however, reminds us not only that it is homodiegetic narration, but that the narrator is in fact one of the main characters, the son of the family:

> Or, that's how I remember it, anyway. Me. Paul. The gab. That's what I remember. And that this story really ends right at that spot. I have to leave Benjamin there with that news . . . and I have to leave myself—Paul—on the cusp of my adulthood, at the end of that *annus mirabilis* where comic books were indistinguishable from the truth, at the beginning of my confessions. I have to leave him and his family there because after all this time, after twenty years, it's time I left. (279)

Heinze runs through the ways in which this revelation might be naturalized, dismissing the illusory, the humorous, and the mnemonic because the narrator does not reveal a natural source for his knowledge or highlight his subjectiveness or speculation, and claims that the authoritative heterodiegetic report can only be the result of unnatural knowledge. He seems to contradict his rejection of naturalization, though, when he asserts that as a result of the revelation "the reliability of everything that has been told has to be reevaluated" (291). In fact, *The Ice Storm* really does belong to Heinze's most "naturalizable" and easily dismissed category: that of illusory paralepsis. Indeed, it would best be described as an example of what Heinze relegates to a footnoted subcase of this type: the cloaked paralepsis, in which "a first person narrator is cloaked for some time in an authorial (heterodiegetic) narrative situation" (294). The reason I say this is because Heinze fails to quote what for me is the key line of the novel, which comes after the narrator describes the uncanny experience of Paul having the exact same dream that his father had years earlier: "This congruency—between Paul and his dad—is sort of like the congruency between me, the narrator of this story, the imaginer of all these consciousnesses of the past, and God" (206).

This line draws attention to the imagination rather than unnatural telepathy of the narrator, and obviously refers to the convention of omniscience with its reference to God. So why does Heinze privilege *The Ice Storm* as an example of the highest degree of unnaturalizability, as a true violation of mimetic epistemology, for which the "paraleptic insights" of the narrator "cannot be explained or rationalized" (289)? It seems to be because he can't accept that the narrator has *imagined* the "consciousnesses of the past" rather than reported them.

If we need to posit and then discard three types of paraleptic narrators then paralepsis is surely not the best term to understand the phenomenon of first-person omniscience. Paralepsis, from structuralist to unnatural narratology, seems to be defined as a case where a first-person narrator does not *justify* his or her possession of knowledge. The absence of modal language is interpreted as an epistemological dilemma, when really this refusal would, in many cases, more productively be approached as a rhetorical strategy of the narrator, along with the decision to maintain a homodiegetic presence from the beginning or to resort to delayed disclosure. So rather than charting different types of paralepses according to degrees of naturalization, we might think about different rhetorical mobilizations of the conventional performative *authority* of omniscience.

It could be argued that in claiming homodiegetic omniscience is the product of the character narrator's imagination rather than impossible knowledge I am practicing another form of naturalization. This is true, and my response would be that this is the most accurate form of naturalization for these texts. However, I would also argue that we have recourse to naturalization as a reading practice only if we first consider a narrative to be unnatural. This first move, of encountering something strange which needs to be explained, is not necessarily a "natural" response of readers, it is the product of the mimetic bias itself. In Genette's formulation, paralepsis relates to momentary or isolated infractions of the governing code of focalization. If a narrative establishes homodiegetic omniscience as the governing code, one cannot point to instances of impossible knowledge as an infraction of this code, unless one invokes the mimetic bias as an external code or cognitive frame. Rather than focusing on the unnatural qualities of first-person omniscience by terming it paralepsis, I suggest an approach which highlights the fictional invention of the narrator.

Paralepsis and Hypothetical Focalization

This brings me to David Herman's work on hypothetical focalization (HF). In his project to bring the theory of possible worlds semantics into dialogue with narratology, Herman suggests a way of building upon the classical structuralist typology of focalization. "My claim is that by examining narratives told from a more or less obviously hypothetical point of view, we can start to rethink narrative mood generally, focalization specifically, in the context of the theory of possible worlds" ("Hypothetical Focalization" 233). He proceeds to outline Genette's categories of zero, internal and external focalization before asking:

> But what about narratives whose development provokes, in a more or less direct or explicit way, speculation about some nonexistent focalizor? At issue are narratives focalized such that we gain as it were illicit access to the materials of the story—materials not in fact focalized, or not focalizable even in principle, in the world(s) of the narrative. (236)

This discussion of "illicit access" sounds very much like a reference to paralepsis, and indeed in a footnote to this passage Herman writes: "Thus, we might want to construe HF as a special case of what Genette terms 'paralepsis,'" arguing that his purpose "is to analyze in detail the specifically paraleptic effects of HF—effects which may suggest less the infraction of a code, than grounds for rethinking the principles on which the code itself is based" (249).

Herman's goal is to reconfigure our understanding of focalization from a distinction between internal and external perspectives on a story (in Bal's understanding of these terms), to a scale of epistemic modalities in which varying degrees of doubt or certainty about the storyworld are encoded in the narrative discourse by grammatical moods. And here he suggests that we can take Genette's application of grammar to narrative not in a loose metaphorical sense, but literally by attending to modal locutions. This approach to what he calls the intensional properties of narrative, Herman argues, will facilitate greater attention to the study of narrative meaning because it posits focalization as a means of establishing propositional attitudes toward the reference world.

This is the context in which he discusses the category of HF, the appeal to a nonexistent or virtual focalizer or focalizing act, marked by modal locutions which offer a counterfactual perspective on what might have been observed or thought. Herman places HF at one end of a scale of "epistemic deixis," marking maximal doubt about the reference world, and zero focalization at the other end, indicating maximal congruence between the expressed and the reference world of the narrative. For Herman, then, "'omniscience' entails an epistemic stance in which a focalizer has absolute faith in the veracity, the actualness or actualizability, of the states of affairs detailed in the narrative" (246).

The question here is, what happens when this omniscience is attached to a character narrator? We have the discursive appearance of certainty, but the narrator's role as a character calls this epistemic stance into doubt, not through the presence of modal locutions, but by the very act of adopting an "external" perspective in the act of narration. So if first-person omniscience is defined as a paralepsis, and if Herman calls HF "a special case" of paralepsis, what is the relation between first-person omniscience and HF?

First-person omniscience, I suggest, offers an epistemic stance in which a "focalizer," which I understand as a perspectival position rather than an agent, may express no doubt about the reference world, but the narrator, in saying more than he or she knows or could know, cannot unproblematically claim the epistemic authority associated with this focal position. As a result, first-person omniscience becomes a performance of knowledge based on the hypothesis of a virtual focalizer: this is what *would* have been perceived by an omniscient narrator if such a perspective were possible. The extent to which readers doubt the epistemic stance of this virtualized zero focalization is dictated by the rhetoric of the narrating agents, their willingness to "justify" this stance, to make light of it, or their decision to conceal it. So the difference between what Heinze calls the "illusory" paraleptic narrator of Jeffrey Eugenides's *Middlesex,* who reminds us that "of course, a narrator in my position (prefetal at the time) can't be entirely sure about any of this" (9) and Moody's local paraleptic narrator who utters third-person authorial pronouncements, is one of rhetorical strategies rather than degrees of knowledge.

As Herman's examples show, isolated passages of grammatically encoded HF operate across a range of narrative categories, from first- to third-person voices, and from internal to zero focalization. While he carefully delineates the different functions of direct and indirect HF in their strong and weak versions, the case of homodiegetic omniscience highlights the importance of demonstrating how these types of HF interact with different modes of focalization and different narrative voices.

For instance, it is obvious that omniscient narrators may deploy HF to demonstrate hyperbolically their own epistemic authority, conjuring a virtual focalizer to speculate about what they already know, as is the case in Herman's example from *Possession:* "An observer might have speculated for some time as to whether they were travelling together or separately" (273). The narrator, of course, knows that these two characters are secret lovers travelling together. In this sense, hypotheticality could be understood as a paralipsis, Genette's term for a narrator saying less than they know. At the same time, the narrator's rhetorical use of this "hypothetical observer" (274) orients contemporary readers to a subject position aware of nineteenth century models of propriety. *The Ice Storm,* on the other hand, has several instances of modal locution which paradoxically serve to solidify its narrative authority by counterfactualizing the already imaginary act of focalization. Here is Benjamin Hood, Paul's father, turning up at a "key" party in the 1970s and realizing that the ascot tie he is wearing is no longer fashionable: "Had Hood been in a mind to comfort himself, he might have approved of his ample shirt collar, spread wide on the wings of his lapels. But how had he managed to get out the door wearing the ascot? How had he let himself?" (107). The modal locution in the first sentence marks the thought as virtual. The conjunction suggests the following questions could easily be an extension of the narrator's HF, even as it takes the form of free indirect thought. In fact, the whole passage of internal focalization is counterfactualized by the revelation that the narrator is this character's son, adopting the privilege of omniscience in the act of narration and describing himself as "the imaginer of all these consciousnesses of the past" (206).

Omniscience across Person

All this is by way of arguing that the relation between voice and focalization is crucial to the effects of HF, and that, like other modes of focalization, HF is a rhetorical strategy of storytelling akin to the strategies of justification employed by first-person omniscient narrators. So my claim is that first-person omniscience is an extension of HF beyond isolated modal locutions to the governing code of a narrative, in which a character, in the act of narration, draws upon the "privilege" of authorial omniscience to posit what could be known or perceived from the epistemic stance of zero focalization. The hypotheticality is not necessarily a propositional attitude of doubt, however, first because in its grammatically encoded manifestations HF can operate as a rhetorical strategy for highlighting epistemic authority (such as in the case of *Possession*), and secondly because the epistemic logic of first-person omniscience is often one of invention. So when the narrator of *Middlesex* undermines his epistemic authority by pointing to the limitations of his knowledge of the past, he is nonetheless asserting his narrative authority to tell the story of his life with conviction, established with this early invocation: "Sing now, O Muse, of the recessive mutation on my fifth chromosome!" (4).

In *The Rhetoric of Fictionality* Richard Walsh argues that positing the idea of a narrator who knows cancels out the fictionality of fictional narratives. "The function of the narrator," Walsh points out, "is to allow the narrative to be read as something known rather than something imagined, something reported as fact rather than something told as fiction" (73). Walsh is not dismissing the idea that someone is telling a story, or arguing that fiction is not a communicative act. His rejection of the narrator is a rejection of the concept of level and its implication of a narrative act outside the frame of representation. In claiming that "the narrator is always either a character who narrates, or the author" (78), Walsh argues that "omniscience is not a faculty possessed by a certain class of narrators, but, precisely, a quality of authorial imagination" (73).

The fictional counterpart to Walsh's argument, I suggest, is Ian McEwan's *Atonement*. This novel employs delayed disclosure to reveal that the apparent third-person omniscient narrator is in fact a character, Briony, herself a novelist, who has written the book we have just read, and admits to having invented the ending of the story she has narrated. Here is Briony's justification for her choice of narrative voice:

> The problem these fifty-nine years has been this: how can a novelist achieve atonement when, with her absolute power of deciding outcomes, she is also God? There is no one, no entity or higher form that she can appeal to, or be reconciled with, or that can forgive her. There is nothing outside her. In her imagination she has set the limits and the terms. No atonement for God, or novelists, even if they are atheists. It was always an impossible task, and that was precisely the point. The attempt was all. (371)

The metafictional game being played here involves the "omniscient" author, McEwan, displacing his novelistic privilege of invention onto a character-narrator. Briony, in fact, can more accurately be described as the author of the first three parts of the novel, employing an omniscient narrator to report this fictionalized narrative of her life, creating an ontological distinction between these parts and her revelations in the final section, "London 1999." In this case, the narrating Briony is enacting the experiencing Briony's desire for the unnatural or impossible knowledge of omniscience. This desire has two competing aspects: to access the thoughts of Cecilia and Robbie which would have afforded her experiencing self the requisite empathy for understanding their motivations; and to assert creative control over the lives of her characters, offering the lovers a happy ending in fiction denied them in life by Briony's misreading of their motivations.

It should be made clear that I am not rejecting the argument that isolated cases of impossible knowledge in many novels throughout history can be understood as paraleptic infractions where the author's desire for exposition "trumps" the dominant focalizing code of first-person narration. I am arguing that the desire of characters to perform omniscience in the act of telling constitutes a global frame in much contemporary fiction, in which narrators invoke the genre of the novel rather than the memoir or the autobiography, which character narration originally mimicked precisely for the purposes of verisimilar authority. First-person omniscience, then, highlights the fact that telling one's story is as much an act of imaginative reconstruction as it is a narrative report by someone who knows. In turn, it highlights what self-reflexive novelists have said for centuries: the capacity to invent fictional truths is part of the author's discursive authority.

What, then, are the ways in which the relation between first-person omniscience and traditional authorial narration have been explained? In considering the "functional design" of first-person omniscience, Heinze concludes that "paralepsis in first-person narrators can then be read as a satiric comment not only on the alleged panopticism of authorial narratives but also on those critiques of these fictions that read them as panoptic" (292). Heinze locates these narrators historically as "the legitimate heirs of the postmodern language games," with the unnatural knowledge of narrators parodically highlighting the fantasy of omniscience in realist fiction: "If epistemic unity—or its pretense—is a form of assuming discursive control, then these narratives assume an impossible control, emphasizing that it has always been illusory anyway" (292). Morton P. Levitt makes a similar claim on behalf of modernism in *The Rhetoric of Modernist Fiction,* arguing that what he calls the "seeming omniscience" at play in the work of Carol Shields and José Saramago demonstrates the triumph of point of view and the subjectivism it entails over the certainties of the form inherited from the Victorian novel.

Can we see omniscient character narration, therefore, as a governing code or frame of hypotheticality which operates as a critique of the epistemological surety of traditional omniscience? Only, it seems to me, if we perpetuate the epistemological fallacy of focalization as a mode of knowing rather than a strategy of telling. While it is certainly true that first-person omniscience produces a metatextual stance on the concept of omniscience itself, I would suggest that it is not a critique of omniscience, but another deployment of omniscience in the wake of postmodern metafiction. I have already argued that metafiction reflexively re-introduced omniscience by highlighting the author's creative power in agonistic rather than triumphalist fashion. I would suggest that first-person omniscience can be characterized as a post-postmodern move beyond metafiction because it draws attention, particularly in examples of delayed disclosure, to the artifice of the fiction, but locates the authorial figure within the diegesis, providing a characterological motivation for the reflexive experimentation with conventions of omniscience. In this way it contributes to the development of a relativized omniscience across person in contemporary fiction.

Here I return to Richard Powers, whose post-postmodern sensibility is characterized as a combination of realism and metafictional experimentation. As reviews of *Generosity* attest, the novel courts uncertainty about the diegetic status of the narrator. The novel opens with the narrator voyeuristically observing the protagonist, Russell Stone, on a train, and attempting to read the notes he is taking, while simultaneously drawing attention to the spatio-temporal distance of the narrating instance from the story:

> A man rides backwards in a packed subway car. . . . He's just thirty-two, I know, although he seems much older. I can't see him well at first. But that's my fault, not his. I'm years away, in another country, and the El car is so full tonight that everyone's near invisible. (3)

At times the narrator assumes the role of an immanent presence in the diegesis, spying on his own creation—"His pen freezes in midair; he looks up. I glance away, caught spying" (5). At other times he indicates that he is recreating the "real" world in fiction: "I watch him twist, the way he did so often in real life" (96).

These intrusions display an anxiety about the extent of the narrator's knowledge of the protagonist, similar to Martin Amis's narrator in *The Information*: "The train sways, he pitches in his seat, and I don't know anything. I stop deciding and return to looking" (4). The narrator's conventional access to consciousness seems insufficient, as he resorts to observation and the documentary traces of Russell's existence (his notes, the books he reads):

> I search for Russell Stone all over. I read the almanac for that year. I read his class textbook, of course. I read back issues of his magazine. I even loot those hall-of-mirrors avant-garde novels whose characters try to escape their authors, the kind he once loved, the kind he thought he'd write one day, before he gave up fiction. (37–38)

The equivocation between creative control—"I have her flip up her window slide and look out the plastic portal" (80)—and lack of insight—"I wish I could make out Stone's students better. I can see how they disturb him. But I just can't see them in any detail. They're hiding in the sullen, shiny performance of youth" (7)—underpins the metafictional commentary on the armature of fiction, from the arbitrariness of plot to the handling of time: "*Time passes,* as the novelist says. The single most useful trick of fiction for our repair and refreshment: the defeat of time. . . . I needed 125 pages to get from Labor Day to Christmas vacation. In six more words, here's spring" (156). There is enough evidence to suggest that this self-reflexive omniscient narrator is less of an authorial figure exposing the artifice of realist fiction and its representational claims than Russell himself writing about his life in a form he has lost faith in: "Just beyond the South Bend, Stone has an epiphany. He knows why he could never in his life or anytime thereafter write fiction: he's crushed under the unbearable burden of a plot" (273). That the narrator is a character separated from his experiencing self by temporal distance (subsequent narration) and by narrative voice (heterodiegetic) can be assumed from a line such as this: "Purveyors and contractors, drug dealers, number crunchers, busboys, grant writers. Just brushing against them in memory makes me panic" (4).

The conclusion suggests that Russell has self-consciously adopted the role of omniscient authorial narrator as he turns his life into a work of fiction to make sense of the death of his student, Thassa. In the final pages, Thassa meets up with the journalist, Tonia Schiff, and it is unclear at first whether this is an actual event in the storyworld, or a fictional encounter in which Thassa remains alive only in the novelist's imagination. In this scene, Thassa wants to return the writing handbook which Russell set for his students to read, *Make Your Writing Come Alive*. The following line suggests an equivalence in identity between narrator and character:

"It's not mine," she says. "Give it to Russell. He will need this."

I will need much more. Endless, what I'll need. But I'll take what I'm given, and go from there. (295)

The novel, then, draws parallels between a heterodiegetic authorial narrator metafictionally commenting on a character he has created but cannot fully know, and a character narrator acknowledging the process of fictionalization involved in reconstructing his life as a narrative: "And I'm here again, across from the daughter of happiness as I never will be again, in anything but story. . . . She's still alive, my invented friend, just as I conceived her, still uncrushed by the collective need for happier endings" (295). In a sense this severs the existential link between narrating and experiencing self which provides the epistemological grounds for a character narrator's focal restriction. To the extent that the novel itself takes the relation between fiction and nonfiction as an object of exploration, *Generosity* shows how Powers has offered omniscient character narration as an extension of his practice of combining metafiction and realism, locating the metafictional elements in the character's self-authorship.

First-Person Omniscience and Narrative Authority

> Many first-person narrators go far beyond transcribing that which they have experienced themselves by letting the narrative arise anew from their imagination.
>
> —Franz K. Stanzel, *A Theory of Narrative* 215

My argument is not simply that "unnatural" narratives can be naturalized, or to provide different interpretations of the texts under consideration. In suggesting hypotheticality as the way to understand first-person omniscience, particularly as it highlights invention rather than speculation and doubt, I want to think more about the relation of first-person to third-person omniscience in contemporary fiction. I have argued throughout this book that omniscient narration is best understood not as a quality of authorial or narratorial knowledge, but as a specific rhetorical performance of narrative authority. As a result of this approach, I have suggested that focalization, the narratological category under which omniscience is typically discussed, must be seen as a rhetorical strategy of narrative voice. Instead of conceptualizing an all-knowing authorial narrator who is already in full possession of all there is to know about the storyworld and who can then deploy different modes of regulating information about this storyworld when representing it to readers, I am suggesting that we think of omniscient narrators as storytellers who generate and perform this knowledge in the act of narration. First-person omniscience "dramatizes" this concept of omniscience. If the impossible knowledge of homodiegetic narrators draws attention to the "unnaturalness" of omniscience assumed by authorial narrators, what it highlights is our willingness to understand the convention of omniscience in terms of narratorial knowledge rather than authorial invention. What is at stake in this form is a tension between two modes of narrative authority which have informed the history of the novel: the verisimilar authority of the eyewitness derived from the nonfictional form of the memoir or autobiography or confession; and the authority of "fictional truth" claimed by the novelist.

My argument about imagination as the central paradigm for homodiegetic omniscience is anticipated by Scholes and Kellogg, who point to an uneasy relationship between empirical and fictional impulses in the history of the novel as a problem of authority associated with the question of point of view. The empirical authority of eyewitness narrators, they argue, is balanced by the fact that they cannot witness everything and can know only one mind: their own. "But the novelist's determination to have the benefits of eyewitness narration without accepting its limitations has been indefatigable" (259). In tracing this determination of novelists, Scholes and Kellogg point to Tristram Shandy whose eyewitness status covers events before his birth, and to the narrator of Madam Bovary who begins as an eyewitness before fading into an omniscient presence (259). They also draw attention to Dickens's "famous resort to a combination of disembodied omniscience and direct reporting in *Bleak House*" (260). In particular, they discuss the work of Proust who "has given us some of the most flagrant cases in all literature of the novelist's insistence on having things both ways" (260). The paralepses in Proust which have become the touchstone of the epistemological fallacy in narrative theory are discussed here in terms of

> Proust's entire esthetic, which continually mentions the limitations of the empirical and asserts the extraordinary power of those insubstantial essences, memory and imagination. He simply rejects the notion that "real" people can be apprehended without the assistance of these esthetic essences. Thus, conversely, as long as the eye-witness is imaginative enough he need not be hindered, like poor Lucius in the stable, by any merely physical bonds. *Since we are all makers, he suggests, creating*

our lives as we go, there is no incompatibility between the narrator as witness and the narrator as creator. Proust's esthetic enables the narrative artist to regain some of the ground he had lost when he abandoned his position as inspired bard for the more empirically oriented positions of eye-witness and *histor.* (260–61, original emphasis)

Unencumbered by the epistemological fallacy, Scholes and Kellogg are able to acknowledge Proust's focal transgressions but discuss them as a function of Marcel's narratorial imagination (as opposed to telepathy). They go on to discuss the peripheral eyewitness narrator in the work of Conrad, claiming that: "Since the imagination plays the central role, the factual or empirical aspect of the protagonist's life becomes subordinated to the narrator's understanding of it. Not what really happened but the meaning of what the narrator believes to have happened becomes the central preoccupation in this kind of narrative" (261). Fitzgerald, Faulkner, and Warren, they claim, "have all worked variations on this basic tactic" (261). The novels which I mentioned at the start of this chapter extend this tradition of emphasizing the role of imagination in narrative report. As examples of ways in which authors construct narrators who deploy omniscience in order to solve the limitations of first-person narration, they are also examples of ways in which first-person narration has extended the possibilities of omniscience in contemporary fiction.

Hypothetical Focalization and the Narrating Instance

I do not wish to reject all claims for impossible knowledge, but the paradox of characters narrating more than they know can be construed as a rhetorical function of voice rather than an epistemological problem of focalization if we pay attention to the distinction between the narrating and experiencing selves of a character. In works of contemporary omniscient character narration, narrators constantly draw attention to the narrating instance, providing a range of justifications for their "impossible" knowledge. These justifications necessarily imply a narratee as the narrators contend self-reflexively with the "mimetic bias," asserting their authority to narrate the story. On the majority of occasions, I suggest, they do so by invoking the importance of the imagination to the narrative act. So, instead of displaying impossible knowledge attributable to an unnatural mind or the (implied) author, these character narrators deploy HF to assume the narrative authority of omniscience. Their narratives are not the product of unnatural narrative acts, but of narratorial invention, drawing authority from the figure of the novelist who creates rather than the memoirist who reports. They self-consciously replicate, in the narrating instance, the determination of novelists to have it both ways, drawing attention in most cases to the fact that they are written narratives.

Classifying omniscient character narration according to a model of paraleptic violations of mimetic epistemology with varying degrees of naturalizability creates a kind of artificial distinction between examples of this form. Instead, we can pay attention to the self-reflexive references to the narrating instance in justificatory statements to establish the rhetorical means by which narrators perform the conventional authority of omniscience as an imaginative heuristic, a search for knowledge. A typology of different modes of omniscient character narration would then focus on strategic deployments of the conventions of omniscience: autobiographical reconstruction of the narrator's past in an attempt to make sense of their lives, narrated in autodiegetic mode (*Midnight's Children, Middlesex, The Lovely Bones*) or in heterodiegetic mode (*The Ice Storm, Atonement, Generosity*), typically employing delayed disclosure; or biographical reconstruction of the lives of other characters, known and unknown to a peripheral narrator, narrated by a singular (*Oscar and Lucinda, Jazz*) or plural (*Ways of Dying, The Virgin Suicides*) homodiegetic narrator.

References to the imagination are common in many of these examples. The first-person plural or "we" narrator of Jeffrey Eugenides's *The Virgin Suicides* speaks for a group of neighborhood boys who are unable to understand the female "point of view" represented by the mysterious Lisbon girls. Their capacity to narrate scenes and thoughts to which they were not privy is not explicitly explained, but readily alluded to early in the novel: "He had a high voice, and when Joe Larson told us how Mr. Lisbon had cried when Lux was later rushed to the hospital during her own suicide scare, we could easily imagine the sound of his girlish weeping" (8). The desire which animates this imagination is evident in their experience of seeing Cecilia Lisbon moments before she commits suicide: "She kept her face to the floor, moving in her personal oblivion, her sunflower eyes fixed on the predicament of her life we would never understand" (29). This is what the boys do witness, at a party they were invited to. They then hear Cecilia walk up the stairs and fling herself out of a window to her death. They will never understand Cecilia or her sisters and this whole narrative, written years after the event in the narrators' adulthood, is an attempt to flesh out what they know in the act of narrating, of imagining, of performing omniscience. "Like us," the narrators say of news reporters, "they became custodians of the girls' lives, and had they completed the job to our satisfaction, we might never have been forced to wander endlessly down the paths of hypothesis and memory" (224).

In Tony Morrison's *Jazz,* the narrator opens with the line "Sth, I know this woman" (3), and proceeds to relay the private life and inner thoughts of the woman, whom she does not actually seem acquainted with, and many other characters, even those in the past. Caroline Rody describes *Jazz* as having "a form of narration we might call the first-person omniscient anonymous" which makes "the identity and the status of the knower a central puzzle of the story" (622). Rody claims that the combination of personal subjective narrator and omniscient knowledge make this an "impossible" and "logically infeasible" voice (622). However, the narrator makes clear the grounds of her knowledge: "Risky, I'd say, trying to figure out anybody's state of mind. But worth the trouble if you're like me—curious, inventive, and well informed. . . . So he didn't know. Neither do I, although it's not hard to imagine what it must have been like" (137). The narrator in fact goes on to make this invention the grounds for a confession to the reader: "How could I have imagined him so poorly? . . . I have been careless and stupid and it infuriates me to discover (again) how unreliable I am" (160); "I believed I saw everything important they did, and based on what I saw I could imagine what I didn't" (221). The concluding section reveals the desire animating the narrator's performance of omniscience: selfishness—"confused in my solitude into arrogance, thinking my space, my view was the only one that was or that mattered" (220); and envy—"I envy them their public love. I myself have only known it in secret" (229).

I will examine in more detail the narrative voice of Salman Rushdie's 1981 novel, the Booker of Bookers, *Midnight's Children,* for this is the earliest of contemporary omniscient character narrators, referred to by Nicholas Royle as evidence for the necessity of recasting omniscience as telepathy, and because it certainly does have "unnatural" elements. In the magic realist world of this novel, the first-person narrator, Saleem Sinai, asks readers to believe that he somehow became a radio receiver when he was nine, able to hear the thoughts of other characters: "Telepathy, then: the inner monologues of all the so-called teeming millions, of masses and classes alike, jostled for space within my head" (168). In an account of how he dealt with this transformation, Saleem gives us a list of different types of focalization: "By sunrise I had discovered that the voices could be controlled—I was a radio receiver, and I could turn the volume up or down; I could select individual voices; I could even, by an effort of will, switch of my newly-discovered inner ear" (164).

And yet, despite this account of the unnatural mind of his younger experiencing self, the act of narration is a "natural" frame, in which the self-consciously unreliable narrator persistently refers to the process of writing in his attempts to reconstruct his past, to fill in the gaps in his knowledge: "Most of what matters in our lives takes place in our absence: but I seem to have found from somewhere the trick of filling in the gaps of knowledge, so that everything is in my head, down to the last detail" (14). This "trick" is the function of memory, "my new, all-knowing memory, which encompasses most of the lives of father mother grandfather grandmother and everybody else" (97). Here we have a magic realist justification for the narrator's mnemonic overkill. If this all-knowing memory is the product of his telepathic access to the memories of his family, however, it does not guarantee the infallible knowledge of omniscience. Indeed telepathy is far less important as both a theme and a mode of knowledge than memory:

> "I told you the truth," I say yet again, "Memory's truth because memory has its own special kind. It selects, eliminates, alters, exaggerates, minimizes, glorifies, and vilifies also; but in the end it creates its own reality, its heterogeneous but usually coherent version of events; and no sane human being ever trusts someone else's version more than his own." (242)

Rushdie's narrator is aware of the role the imagination plays in the function of memory, thus recognizing that distortions and factual errors are inevitable in his narration: "I reply across the unreliable years to S. P. Butt, who got his throat slit in the Partition riots and lost interest in time: 'What's real and what's true aren't necessarily the same'" (87). This awareness is built into the act of narration itself: "as my decay accelerates (my writing speed is having trouble keeping up), the risk of unreliability grows" (310).[3]

Furthermore, the act of narration is not informed by telepathic access to other character's thoughts. In the following passage Saleem discusses the differences between his (older) narrating self and his (younger) experiencing self:

> Then as now, someone was awake in the dark, hearing disembodied tongues. Then as now, the one deafened ear. And fear, thriving in the

heat . . . it was not the voices (then or now) which were frightening. He, young-Saleem then, was afraid of an idea—the idea that his parents' outrage might lead to a withdrawal of their love; that even if they began to believe him, they would see his gift as a kind of shameful deformity . . . while I, now, Padma-less, send these words into the darkness and I am afraid of being disbelieved. He and I, I and he . . . *I no longer have his gift; he never had mine.* (190, original ellipses, emphasis added)

This suggests that Saleem's narrating self no longer possesses his youthful gift of telepathy and must rely upon his memory. In this sense, then, the narrator is paradoxically paraliptic, saying less than he knew. The "disembodied tongues" that he hears in this passage are present only in his confusion of past and present self: "Different and similar, we are joined by heat. A shimmering heat-haze, then and now, blurs his then-time into mine . . . my confusion, travelling across the heat waves, is also his" (191). Although Saleem discusses how as a child he would enter a person's mind, he typically refrains from relaying the contents of that mind. To cope with his telepathic gift, he tells us, he had to assume some sense of control:

Because the feeling had come upon me that I was somehow creating a world; that the thoughts I jumped inside were *mine,* that the bodies I occupied acted at my command; that, as current affairs, arts, sports, the whole rich variety of a first-class radio station poured into me, I was somehow making them happen . . . which is to say, I had entered into the illusion of the artist, and thought of the multitudinous realities of the land as the raw unshaped material of my gift. "I can find out any damn thing!" I triumphed, "There isn't a thing I cannot know!" (199)

This admission, of course, raises the specter of doubt regarding the young Saleem's "gift" within a global narrative framework of unreliability. The story being narrated is an imaginative reconstruction rather than a reliable paraleptic account, and subject to the dictates of the narrative act itself: "And now I, Saleem Sinai, intend briefly to endow myself-then with the benefits of hindsight; destroying the unities and conventions of fine writing, I make him cognizant of what was to come, purely so that he can be permitted to think the following thoughts" (270). This narrator is liberated from the mimetic bias not by virtue of his unnatural mind, but by his self-reflexive awareness of narrative as an act of invention.

Writing about *Midnight's Children* in his 1982 essay, "Imaginary

Homelands," in the context of his status as an Indian writer, Rushdie claims:

> Writers are no longer sages, dispensing the wisdom of the centuries. And those of us who have been forced by cultural displacement to accept the provisional nature of all truths, all certainties, have perhaps had modernism forced upon us. We can't lay claim to Olympus, and are thus released to describe our worlds in the way in which all of us, whether writers or not, perceive it from day to day. (12–13)

Midnight's Children can thus be seen as the refracted voice of Rushdie's cultural authority in the relativized omniscient voice of Saleem Sinai. That Rushdie chose, several years later, to write *The Satanic Verses* with an omniscient "satanic" narrator, suggests another experimental attempt to lay claim to Olympus.

Authorship and Homodiegetic Omniscience

I have pointed out how Genette attributes Marcel's paraleptic statements to the transgressive polymodality of the "omniscient author," and how Phelan attributes similar statements in other works to the implied author operating along a different track of communication from the narrator. More recently, Henrik Nielsen has drawn upon the premises of unnatural narratology to assign paraleptic statements to an impersonal first-person voice separate from the character narrator ("The Impersonal Voice") or to a kind of authorial intrusion in a character's narrative, both of which expose the logical unity of the narrating instance as an anthropomorphic projection. The latter argument is made in "Natural Authors, Unnatural Narration," in which Nielsen suggests the need to reconsider the importance of authorship in narrative theory. Nielsen refers to Richard Walsh's argument that to employ the concept of narration as report, and thus posit the figure of a narrator who knows rather than invents, cancels out the fictionality of a work. He draws upon this insight to investigate works which problematize distinctions between fiction and nonfiction, and he does so to suggest that we need to pay more attention to how authors communicate information to readers through local manifestations of unnatural narration.

Any attempt to acknowledge the importance of craft-based decisions by authors is productive. However, such a move seems again to rely upon the epistemological fallacy and its logic of deferred attribution. This is because Nielsen wants to describe a narrative, or a moment of narration, as unnatural if its narrator could not know what is being reported. "Since narrators as 'agents' do not invent, they cannot help to explain passages that are—inside fiction itself—obviously invented and not reported" (298). Hence Nielsen's recourse to the author to explain this invention. Yet surely the point of Walsh's insight is that we don't need to rely upon a model of narration as report, of a narrator who knows. If the author directly narrates a fictional invention, then why can't a character narrator also invent a narrative report? Not, by virtue of the same logic of naturalization, an unreliable report, but simply a fictional narrative. That is, in many cases it may be profitable to read a character narrator's story as a novel about their lives with all the conventions of novelistic storytelling available to them, rather than a memoir or autobiography, with the attendant focal restrictions accompanying the narrating instance of these forms. Only if we understand memoir or autobiography as the global generic frame of first-person narration will we deem instances of "impossible" knowledge as unnatural.

The problem of unnatural narratology is the assumption it shares with cognitive approaches to theories of naturalization: that only a "naturally" occurring form of oral conversational storytelling in the real world can be considered natural, and that this is the default mode of communication by which fictional narratives are understood. According to Nielsen:

> While the narrative in texts of this nature can *globally* be considered a form of communication from author to reader, this global narrative may include local noncommunication rather than a report from an unwitting narrator. It may, for example, include narration that is unnatural, in the simple sense that it transcends the norms of everyday conversation and communication, and in the sense that it is without sender or receiver, without narrator or narratee. (297)

So unnatural narration is seen here as non-communication if it cannot be assimilated to the knowledge of the narrator. Nielsen provides a line from James Frey's *A Million Little Pieces* which he says is unnatural because it cannot be communicated by a narrator: "I fade in and out. The TV is narcotic. In and Out. In. Out. In. Out." For Nielsen, "there is no one to tell, and no one with a conscious mind able to do the telling" (297). Hence the line must be a global communication from the author, a fictional invention which "violates the limits of narratorial communication" rather than a local report from the narrator (298). But if, as Nielsen points out, "written narrative lends itself more easily to non-communication" (297), and the character narrator is authoring his own life, why can he not have *written* this? For Nielsen it is because rather than two tracks of communication, in which the author communicates through the narrator, we have two voices:

> My proposal has the advantage of acknowledging the ability of authors to employ such features of their choosing, as well as their ability to transcend normal communication and the rules governing conversation or storytelling from narrator to narratee. This ability to go beyond communicational models is paradoxically, yet completely logically, possessed by no narrator understood within the framework of the very same communicational model. (299)

My argument in this chapter has been that such claims deny the capacity of authorial invention to character narrators when this capacity would seem to be a central rhetorical element of the narrative. Nielsen, at least, directs the epistemological preoccupations of unnatural narratology to questions of authorship, concluding that "narration cannot always be understood according to the rules of communicational discourse. Furthermore, this fact ties narration more closely to its flesh-and-blood author" (299). In my final chapter I will address the question of global communication between author and reader in terms of fiction as a mode of public discourse.

CHAPTER 8

Real Authors and Real Readers

A Discursive Approach to the Narrative Communication Model

IF NARRATIVE AUTHORITY is the contingent product of a relational exchange between textual agents, and of the institutional and cultural conditions of production and reception, I want in this final chapter to elaborate the broader narratological ramifications of investigating the formal category of narrative voice in a discursive context. In doing so I will discuss how narrative theory can address its most significant lacuna: attention to the role of real authors in the structure of narrative communication. Acknowledging authorship is crucial to the function of narrative authority in contemporary omniscient narration.

The foundational claims of *Narrative Discourse,* Genette's "essay in method," is that a narrative "can only be such to the extent that it tells a story" and "to the extent that it is uttered by someone" (29). This definition informs Genette's study of the ways in which a narrator reports information about the story in the narrative discourse. In *The Rhetoric of Fiction,* on the other hand, Wayne Booth is interested in "the technique of non-didactic fiction, viewed as the art of communicating with readers," in the "rhetorical resources" which writers employ to "impose [their] fictional world upon the reader" (xiii). Booth's study is concerned with understanding how fictional form conveys the values of (implied) authors.

Narrative text
Real author - - - > | Implied author —> (Narrator)—>(Narratee)—> Implied reader | - - - > Real reader

FIGURE 1   Narrative text

Adopting Roman Jakobsen's linguistic account of the act of verbal communication—in which an addresser sends a message to an addressee—as its basic model, narrative theory incorporated Genette's narrator, Gerald Prince's narratee, and Booth's implied author and the reader he "makes" (named by Iser as the implied reader) to facilitate the study of narrative communication. Peter Rabinowitz's 1977 "Truth in Fiction" drew these figures into a typological account of the relations between narrative agents, focusing on the receptive roles a text invites, such as the narrative audience and the authorial audience. Seymour Chatman's diagrammatic model of narrative communication, proposed in his 1978 book, *Story and Discourse,* remains the standard (see figure 1).

Thus, classical narratology posited as its object of study a series of agents immanent to a work of narrative fiction while leaving aside the agents which bracket this formulation: the author and the reader. As Shlomith Rimmon-Kenan argued in *Narrative Fiction*: "the empirical process of communication between author and reader is less relevant to the poetics of narrative fiction than its counterpart in the text" (90).

There have since been any number of variations and revisions of this basic model, depending on the methodological focus of individual scholars. In a 2005 book chapter titled "Why Don't Our Terms Stay Put? The Narrative Communication Diagram Scrutinized and Historicized," Harry E. Shaw makes two points: first that "users of the diagram bring to it two different implicit models of the communication situation; and second that the terms the diagram seeks to describe necessarily become hazier as we move from left to right" (299). If the communication diagram evokes "the image of someone telling a story to someone else" (300), Shaw claims, the first model emphasizes the flow of information between the various communicative agents, while the second emphasizes the "effects and purposes the teller wishes to achieve" (300).

For me, two important points arise from this account. First, Shaw's distinction between an emphasis on the flow of information and an emphasis on the rhetorical features of telling can be seen as a difference in analytical focus between focalization and voice. Information theorists would see the narrating as the *medium* by which a focalized story is accessed or constructed by readers. Rhetoric theorists would see the focalized story as a vehicle for establishing a narrative effect. Given critical consensus that story is an effect of discourse, I think the latter must be privileged. Secondly, despite Shaw's emphasis on the importance of the narrator, postclassical narratology has engaged primarily with the hazier right-hand side of the diagram. The story of postclassical narratology may be seen as an attempt to take up the challenge of theorizing the bracketing agent on the far right of the diagram, what is variously called the real reader, the actual reader, the empirical reader and the flesh-and-blood reader. Two prominent approaches to this challenge are the rhetorical-ethical and the cognitive. One focuses on the ethical judgments readers make in response to the rhetorical techniques employed in a narrative; the other investigates how readers process and make sense of narrative elements to construct mental storyworlds. Both betray a tension between academic and general readers even as they try to elide the distinction.

In the rhetorical approach, the critic stands in as a test case for this flesh-and-blood reader, one capable of entertaining a range of cognitive, emotional, aesthetic, and ethical responses, while still asserting a final critical judgment. For instance, in applying his model of rhetorical poetics to Ian McEwan's *Atonement,* James Phelan writes: "I believe that flesh-and-blood readers who respond in these ways are missing some of the intricacies of McEwan's communication, but I also believe that in McEwan's strategies they have good reasons for their responses" (*Experiencing* 131). This emphasis on readers begs the question: how do we know the ways in which readers respond to a narrative?

This question has animated criticisms leveled at the related field of reader response theory, in which it has been pointed out that the reader under study is typically an idealized version of the (androcentric) critical self. For instance, in a 1982 essay Mary Louise Pratt argued that "given the autobiographical bent of his recent book, *Is There a Text in This Class?,* it is fair to see [Stanley] Fish's theoretical work partly as a personal quest to examine, and with any luck to validate, the bases of his own critical and pedagogical practice" (221–22). In a review of Phelan's *Living to Tell about It,* Michael Eskin claims that Phelan cannot generalize into a theory of narrative his claims about the range of readers' responses to narratives unless he incorporates an empirical approach into his critical practice. It should be pointed out, though, that in many instances Phelan is dealing with well-established public responses to narrative texts, evidence for which can be found in reviews and essays about these texts. Responses to the revelation at the end of *Atonement* provide one clear example. At any rate, Phelan would legitimately claim that while his approach is reader oriented, it is nonetheless focused on the rhetorical strategies designed to evoke particular responses.

The cognitive approach in narrative theory attempts to address this empirical shortcoming by overtly drawing its theoretical authority from research in cognitive science. In doing so, it collapses reader responses to a narrative into universal shared mental processes—such as "our evolved cognitive capacity for mind-reading" (10), in Lisa Zunshine's words—while still retaining a scholarly distance able to apprehend these processes in operation and articulate their relation to the narrative text. Manfred Jahn, in his cognitive approach to third-person narration, warns against the distinction between professional and general readers, arguing that to juxtapose "a sophisticated narratologist's reading and a general reader's reading highlights in a rather unflattering way the detrimental effect of mainstream narratology's failure to account for what should be one of its prime considerations, the cognitive mechanics of reading" (464). Jahn goes on to argue that narratological readers not only share the same cognitive mechanics as general readers, but they must embrace this shared process of reading in order to generate more sophisticated textual analysis:

> Despite the fact that recourse to readers, readers' intuitions, and reading plays an important part in narratological argument, the contribution of mainstream narratology is preoccupied with bottom-up analyses, often assuming determinacies in violation of the Proteus Principle and indeterminacies in the presence of established cognitive preferences. (465)

To what extent does a theoretical and empirical focus on real readers affect the validity and usefulness of the narrative communication model, and what sort of attention should be paid to real authors? While rhetorical approaches to the effects of narratives on readers necessarily require a theory of narrative communication which attends to the agential function of narrators and (implied) authors, these occupants of the left-hand side of the communication diagram have been less important to cognitive studies. The overwhelming focus on the cognitive mechanics which enable readers to make sense of stories has shifted attention firmly onto the constructivist role of reception. David Herman's account of his cognitive approach in *Story Logic* makes clear this focus on reception. "In the approach outlined in the present book," Herman explains, "the real target of narrative analysis is the process by which interpreters reconstruct the storyworlds encoded in narratives" (5).

We can see that a focus on how readers process narrative, rather than how authors construct them, would lend itself more easily to a concern with focalization or perspective because this will yield the ways in which information about the storyworld is conveyed to readers.[1] In cognitive narratology, the role of the narrator tends be subordinated to this function of narrative. I will focus here on two challenges to the concept of the narrator and narrative communication offered from cognitive perspectives. In the "psychonarratological approach" of Marisa Bortolussi and Peter Dixon, the narrator is seen as a reader construct, the mental representation of a speaker in the reader's mind derived from textual features. For Monika Fludernik's "natural narratology," the narrator is the illusory product of an interpretive strategy based on a false presupposition that a narrative must be told by someone. For both, the communication model of narrative which accepts the textual existence of a narrator must be discarded because the postulation of a fictional narrator derives from the application of real world frames of conversational storytelling to a written narrative.

"In our view," Bortolussi and Dixon claim in *Psychonarratology*, "it is common sense to analyze the words of the narrative as presented by a narrator, and a departure from this view strikes us as nonintuitive" (63). However, they are at pains to stress that the relation between readers and the narrators they construct can only be understood analogically: "although there is no real communication in the linguistic, conversational sense, we argue that readers treat narrators *as if* they were conversational participants" (73). Bortolussi and Dixon claim that focusing on "the essential communicative transaction between the narrator and reader" (69) is necessary because there is no actual communication between author and reader in written narratives, there is no "direct contact between interlocutors" and hence no "feedback loop and progressive interchange of utterances" (70).

The inapplicability of oral conversation to narrative fiction would appear to be obvious and common sense. Bortolussi and Dixon take the odd position of claiming author–reader relations cannot be understood in terms of a communicative model of oral conversation, before asserting that narrator–reader relations operate precisely according to this model. Yet if reader and author "do not share common perceptual ground" and "cannot engage in the communicative process of confirmation and error correction" (74), these problems surely also apply to the reader and the narrator. So if, as they postulate, readers construct narrators as interlocutors, why can they not do the same with authors? Bortolussi and Dixon will admit that they do, and it would seem remiss to disregard this aspect of the reading experience.

Bortolussi and Dixon seem to be quibbling over an analogy they themselves have introduced, particularly in regard to the question of intentionality: "suggesting that readers can be concerned with the historical author's intention is not the same thing as suggesting that there is a substantive communicative interaction between the author and the reader analogous to what transpires in conversation" (70). But what proponent of narrative fiction as communication has made this suggestion? James Phelan defines his rhetorical account of narrative as "somebody telling somebody else on some occasion and for some purpose(s) that something happened," but he emphasizes a double communicative situation in fictional narrative, with both author and narrator addressing different audiences. Bortolussi and Dixon claim that "readers perceive that the narrator addresses them for some purpose, and they feel naturally motivated to discern this purpose" (73). This would seem to tally very much with Phelan's conception, yet while Phelan focuses on the intentionality behind "textual features," they would like to keep reading at the solipsistic level of an imagined communication.

The problem is a conception of reading as a private individual act analogous to a conversation unfolding in real time. To say that narrative fiction is not a form of communication because it is not the same as conversation is to operate with a very restrictive definition of communication. As I will argue later in this chapter, if we conceive of narrative fiction as a mode of public discourse, "real" communicational exchange between author and reader does in fact take place extratextually in interviews, reviews and responses to reviews, and so forth, which calls for a different formulation of communication.

In the case of Bortolussi and Dixon, the analogy of the narrator as a conversational participant has analytic force for the empirical study of how readers engage with the narrator. Fludernik's concept of a natural narratology, first proposed in *Fictions of Language and Languages of Fiction* and elaborated in *Towards a "Natural" Narratology*, is far more complex and sophisticated than psychonarratology, while still retaining the central focus on how readers apply cognitive frames to make sense of texts, or, in Fludernik's words, to narrativize them. Fludernik describes narrativization as an interpretative practice by which readers process a work as a narrative. She defines narrative, at the base level, as the presentation of experientiality through the mediating function of consciousness, whether a character's or a narrator's.

On this basis, Fludernik claims, cognitive frames allow us to establish a continuum from naturally occurring spontaneous storytelling to experimental postmodern fiction, and this continuum can be the basis of a diachronic account of the ways in which new modes of narrative develop throughout history. This enables her to trace the development from oral to written narratives, and the absorption of non-natural modes of storytelling into narrative fiction. The model of natural narratology thus allows her to criticize the narrative communication model as a theoretical fallacy produced by the reification of cognitive frames. Like Bortolussi and Dixon, however, Fludernik criticizes a model for which she has provided an explanation, claiming for example that "one can now comprehend Stanzel's narrative situations as a direct development from natural categories" (47).

In relation to the concept of teller figures, Fludernik writes: "One can thereby explain the entire communicative analysis of fiction as an (illicit) transfer of the frame of real-life conversational narrative onto literary personae and constructed entities (such as that of the notorious 'implied author')" (47). This supports her argument, along the same lines as Ann Banfield in *Unspeakable Sentences,* that the persistent investment of narratologists in this illicit transfer operates against the grain of their own theoretical distinction between author and narrator, and, crucially, of the implications of modernist fiction:

> Even more absurd, since the earlier (script-logical) tendency to identify the non-personalized narrator with the (historical) author has become untenable in the wake of the Modernist aesthetic, the responsibility for the telling has now been transferred to the (covert) narrator, or the implied author, and that even in narratological circles. The persistence of this preconceived notion that *somebody* (hence a human agent) must be telling the story seems to derive directly from the frame conception of storytelling rather than from any necessary textual evidence. (47)

If Fludernik devotes four hundred pages to explaining how narratives are interpreted according to cognitive frames derived from real-life storytelling, why criticize narratology for doing the same thing which "readers" do? At stake seems to be a supposed misreading of the privileged mode of modernist fiction. Fludernik deploys cognitive science and linguistics to provide theoretical grist for the modernist aesthetic mill that

Lubbock codified in *The Craft of Fiction,* from his idea of the creative reader reconstructing a fictional world from the shadowy phantasm of the book, to the ideal of an effaced authorial presence deriving from the distinction between telling and showing. The difference being that what Lubbock addressed in terms of an author's methods Fludernik describes as scripts and schema brought to bear on a text by readers:

> Figural or reflectoral narrative allows them [readers], instead, to experience the fictional world from within, as if looking out at it from the protagonist's consciousness. Such a reading experience is structured in terms of the natural frame of EXPERIENCING, which includes the experiences of perception, sentiment and cognition. (48)

Two points must be made in relation to these cognitive approaches to narrative. First, postulating a narrator is not simply an interpretive strategy of readers that narratologists have illegitimately replicated; it is a viable method for addressing the rhetorical features of narrative, and it is surely strengthened by the very fact that "readers" approach narrative in the same fashion. Hypostasizing the narrator as a formal element of narrative strikes me as no less viable than arguing that we can understand narrative in terms of how readers construct narrators as conversational participants. Most importantly, like cognitive narratology in general, the paradigm of the natural is based on a study of the private individual reading experience as a cognitive processing reliant on a facsimile of one on one communication, neglecting the crucial public dimension of the reception of literature in which narrative fiction is understood as a written artifact to be discussed. It cannot help address the interrelation of narrative voice and authorial discourse that is at the heart of omniscient narrative authority.

Defining the Reader: How "Real" Is Real?

The cognitive study of narrative most reliant on empirical research is the psychonarratological approach offered by Bortolussi and Dixon. This approach is founded on their view that "[h]ow readers process narrative is essentially an empirical question that can only be answered by systematic observation of actual readers reading actual texts" (13). In distinguishing between "textual features (i.e., objective and identifiable characteristics of the text) and reader constructions (i.e., subjective and variable mental processes)" (37), Bortolussi and Dixon make a series of hypotheses about how readers will respond to a particular text feature and then test out these hypotheses by conducting "*textual experiments,* in which particular features of a text are identified and manipulated by the researcher" (51). This method provides the bridge between narrative theory concerned with "real" readers and broader empirical studies of readers and the process of reading.

In a 2006 article titled "Empirical Approaches to Studying Literary Readers: The State of the Discipline," David Miall locates the work of Bortolussi and Dixon in this field, claiming that the "serious commitment to the examination of reading and the testing of hypotheses about reading with real readers . . . differentiates it clearly from the reader-response studies of the last thirty years, from Fish to Wolfgang Iser" (307). An important part of this differentiation, for Miall, is that real readers are to be sharply distinguished from "professional" readers who produce published interpretations of literary texts. Real readers are "nonprofessionals" whose "ordinary literary reading" (294) may not be concerned with interpreting literature. Significantly, while acknowledging the importance of "a reader's particular identity and cultural situation," Miall claims that that the processes which precede and support any act of interpretation "themselves are constituted by the cognitive and affective equipment that we possess in common with our reading ancestors" (293).

For Miall, "empirical studies of readers and reading" offer the potential to "provide new landmarks for a more socially responsible and ecologically valid form of scholarship" (307). The problem with this sort of claim, I would argue, is that the empirical approach remains open to the charge that it does not study real readers so much as lab-rat readers. Miall points out that "often experimental methods involve laboratory conditions in which acts of reading can be controlled and monitored" and that "typically, the readers studied will be drawn from the student population" (292). The category of the "real" reader can then be seen as a *virtual* construct of literary theory, which seeks to corroborate and universalize the professional theorist's critical response to a text under the guise of testing how readers *actually* read.

The limitations of this approach are taken up in a 2009 special issue of *Language and Literature* which collects articles devoted to a more ethnographically oriented and thus, it is claimed, more ecologically valid study of reading. In this issue, Joan Swann and Daniel Allington distinguish between two approaches to the empirical study of real readers: the "experimental" and the "naturalistic." The first, they suggest, involves "the artificial environment of a reading experiment," generally taking students and testing "pre-specified and isolated aspects of reading" (248). The second approach, which they favor, involves observing readers "in their usual environment, engaged in habitual reading behaviour" (248). The case study of "social reading" which Swann and Allington provide in this article is of reading groups, and their focus is on the interpretations and evaluations of literary texts which readers make in these environments. This allows them to emphasize the importance of interpersonal discussion and the "culturally and historically contingent" nature of specific reading contexts.

While Swann and Allington draw a contrast "between experimental and naturalistic studies of 'real' readers in terms of research design and focus" (260), what these two empirical approaches share is their attention to a certain type of reader, which they characterize as "'ordinary readers'—i.e. readers other than academic critics and professional reviewers" (248). However, if we are serious about the "ecological" value of empirical studies of reading, it would seem unproductive to dismiss published "interpretations" by professionals in favor of ordinary acts of reading by nonprofessionals, especially given the influence of "unreal" professional critics and reviewers on the publication and reception of literature, and hence upon practices of social reading. Swann and Allington do acknowledge this briefly, pointing out how reading group participants respond to reviews of the books they are discussing. Therefore, a comprehensive account of the ecology of literary reading might distinguish between different types of readers, but it would then need to incorporate all these types in its analysis.

Public Readers

Ultimately it must be recognized that the reader is a methodological construct, emerging out of the specific research questions being posed. So how would I theorize the real reader when trying to account for the narrative authority of contemporary omniscience? The empirical approaches outlined above are concerned with the cognitive and affective mechanics of reading and the social interpersonal discussions of reading. My concern is with the public reception of literary works. This derives from my intention to reconsider the narrative communication model by articulating an approach to the study of narrative founded on the recognition of fictional narratives as public statements in a broader discursive formation, and therefore as vital elements of public discourse. By doing so, I wish to proceed not from a distinction between what is inside a narrative text and what lies outside, but from an approach to the narrative *discourse* of fictional texts *alongside* other nonfictional and nonliterary discourses in the public sphere. Here I am betraying the influence of Bakhtin and, especially, Foucault. In one sense I'm trying to negotiate a link between Bakhtin's belief in authorial agency, that person who orchestrates public discourses *in* the novel, and Foucault's claim that we must avoid seeing literature as a substitute or "general envelope for all other discourses" ("Functions" 308). This leads to my second aim: to investigate the ramifications of this discursive approach for a narratological theory of authorship, particularly one which takes into account the question of authorial responsibility and narrative authority in relation to contemporary omniscient narration.

Recognizing the literary ecology which I outlined in the introduction makes it necessary to approach fictional narratives not as a medium for private or abstract communication between the individual entities of author and reader, but as a public "zone of transaction" between a range of subject positions. In doing so, I wish to develop a model of narrative communication which situates the various agents of this model as subject positions anchoring textual utterances in the public sphere. In "Estranging Unreliability, Bonding Unreliability, and the Ethics of *Lolita*" James Phelan proposes to discuss the unreliable narration of *Lolita* in order to "account for two especially notable groups of readers": those who are seduced by Humbert's narrative voice and those who are not (223). What is implicit in Phelan's rhetorical approach to readers' responses is what I want to make explicit. I'm interested in the actual public textual responses of readers as concrete evidence to be situated alongside the narrative discourse. The *textual* forms of this public response would range across three overlapping forums: the *literary establishment* in the form of reviews and feature articles; *academia* in the form of scholarly essays and monographs; and the *general public* in the form of letters, blogs, online forums, and customer reviews. This would constitute empirical textual evidence of the reader as a *public* reader, a figure which has the most material impact on the survival of a book. Such an approach is important for understanding that narrative authority is not something which is purely immanent to a text, to be recuperated from a formalist study of narrative conventions such as privilege or level. And if, culturally speaking, narrative authority must be granted by readers, it must not reside only in the cognitive processes of readers as individual agents of textual perception. This authority is contingent upon the collective public textual response to the narrative in question.

The Author in Narrative Theory

The corollary of this approach is that to understand the modes of narrative authority specific to contemporary omniscient narration we must investigate the rhetorical strategies employed by authors as public figures, not just those employed by narrators. Narratology has long eschewed consideration of authorship, except in the controversial guise of the implied author, originally proposed to unyoke the question of "intentionality" from its relation to authorial biography. The implied author is a way of providing an anthropomorphic center for a narrative, even if there is no narrator or an effaced narrator, for it attributes implicit personal values and norms to the design of the narrative itself, or at least acknowledges that readers construct a sense of the authorial persona out of the text. Theories of implied authorship have undergone a range of permutations since Wayne Booth's original formulation, and in many cases have moved so far from questions of authorial *agency* that we can have claims that each reader constructs a different implied author to guide and affirm his or her reading. For instance, Wolf Schmid writes in his survey of debates over the concept: "it must be remembered that, like the readings of different recipients, the various interpretations of a single reader are each associated with a different implied author" (161). We can even have a claim such as Ansgar Nunning's that "a pederast would not find Humbert Humbert, the fictitious child molester and narrator of Nabokov's *Lolita,* unreliable" (97). Such claims leave us with the problem of weighing up the relative significance of the individual private act of reading, and the general public reception of a text.

My question here is: when readers infer an authorial persona from a fictional text do they "know" that this persona is only that of an implied author? That is, are they complicit in their own construction of an imagined entity, or do they infer what they think *is* the real author? If we wish to posit an implied author as a mediating entity between author and narrator, we need to define what we actually mean by a *real* author. We typically define the author as the historical figure who wrote the book, and then spend our time debating the existence of narrators and implied authors.[2] The author emerges as an aporia, granted both an existential solidity and an epistemological evanescence, disappearing from our knowledge in the act of reading. The problem, I think, is that we're dismissing a straw man concept of authorship: a figure with singular intentions and coherent values and norms.

Sometimes, in defense of the idea of an implied author, we have the claim that of course an author is assuming a particular persona when writing a book, in the way that we assume a professional persona when we are writing a job application, and that we must therefore be careful to distinguish this ideal, or at least different, self from the real author. Discussing the implied author as a way of thinking about how authors present themselves, Peter Rabinowitz writes: "think of your own implied authors as you write letters of applications, ads for dating services, thank-you notes, even academic articles" ("'The Absence'" 102). In promoting the continued ethical importance of the implied author, Wayne Booth writes: "In every corner of our lives, whenever we speak or write, we imply a version of our character that we know is quite different from many other selves that are exhibited in our flesh-and-blood world" ("Resurrection" 77). This, for me, is a kind of endless deferral of the "real" to a zero point of an essentialized private self, only ever accessible in the "flesh and blood." Or, it is the opposite, evacuating any sense of a knowable self in favor of a series of performative selves which we all construct for different social occasions. In which case an authorial persona cannot be any less "real" than any other self that writers adopt in their lives, or those of a real reader. Either way, surely the figure which readers infer is that of an *author*, a public figure whom they hold responsible for the book which they are reading, rather than simply a private citizen whose personal values and norms underpin the narrative. And readers construct a sense of this public figure not only from the narrative text, but from extratextual elements.

The rationale for positing an implied author is that communication between authors and readers is mediated by the narrative text, and hence there is no direct access to an author's intentions. But, as I have pointed out, in the actual world of the public sphere such access is available, and there is enormous interest in hearing the voice of the author, from writers festivals and readings through to interviews and essays. These are part of the empirical reading experience. So, what James Phelan (*Experiencing*) calls the "recursive relationship" between authorial agency and reader response is facilitated not just by textual phenomena, but by the author's and readers' extratextual statements which circulate alongside the fictional text in the public sphere. If readers do construct an implied author, I'm suggesting, it is only to facilitate their response to the real author. Once we accept this, it means we need to attend to the crucial function of real authors, not simply as producers of a narrative text, but as active participants in the process of reception.

A Discursive Narratology

A discursive approach begins with the assumption that a key challenge of contemporary narratology is how to negotiate methodological relations between formalist approaches to textual features, and contextualist approaches to the contingencies of textual production and reception. Proceeding from an understanding of fiction as public discourse, how might we incorporate extratextual public statements of authors and readers in the narrative communication model to develop a theory of authorship? My aim is to achieve this by refining the two major narratological approaches to fictional texts as published books active in the public sphere, rather than static formal artifacts: that proposed by Susan Lanser in *The Narrative Act* and that proposed by Gerard Genette in *Paratexts*.

The authority of a published text, Lanser argues, is vested in what she calls its extrafictional voice, "the most direct textual counterpart for the historical author," which "carries all the *diegetic authority* of its (publicly authorized) creator and has the ontological status of historical truth" (122). Now this formulation, as Lanser points out, is very similar to the implied author; however, she locates its manifestation not in the narrative discourse, but in extrafictional elements of the material book itself, from chapter divisions to authorial prefaces and publication details. Lanser is content to speculate about how readers respond to this extrafictional voice, but the very concept, I think, provides the methodological point of departure for theorizing authorship more broadly in relation to the narrative communication model. It enables us to approach the author not as a private citizen speaking to readers through the narrative text in order to convey personal values and norms, but as a public intellectual discursively engaging the reader via the link between narrative and extrafictional voice. "The extrafictional voice," Lanser argues, "is the most immediate vehicle available to the author, and although most novelistic communication does not take place on the extrafictional level, the extrafictional voice carries more than its quantitative proportion of impact" (128).

Lanser indicates that this extrafictional voice, which can be reconstructed from textual information within the book itself, is different from "*extratextual* sources of information about the author or the book" (124, original emphasis). I would argue, however, that if this extrafictional voice frames the text and its narrative discourse, it also turns the text outwards to the broader public sphere and its range of extratextual sources. Here we find other vehicles of communication available to authors: public statements ranging from essays to manifestos to interviews and opinion articles, which together constitute a rhetorical strategy to establish their literary authority in public discourse. For Lanser, the "author" is "a textually encoded, historically authoritative voice kin to but not identical with the biographical person who wrote the text" (152). In which case, this textually encoded authorial voice must be constituted by both the extrafictional voice of a book, and the author's extratextual material. But it is also constituted by the narrative voice of the author's various fictional works, for these feed back into the author's status as a public figure. Here we see the value of Foucault's author function, not necessarily as the basis for a critique of authorial criticism, but as an anatomization of the ways in which an author's name "points to the existence of certain groups of discourse and refers to the status of this discourse within a society and culture" ("What Is an Author?" 123).

A founding premise of the "discursive narratology" I'm attempting to elaborate is that a work of fiction is a public statement which circulates in the same discursive formation as its author's nonfictional statements. Furthermore, narratives are not static for they are read differently each time according to their context of reception. Narrative authority, then, operates via a continuum between narrative voice, extrafictional voice and authorial voice, and establishes a dialogue with the public response. These voices have different textual forms and diegetic levels, but they co-exist as public statements in the same discursive field, and operate as interrelated rhetorical strategies for asserting the cultural significance of the novel to public life which establish a dialogue with the public response.

A theoretical framework for studying this continuum of voices can be derived from Genette's theory of the paratext.[3] For Genette, the "verbal or other productions" that frame and present a literary work to its readership constitute the paratext: "what enables a text to become a book and to be offered as such to its readers and more generally, to the public" (*Paratexts* 1). This paratext is a threshold between the text and its frame "that offers the world at large the possibility of either stepping inside or turning back" (2). Genette works with a spatial relationship between text and paratext, so that the location of a paratextual element "within the same volume" (4) can be defined as a peritext, while the elements which are "located outside the book, generally with the help of the media" (5) can be defined as the epitext. "In other words," Genette writes, "for those who are keen on formulae, *paratext = peritext + epitext*" (5; original emphasis). Genette also works with a temporal relationship between text and paratext, pointing out prior, original, and later or delayed paratexts, defined in relation to the date of the text's original publication.

The significance of the paratext to my work is the emphasis Genette places on its pragmatic status as a form of authorial communication in which the addressee is the public. "By definition," Genette claims, "something is not a paratext unless the author or one of his associates accepts responsibility for it, although the degree of responsibility may vary" (9). Of most importance is Genette's emphasis on the functionality of the paratext, arguing:

> Indeed, this fringe, always the conveyor of a commentary that is authorial or more or less legitimated by the author, constitutes a zone between text and off-text, a zone not only of transition but also of *transaction:* a privileged place of a pragmatics and a strategy, of an influence on the public, an influence that—whether well or poorly understood and achieved—is at the service of a better reception for the text and a more pertinent reading of it (more pertinent, of course, in the eyes of the author and his allies). (2)

My approach has two crucial points of departure from Genette's model. First is the claim that this paratext is not only the author's attempt to frame a positive interpretation of the fiction, but an attempt to establish the fictional text as the basis for the cultural authority of the author as a public figure. For my purposes, Lanser's extrafictional voice will be located within the peritextual elements of the book, and linked via a discursive continuum to the authorial voice that is manifested in what Genette calls "the public authorial epitext," comprised of interviews, essays, etc. Secondly, I will define paratext more broadly than Genette in the sense that if it constitutes "a zone of transaction," an attempt to influence the public, this zone must also include textual phenomena produced by the reading public as the other party in this transaction. The interview, for instance, a key feature of the "public authorial epitext," necessarily includes readerly responses in the form of the interviewer's questions, and itself is an example of a transaction between author and reader over the significance of the text. The paratext, then, I am arguing, is a type of discursive formation, a set of textual statements in which the relations between these statements construct the text as its object. This leads to my

Paratext

| epitext (Author) <—> peritext (extrafictional voice) <—> text (narrator > narratee) <—> epitext (reader) |

FIGURE 2   Paratext

discursive reformulation of the diagram of narrative communication, as shown in figure 2.

A discursive approach to the narrative communication model situates the narrative text in a broader discursive formation to investigate how narrative authority emerges out of the relations between subject positions within this formation. So the epitext (author and reader), the peritext (extrafictional voice) and the text (narrative voice) contain the discursive sites at which these subject positions are articulated, and together the three sites constitute the paratextual zone of transaction, the discursive formation, in which what is being "transacted" is not so much textual meaning, but the significance of the text to public discourse. I have excluded the implied author and the implied reader from this model because, while they may be legitimate critical/cognitive constructs which facilitate reading, they are not concrete subject positions within or without the text so much as they are anthropomorphic postulations of the act of reading. I have retained the narratee as a fictional subject position because, especially in omniscient narration, it is given textual form by virtue of a specific narratorial address. The two-way arrows indicate that each discursive site facilitates a dialogue between the subject positions, that communication is always ongoing, drawing into play the temporal relations of a zone of transaction, and that the text itself always gestures outwards or beyond to public dialogue on the paratextual level.

Omniscient Authority

A key reason for postulating an implied author has been the need to retain the valuable theoretical distinction between author and narrator. Susan Lanser points out, though: "If an author–narrator separation is true in the abstract, it is nonetheless not abstractions that determine the reading of literature, but the conventions governing linguistic and literary use" (*Narrative Act* 149). She goes on to argue that "in the absence of direct markings which separate the public narrator from the extrafictional voice, so long as it is possible to give meaning to the text within the equation author = narrator, readers will conventionally make this equation" (151). Omniscient narration is one fictional form for which such an equation is traditionally made, and recognizing this is crucial for understanding omniscient narrative authority beyond that of a literary convention. Hence the need to frame the relationship between narrator and author in pragmatic and flexible terms beyond the binarism of formalist distinctions if we are to understand the historical contingency of omniscient narration. The narrator and the author may be separate entities, but the act of narration, while fictional, nonetheless constitutes a statement within public discourse which is attributed to the author. The intrusive commentary of omniscient narration draws attention to this relationship, so that the "fictionality" of its discourse can be seen as a rhetorical device for asserting the importance of the novelist in public intellectual life, particularly when this narrative voice resonates textually with the extrafictional and extratextual voices of the author. As Lanser points out, "the equivalence of author and narrator implies an authorial responsibility that is similar to an author's responsibility for his or her nonfictional work" (153).

So if omniscient authority is not so much a textual phenomenon, the narrator's complete knowledge of the fictional world, but a type of narrative performance articulated through commentary, it gestures outwards, extratextually, to a particular figure of authorship. And if the narrative authority of contemporary omniscience no longer relies, as it did in previous centuries, on the consonance of its formal conventions with the cultural authority of the novel itself, this performance must necessarily operate with a tension between its form and its status. The narrators of contemporary omniscience, I am suggesting, must gesture outwards to the broader realm of public discourse, in which less "universal" modes of public address circulate, in order to gain traction for their commentary. And here a knowledge of authorial voice becomes important, not for anchoring a biographical reading of a book, but for understanding how contemporary omniscient narration engages with the very question of novelistic authority.

The Paratext of David Lodge's *Author, Author*

I will conclude with a discussion of David Lodge's *Author, Author*, which provides a good example of how contemporary omniscient authority operates along a discursive continuum from narratorial to authorial voice, and of a narrative text whose paratext stages an ongoing debate over the status of contemporary fiction. This book, which operates in the mode I have labeled the *literary historian,* self-consciously situates itself in the generic boundaries between novel and biography as it reconstructs a period in the life of Henry James: his relationship with George Du Maurier, and his forays into writing for the theatre. The rhetorical purpose of the narrator is clear: to demonstrate the influence of James's catastrophic attempts at writing for the theatre on both his life and his novelistic output. This is in the service of demonstrating the importance of James to the history of the novel. *Author, Author* opens with a present-tense account of James on his deathbed, immediately establishing the narrator's diegetic authority through historical detail and asserting his moral authority through commentary:

> London, December 1915. In the master bedroom (never was the estate agent's epithet more appropriate) of Flat 21, Carlyle Mansions, Cheyne Walk, Chelsea, the distinguished author is dying—slowly but surely. In Flanders, less than two hundred miles away, other men are dying more quickly, more painfully, more pitifully—young men, mostly, with their lives still before them, blank pages that will never be filled. The author is seventy-two. He has had an interesting and varied life. (3)

A biographical summary completes the paragraph, underpinning the right of the narrator to place James's comparatively rich life in immediate historical context. The rest of this opening frame narrative is variably focalized through James's deathbed companions, but the bulk of the novel, which revisits his life, is internally focalized through James, although the preponderance of summary means the guiding presence of the narrator-biographer is palpable. The major exception to this structure is a chapter covering the key scene of the opening night of James's stage play, *Guy Domville.* The chapter begins: "In his practice as a novelist and short story writer, Henry had developed a firm faith in the superior expressiveness and verisimilitude of the limited point of view" (230). The narrator amplifies this comment with an account of the technical means by which James felt the limited point of view could be realized. "The antithetical method," the narrator continues, "was well exemplified by *Trilby,* in which the authorial narrator, in Thackerayan fashion, took out his puppets from the box, and set them capering, and told you in his own confiding ruminating voice exactly what they were all thinking at a given moment" (230). The narrator, then, is highly self-conscious of James's position in literary history, his contribution to the diminishment of the authority of the nineteenth-century omniscient narrator.

This discussion of narrative form serves to justify a structural shift to multiple focalization, providing a comprehensive account of the fateful opening night of *Guy Domville* from the perspective of a range of different participants. The narrator has James speculating that to do justice to the events of the evening which he later pieced together from second-hand information, he would have to imagine that "while his story, with its drastically limited point of view, was proceeding, other connected stories were in progress, other points of view were in play, at the same time, in parallel, in brackets as it were" (231). The narrator dutifully provides readers with these stories, replete with brackets and amplified by his omniscient knowledge.

The novel concludes by returning to the present-tense frame narrative of James's death bed. In this last section the narrator intrudes overtly to draw attention to the narrating instance: "*as I conjure up this deathbed scene, looking at it as through the curved transparency of a crystal ball*" (373, original emphasis). It is obvious then that the narrator's omniscient knowledge is a conflation of historical research and fictional speculation, and his authority relies not only on making this manifest, but on explaining why. In one of these italicized interpolations, the narrator clearly establishes his temporal distance from the story:

> *It is therefore tempting to indulge in a fantasy of somehow time-travelling back to that afternoon of late February 1916, creeping into the master bedroom of Flat 21, Carlyle Mansions, casting a spell on the little group of weary watchers at the bedside, pulling up a chair oneself, and saying a few reassuring words to HJ, before he departs this world, about his literary future.* (375)

Omniscient commentary in this novel is not geared to a moral evaluation of character so much as it is to James's contribution to literary history, and the "communal mind" invoked is that established by the evidence of canonization, scholarly interest and popular cultural adaptation. The obvious conflation of narratorial with authorial voice encouraged by this commentary, linking the narrator to the extraliterary world, is given weight by the prefatorial comment in the extrafictional peritext:

> Sometimes it seems advisable to preface a novel with a note saying that the story and the characters are entirely fictitious, or words to that effect. On this occasion a different authorial statement seems called for. Nearly everything that happens in this story is based on factual sources. With one insignificant exception, all the named characters were real people. Quotations from their books, plays, articles, letters, journals, etc., are their own words. But I have used a novelist's licence in representing what they thought, felt, and said to each other; and I have imagined some events and personal details which history omitted to record. So this book is a novel, and structured like a novel.

Here Lodge claims the authority of the historical record as well as that of novelistic convention in his biographical treatment of Henry James's life. Clearly the omniscient authority of this narrator is bound up in the contemporary "postmodern" debate about the generic boundaries and discursive status of history and fiction. The extrafictional voice operates not only to underpin the narrator's omniscient knowledge, but to link it with the professional status of Lodge himself, a well-regarded critic and theorist of the novel. The peritextual acknowledgments which follow the text shore up this status, providing bibliographic references and archival sources, as well as identifying the invented sections of the novel. The acknowledgements conclude by pointing out that only when he had completed the manuscript of *Author, Author,* did Lodge discover that Colm Tóibín's novel about Henry James, *The Master,* would be published in the same year. "I leave it to students of the zeitgeist to ponder the significance of these coincidences" (389). Hence Lodge anticipates the reception of his novel by "real" readers in the epitextual public sphere.

A survey of the reviews of *Author, Author* indicates that the novel was received and evaluated according to the coordinates established by Lodge's extrafictional voice: its hybrid generic status, and its comparison with Tóibín's *The Master*. Here I turn to James Wood's review as an exemplar because it provides a critique common to many reviews: the novel's lack of convincing interiority resulting from the language and form of biographical writing. Wood goes further, though, and links this problem specifically to the question of point of view. Like many reviewers, Wood points out the dilemma of writing a novel about Henry James, the "novelist of consciousness," before asserting:

> It is not only that Lodge's prose must be judged by James's. The larger

difficulty is that it is not always clear from whose point of view Lodge is writing. "Point of view," of course, was an obsession for James, because he had come to the conclusion, rightly, that there is no such thing in fiction as "omniscient narration." ("The Spoils" 3)

Ultimately, then, his aesthetic critique of Lodge's craft as a writer is based on an ideological critique of the narrator's omniscient presence, his display of unfocalized knowledge. Wood criticizes this omniscience not only for violating James's own aesthetic creed, but for being based less on accepted novelistic convention than on an appeal to an extraliterary figure of authorship: the biographer. On these grounds he compares Lodge's work unfavorably to Tóibín's, arguing that "Tóibín's willingness to take his novel seriously as a novel fruitfully detaches it from its historical referent; but Lodge's unwillingness to do so manacles it to mere record" (1).

One might say, then, that on balance, Lodge's extrafictional bid for the omniscient authority of his narrator was unsuccessful, with his novel generally seen to have failed in comparison with that of Tóibín, who employs the more favored internal focalization to explore James's interior life. As Wood points out, though, Tóibín is inventing a fictional character (while still historically grounded, as evidenced by his own list of references), whereas Lodge is attempting to imagine the real historical figure. Wood's review is a defense of the novel over any generic incursions on its terrain. And yet *Author, Author,* it could be argued, is concerned more with asserting the cultural authority of the novelist to contribute to contemporary critical and biographical scholarship on James than with simply drawing on this scholarship for verisimilitude.

Turning to academic articles as another form of paratextual public response by readers, we can see that these articles locate both novels within a particular discursive formation—academic scholarship on James—and argue that their form, the biographical novel, is what enables this link. Indeed, scholarly articles on these books tend to discuss them precisely in terms of the plausibility of their biographical speculation. In *The Cambridge Quarterly,* Max Saunders claims that

> the way for these novels was prepared by very specific developments in James biography and criticism. They didn't come out of nowhere, or out of a generalised "Zeitgeist," but out of recent rethinking of James's friendships with men and women. Where Lodge might be right, though, in that they might be a sign of our postmodern times, is in the fact that

these biographical explorations of James are presented as novels, not biographies, and that their autobiographical dimension is also emphasised. (125)

Saunders does, however, replicate Wood's aesthetic judgment on these novels: "where Tóibín allows fictional biography to do the work of literary criticism, Lodge increasingly fuses novel with lecture on literary technique in *Author, Author,*" suggesting that Lodge "is better at theorizing literary consciousness than representing it" (126). Again we see extraliterary claims to narrative authority established by Lodge's omniscient narrator judged in terms of the modernist aesthetic of impersonality.

John Harvey follows a similar line of comparison, in the *Yearbook of English Studies,* yet still discusses both novels in terms of their contribution to Jamesian biographical and critical scholarship, speculating as to whether they have captured the "real" Henry James or the myth of Henry James, whether they have managed to reveal anything about his works themselves. In the *Journal of Modern Literature,* Daniel Hannah treats the narratorial intrusions in *Author, Author* as a conscious intervention in current literary-critical discourse: "Against these two forms, Lodge calls on fictional biography as a form that might both more graciously reclaim (rather than merely expose) James on a popular stage and reposition "queer" James as an author of consciousness and style (rather than an author of erotic subtexts)" (80). Like reviewers in the mainstream press, these academic articles have little interest in a rigid distinction between author and narrator, and no theoretical need for the implied author. Saunders points out that Lodge concludes his novel "in his own authorial first person" (126), and Karen Scherzinger, in the *Henry James Review,* indicates that: "As his novel draws to an end, Lodge finally gives up all pretense of disguising his own presence and seeks to recuperate James one last time" (191).

If these reviews and articles constitute the readerly epitext in a broader paratextual discursive formation which constructs *Author, Author* as its subject, and circulate around the authority of Lodge's omniscient narrator, the other side of this zone of transaction is represented by Lodge's *The Year of Henry James: The Story of a Novel,* which was published two years after *Author, Author* appeared to "mixed" reviews. This book constitutes what Genette would call a "later epitext," and specifically an authorial response. If the narrative voice of *Author, Author* gestures outwards to the authority of its extrafictional voice, this discursive continuum can be traced further to the authorial voice in *The Year of Henry James* where Lodge draws upon his authority as a literary critic to contextualize his aesthetic choices in relation to point of view. One of his strategies is to provide extracts from his private notebooks, demonstrating an awareness of the relevance of his choices beyond the artistic integrity of his treatment of the subject:

> A persistent theme in many of the notes, widely separated in time, is an anxiety that the novel should not read like a biography, and the hope that I could avoid this effect by foregrounding the machinery of narration itself, through abrupt time-shifts, switches of point of view and "postmodernist" authorial interpolations. (50)

Lodge proceeds to quote a section from his notebook which reads: "*On reflection I think it would be a mistake to draw attention to myself as the 'real' author in this way. I couldn't then 'invent' freely. The authorial narrator must have authority*" (52). He then comments that

> what this first attempt revealed to me was that I really wanted to write a novel in which the joins between documented facts and imaginative speculation would be seamless and invisible, and that drawing attention to myself as narrator would entail coming clean about the extent to which I was selecting from and embellishing the historical record. (52)

It seems, though, that Lodge did end up "foregrounding the machinery of narration itself" through his omniscient narrator, but saved coming clean about his embellishments for the acknowledgements, thus dividing the authorial narrator's authority between the narrative and the extrafictional voice of the text. *Author, Author,* by virtue of this epitextual authorial response, becomes a discursive site at which its narrative voice enacts the struggle of contemporary fiction for cultural authority, and part of the paratextual zone of transaction regarding the significance of the novel in public discourse.

I have argued throughout this book that the emergence of contemporary omniscience alongside cultural anxieties about the relevance of the novel in the new millennium can be read as symptomatic of a broader desire to reclaim the cultural authority of nineteenth-century novelists. At the same time, novelists aware of the legacy of postmodernism have developed new modes of omniscient narration. In another public authorial epitext, a 2005 interview for *Sources* magazine (Gallix et al.), Lodge provides a similar context for his novel:

There are lots of people who openly say that they cannot be bothered reading novels but they read biographies all the time. It is a pity but I think it may also have something to do with the lack of a coherent body of shared values in the reading community. If you think of the great nineteenth-century novelists, they could assume their readers shared basically the same beliefs, the same values, the same ideals of what the good life was, what evil was. In a much more relativistic age, a multicultural society with different ethical systems competing or coexisting, it is very difficult to create a fictional world in which you have the kind of moral authority which the classic novelists used to have. But if you say: "this is how it was, this is what happened," it does not raise the same expectations. Instead of trying to persuade readers to share your view of life, you just say: "this is a human record: make of it what you will. (21)

The rhetorical strategy of the omniscient narrator of *Author, Author* is thus simultaneously to draw upon the contemporary popularity and cultural authority of biography and to reassert the novel as a pre-eminent mode of exploring historical figures. This narrative voice cannot be understood in purely formalist terms, it must be located in a broader discursive context which recognizes the significance of extrafictional and extratextual subject positions to the performance of narrative authority.

CONCLUSION

MY AIM in this book has been to reconsider the prevailing view that omniscient narration is no longer aesthetically viable in literary fiction or prominent in the contribution of novelistic discourse to cultural debate. I have argued that contemporary omniscience should not be characterized as a nostalgic revival or parodic critique of an archaic form, but as a legacy in mainstream fiction of postmodern experiments with narrative voice. This has led me to investigate what distinguishes "post-postmodern" modes of omniscient narration from classic examples of the form in eighteenth- and nineteenth-century fiction, and what this might reveal about the cultural status of the novel in contemporary public discourse. In doing so, I have located the emergence of new modes of omniscient narration in the context of millennial anxieties about the decline of book culture and argued that omniscient narration is best understood as a rhetorical performance of narrative authority that simultaneously invokes and projects an historically specific figure of authorship.

To investigate this figure of authorship, I have analyzed the narrative voice of a work of fiction in relation to its author's nonfictional commentary in the public sphere. These statements, as I have shown, typically lament the loss of cultural authority supposedly invested in the omniscient voice of nineteenth-century fictional narrators while recognizing the need to relativize this voice in contemporary fiction. I have further argued that the narrative voices of contemporary omniscience self-reflexively demonstrate an agonistic awareness of the diminished "universality" of authorial narration, drawing authority not from the novelist as observer of human nature and guide to ethical conduct, but from the writer as public intellectual both competing with and deploying other nonliterary discourses of "knowledge": journalistic, historical, scientific, critical, and so on.

Another aim of this book has been to employ this investigation of contemporary omniscience to engage with ongoing theoretical debates about the formal category of omniscient narration itself and develop a model of narrative voice more sensitive to the historical contingency and cultural contexts of fictional form. In formalist terms, omniscient narrators are invested by convention with the highest authority to tell a story because they possess reliable knowledge about the storyworld, particularly through their "privileged" access to the consciousness of characters. I have pointed out the need to reconceive narrative authority in more dynamic terms, as performance (the actual use of knowledge) rather than as competence (the possession of knowledge). I have thus approached focalization as a rhetorical strategy which narrators employ to perform their authority, a performance which generates "omniscient" knowledge in the act of narration in order to assert the significance of a story.

To avoid reducing omniscience to a synonym for third-person narration, I have argued that the term ought to apply to narrators who not only report the thoughts of characters, but who narrate what characters do not know (zero focalization), typically aspects of consciousness which characters themselves are unaware of (psychonarration), or information which none could be privy to (prolepses, unwitnessed events). Furthermore, this performance of knowledge ought to contribute to an intrusive narratorial presence established by devices such as direct addresses, commentary, self-reflexive statements, and stylistic expressivity. This intrusiveness can also be a form of zero focalization, in the sense that to offer commentary is to provide insight beyond the awareness of characters, and that references to the act of narration itself are obviously at a higher diegetic level than characters. At the same time, instances of zero focalization are intrusive to the extent that they draw attention to the narrator's capacity to tell rather than show.

I have also used this study of contemporary omniscience to argue for greater narratological attention to authorship, suggesting that authorial voice can be approached as a formal textual feature of narrative communication if we approach narrative fiction as a mode of public discourse. This contextualist approach has been designed to show that narrative theory offers more than just a "toolkit" for textual analysis, that attention to narrative form can be the basis for engaging with critical debates about the cultural status of contemporary fiction. Finally, I hope that this book contributes to broader studies of the novel today, particularly in relation to the legacy of metafiction, the historical novel, and the stylistic and encyclopedic features of maximalism, by demonstrating that new modes of omniscient narration have emerged as a vital feature of fiction after postmodernism.

NOTES

Introduction

1. See Dawson ("Historicising") for a critique of this "pros and cons" approach to the teaching of writing and how it perpetuates a prejudice against omniscient narration. See McGurl for an account of the relationship between American fiction and creative writing programs.

2. The only references I have found to contemporary omniscience in fact come from writers and teachers of writing. See Kress, Anderson, and Boulter. All three suggest omniscience has made a "comeback," listing novels by Isla Dewar, John Irving, and Mary Wesley (Kress), Rick Moody's *Purple America* (Anderson), and the novels of A. S. Byatt (Boulter). Byatt, Pullman, Boswell, Russo, and Dunning also offer defenses of omniscience as a narrative technique.

3. This intellectual enterprise draws its main inspiration from the scholarship of Friedrich Kittler in works such as *Grammaphone, Film, Typewriter*. Daniel Punday more explicitly relates this enterprise to narratological concerns, such as the story/discourse distinction.

4. Some of the books of nonfiction by these writers include Zadie Smith's *Changing My Mind*, which includes her review essay, "Two Paths for the Novel"; David Foster Wallace's *A Supposedly Fun Thing I'll Never Do Again*, which includes his essay "E Unibus Pluram: Television and U.S. Fiction"; Jonathan Franzen's *How to Be Alone*, which includes the *Harper's* essay; Salman Rushdie's *Imaginary Homelands* and *Step across This Line*, which includes his "In Defense of the Novel, Yet Again"; Martin Amis's *The War against Cliché* and *The Second Plane: September 11: Terror and Boredom*. David Lodge is also a literary critic, but some of his important works since he retired from the academy include *The Practice of Writing, Consciousness and the Novel*, and *The Year of Henry James*.

5. Ross Chambers offers a psychoanalytically informed account of the dynamics of the narrative act as a form of seduction. For Chambers, narrative authority is based on

the possession of information, but it is authorized by the interest of the narratee who seeks this information, and narrators must yield their authority in exchange for this interest.

Chapter 1

1. Also see Ermarth, who argues that if we understand omniscient privilege as the product of the collective consciousness of the characters, we can dismiss the problem of how to account for impossible knowledge.

2. Amis has encouraged this autobiographical correlation in an interview about *The Information:*

> There's an "I" in the first sentence. The narrator is me but he disappears halfway through the book. I wondered about that: I think that I wanted to tell the reader where I was coming from. It is a book about mid-life, and for me the mid-crisis came in the form of blanket ignorance, I felt. I just didn't know anything about the world. . . . I felt that I had to open up to the reader about that and say "How can I be an omniscient narrator when I don't know anything." Which is what it felt like. (Laurence and McGee)

3. See "From Imagination to Creativity" in my book *Creative Writing in the New Humanities* for an account of the historical development of theories of creativity.

4. Dorothy Hale brilliantly anatomizes the formalist circumscription of James's ideas in Lubbock's book.

5. Our modern understanding of omniscience is mapped out in Clayton Hamilton's 1908 book *Materials and Methods of Fiction,* which provides the first account of "limited omniscience" that I have found. This book provides a comprehensive overview of point of view long before it was made prominent by Percy Lubbock. In his chapter "The Point of View in Narrative," Hamilton writes that aspects of narrating a story "are all dependent directly on the answer to the question, who shall tell the story?" (117).

6. William Nelles ("Getting") aptly suggests we rename zero as "free" focalization precisely to demonstrate that all other types are contained.

7. Jaffe similarly argues that "omniscience is not so much evidence for the possession of knowledge as an emphatic display of knowledge, a display, precisely, of what is not being taken for granted." From an overtly post-structuralist interest in how transgressions define the limits they exceed, particularly how Dickens's Asmodean figure negotiates the boundaries between the public and the private, Jaffe suggests that "a narrative mode that has traditionally signified an unquestioned assertion of authority may be understood instead to interrogate the grounds of its authority." She thus locates omniscience in the tension at play between the authorial presence which earlier critics bemoaned and the absence of a unitary voice which contemporary theorists argue for.

Chapter 5

1. Nicholas Dames, in *The Physiology of the Novel,* sets out to prove that the long Victorian novel was in fact designed to train readers to adapt their consciousnesses to the new rhythms of industrial life.

Chapter 6

1. Dorrit Cohn (*Transparent*) more accurately places stylistic contagion under the category of psychonarration, demonstrating how it facilitates a move from psychonarration to narrated monologue.
2. Cognitive narratology offers the next iteration of social formalism. *In Why We Read Fiction,* Lisa Zunshine draws upon scientific research into the Theory of Mind to explain the reading process as a stimulation and test of our mind-reading capacities which have evolved to aid social interaction. Zunshine does not specifically discuss FID, for this feature can be collapsed into our larger evolved cognitive ability to attribute (source monitoring) and keep track of states of mind (metarepresentation) when reading fiction.
3. Compare this character's simultaneous fascination and repellence to the omniscient narrator's internal analysis of Isabel Archer in the opening to chapter 53 of Henry James's *The Portrait of a Lady:*

> She had plenty to think about; but it was neither reflexion nor conscious purpose that filled her mind. Disconnected visions passed through it, and sudden dull gleams of memory, of expectation. The past and the future came and went at their will, but she saw them only in fitful images, which rose and fell by a logic of their own. It was extraordinary the things she remembered. (581)

The narrator's wonder at the workings of the mind becomes in contemporary fiction a character's wonder at their own mental processes.

Chapter 7

1. See Alber and Heinze, Hansen et al., and Alber, Nielsen, et al. .
2. Fludernik ("Naturalizing") draws on the latest craze of blending theory to supplement her natural narratology, arguing that it can help explain how new storytelling frames arise. In this view, first-person omniscience, a form which she traces to *Midnight's Children,* emerges when the source domain of omniscient narration is blended with the target domain of first-person narration, although it is possible to see the form as a double-scope blend. The explanatory power of blending theory strikes me as underwhelming in this instance. Also see Alber 89–91.
3. In "Imaginary Homelands," Rushdie draws an autobiographical link between himself and Saleem Sinai, revealing that the motivation for writing the novel was his desire as an expatriate to somehow recover the history of Bombay for himself: "what I was actually doing was a novel of memory and about memory. . . . I tried to make it imaginatively true, but imaginative truth is simultaneously honourable and suspect. . . . This is why I made my narrator, Saleem, suspect in his narration; his mistakes are the mistakes of a fallible memory compounded by quirks of character and of circumstance, and his vision is fragmentary" (10).

Chapter 8

1. Herman has recently affirmed the importance of intentionality to the study of narrative. In "Narrative Theory and the Intentional Stance," he explains the intentional

stance as an evolved human predisposition to attribute intentionality to persons, objects, and artifacts, a heuristic strategy along the lines of folk psychology which we all employ to solve problems.

2. Brian Richardson offers an insightful account of the possible relations between historical authors, implied authors, and narrators, emphasizing that each category is valid if it performs a useful function in the analysis of texts.

3. Marilyn Edelstein points out that Genette's *Paratexts* makes no reference to Lanser's earlier pioneering work on the significance of extrafictional elements to narrative theory and that critics have tended to refer more to Genette's work than to Lanser's. According to Edelstein, what Lanser calls "extrafictional elements" Genette would call the "peritext," since they are part of the book, and what she would call "extratextual elements," framing discourses such as authorial interviews, Genette calls the "epitext."

WORKS CITED

Aczel, Richard. "Hearing Voices in Narrative Texts." *New Literary History* 29 (1998): 476–500.
Alber, Jan. "Impossible Storyworlds—and What to Do with Them." *Storyworlds: A Journal of Narrative Studies* 1 (2009): 79–96.
———, and Ruediger Heinze, eds. *Unnatural Narratives—Unnatural Narratology.* Berlin: De Gruyter, 2011.
———, Stefan Iversen, Henrik Skov Nielsen, and Brian Richardson. "Unnatural Narratives, Unnatural Narratology: Beyond Mimetic Models." *Narrative* 18.2 (2010): 113–36.
———, Henrik Skov Nielsen, Brian Richardson, and Stefan Iversen, comp. and eds. *Dictionary of Unnatural Narratology.* Institut for Æstetik og Kommunikation, Aarhus University, Aarhus, Denmark. http://nordisk.au.dk/forskning/forskningscentre/nrl/undictionary/ (accessed 28 May 2013).
Alexander, Jan. "Happy People Need Love Too." Review of *Generosity* by Richard Powers. *Neworld Review* 2.7 (2009). http://neworldreview.com/vol_2No_7/happyPeople.html (accessed 12 August 2010).
Allende, Isabelle. "Phantom Palace." *The Stories of Eva Luna.* Trans. Margaret Sayers Peden. London: Penguin, 1992. 201–15.
Amis, Martin. *The Information.* London: Flamingo, 1995.
———. *The Second Plane: September 11: Terror and Boredom.* New York: Vintage: 2008.
———. *The War against Cliché: Essays and Reviews, 1971–2000.* London: Vintage, 2002.
Anderson, Linda, ed. *Creative Writing: A Workbook with Readings.* Abingdon, Oxford: Routledge, 2006.
Antrim, Donald. "Jonathan Franzen." *Bomb* 77 (Fall 2001). http://bombsite.com/issues/77 (accessed 29 March 2011).

Aubry, Timothy. "Middlebrow Aesthetics and the Therapeutic: The Politics of Interiority in Anita Shreve's *The Pilot's Wife.*" *Contemporary Literature* 49.1 (2008): 85–110.
Austen, Jane. *Northanger Abbey.* 1818. London: Penguin, 1995.
Bakhtin, Mikhail. *The Dialogic Imagination.* Trans. Caryl Emerson and Michael Holquist. Austin: University of Texas Press, 1981.
Bal, Mieke. "The Narrating and the Focalizing: A Theory of the Agents in Narrative." 1977. *Style* 17.2 (1983): 234–69.
———. *Narratology.* 1985. 2nd ed. Toronto: University of Toronto Press, 1997.
Banfield, Ann. *Unspeakable Sentences: Narration and Representation in the Language of Fiction.* Boston: Routledge and Kegan Paul, 1982.
Barbauld, Anna Laetitia. "Life of Samuel Richardson with Remarks on his Writing." *The Correspondence of Samuel Richardson: Selected from the Original Manuscripts Bequeathed by Him to His Family: To Which Are Prefixed a Biographical Account of That Author and Observations on His Writing.* 6 vols. Ed. Anna Laetitia Barbauld. London: Richard Phillips, 1804. Vol. 1: vii–ccxii.
Barker, Nicola. *Darkmans.* 2007. London: HarperPerennial, 2008.
Barth, John. "The Literature of Exhaustion." *The Atlantic* 220.2 (1967): 29–34.
———. "Lost in the Funhouse." *Lost in the Funhouse: Fiction for Print, Tape, Live Voice.* 1968. New York: Doubleday, 1988. 72–97.
Bassard, Katherine Clay. "Imagining Other Worlds: Race, Gender, and the 'Power Line' in Edward P. Jones's *The Known World.*" *African American Review* 42.3–4 (2008): 407–19.
Beach, Joseph Warren. *The Method of Henry James.* New Haven: Yale University Press, 1918.
———. *The Twentieth Century Novel: Studies in Technique.* New York: Appleton-Century-Crofts, 1932.
Belsey, Catherine. *Critical Practice.* London: Methuen, 1980.
Berube, Michael. "Teaching Postmodern Fiction without Being Sure That the Genre Exists." *The Chronicle of Higher Education* 46.37, 19 May 2000. B4–B5.
Bikerts, Sven. *The Gutenberg Elegies: The Fate of Reading in an Electronic Age.*1994. 2nd ed. New York: Faber and Faber, 2006.
Booker, M. Keith. "Beauty and the Beast: Dualism as Despotism in the Fiction of Salman Rushdie." *English Literary History* 57.4 (1990): 977–97.
Booth, Wayne. "Resurrection of the Implied Author: Why Bother?" *A Companion to Narrative Theory.* Ed. James Phelan and Peter J. Rabinowitz. Malden, MA, and Oxford: Blackwell, 2005. 75–88
———. *The Rhetoric of Fiction.* 1961. Rev. ed. Chicago: University of Chicago Press, 1983.
Bortolussi, Marisa, and Peter Dixon. *Psychonarratology: Foundations for the Empirical Study of Literary Response.* Cambridge: Cambridge University Press, 2003.
Boswell, Robert. *The Half-Known World: On Writing Fiction.* Saint Paul, MN: Graywolf Press, 2008.
Boulter, Amanda. *Writing Fiction: Creative and Critical Approaches.* Houndmills: Palgrave Macmillan, 2007.
Boyd, William. "The Course of True Life." Review of *Underworld* by Don DeLillo. *The Observer,* 1 November 1998. http://www.guardian.co.uk/books/1998/nov/01/fiction.reviews (accessed 12 July 2010).
Brooks, Cleanth, and Robert Penn Warren. *Understanding Fiction.* New York: Appleton-Century-Crofts, 1943.

Burn, Stephen J. "The End of Postmodernism: American Fiction at the Millennium." *American Fiction of the 1990s: Reflections of History and Culture.* Ed. Jay Prosser. London: Routledge, 2008. 220–34.
———. *Jonathan Franzen at the End of Postmodernism.* London: Continuum, 2008.
Byatt, A. S. *The Children's Book.* 2009. New York: Vintage, 2010.
———. *Possession.* New York: Random House, 1990.
———. "True Stories and the Facts of Fiction." *On Histories and Stories: Selected Essays.* 2000. London: Vintage, 2001. 91–122.
Chambers, Ross. *Story and Situation: Narrative Seduction and the Power of Fiction.* Minneapolis: University of Minnesota Press, 1984.
Chatman, Seymour. "Characters and Narrators: Filter, Center, Slant, and Interest-Focus." *Poetics Today* 7.2 (1986): 189–204.
———. *Story and Discourse: Narrative Structure in Fiction and Film.* Ithaca: Cornell University Press, 1978.
Chialant, Maria Teresa. "Dickensian Resonances in the Contemporary English Novel." *Dickens Quarterly* 28.1 (2011): 41–53.
Clark, Roger Y. *Stranger Gods: Salman Rushdie's Other Worlds.* McGill-Queens University Press, 1991.
Cohn, Dorrit. *The Distinction of Fiction.* Baltimore: Johns Hopkins University Press, 1999.
———. *Transparent Minds: Narrative Modes for Presenting Consciousness in Fiction.* Princeton: Princeton University Press, 1978.
Culler, Jonathan. "Omniscience." *Narrative* 12.1 (2004): 22–35.
Dames, Nicholas. *The Physiology of the Novel: Reading, Neural Science and the Form of Victorian Fiction.* Oxford: Oxford University Press, 2007.
Damrosch, Leopold. Jr. *God's Plot and Man's Stories: Studies in the Fictional Imagination from Milton to Fielding.* Chicago: University of Chicago Press, 1985.
Davidson, Jenny. "Great Jones." *The Village Voice Books,* 29 August 2006. http://www.villagevoice.com/2006-08-29/books/great-jones/ (accessed 13 November 2010).
Dawson, Paul. *Creative Writing and the New Humanities.* London: Routledge, 2005.
———. "Historicising 'Craft' in the Teaching of Fiction." *New Writing: The International Journal for the Practice and Theory of Creative Writing* 5.3 (2008): 211–24.
———. "Thomas Pennington's Fetich." *Meanjin* 63.1 (2004): 200–210.
DeLillo, Don. "The Power of History." *The New York Times Book Review,* 7 September 1997. http://www.nytimes.com/library/books/090797article3.html (accessed 5 July 2010).
———. *Underworld.* New York: Scribner, 1997.
DePetrio, Thomas, ed. *Conversations with Don DeLillo.* Jackson: University of Mississippi Press, 2005.
Dickens, Charles. *Bleak House.* 1853. London: Penguin, 2003.
Donatelli, Joseph, and Geoffrey Winthrop-Young. "Why Media Matters: An Introduction." *Mosaic: A Journal for the Interdisciplinary Study of Literature.* 28.4 (1995): v.
Dunning, Jenny. "Reconsidering Omniscience in Contemporary Fiction Writing." *The Writer's Chronicle* 40.4 (2008): 19–22.
Duvall, John N. "Baseball as Aesthetic Ideology: Cold War History, Race and DeLillo's 'Pafko at the Wall.'" *Modern Fiction Studies* 41.2 (1995): 285–313.
Dye, Robert Ellis. "Friedrich von Blanckenburg's Theory of the Novel." *Monatshefte* 60.2 (1968): 113–40.
Edel, Leon. *The Modern Psychological Novel.* 1955. New York: Grove Press, 1959.

Edelstein, Marilyn. "Before the Beginning: Nabokov and the Rhetoric of the Preface." *Narrative Beginnings: Theories and Practices.* Ed. Brian Richardson. Lincoln: University of Nebraska Press, 2009. 29–43.
Eliot, George. *Middlemarch.* 1871–72. London: Penguin Classics, 1994.
Ercolino, Stefan. "The Maximalist Novel." *Comparative Literature* 64.3 (2012): 241–56.
Ermarth, Elizabeth Deeds. *Realism and Consensus in the English Novel: Time, Space, Narrative.* Princeton: Princeton University Press, 1983.
Eskin, Michael. "Narratology Made User-Friendly: Rhetoric, Ethics, Storytelling." Review of *Living to Tell about It* by James Phelan. *Poetics Today* 28.4 (2007): 795–805.
Eugenides, Jeffrey. *Middlesex.* 2002. New York: Picador, 2003.
———. *The Virgin Suicides.* 1993. London: Bloomsbury, 2002.
Faber, Michel. *The Crimson Petal and the White.* Edinburgh: Canongate, 2002.
———. "Eccentricity and Authenticity: Fact into Fiction." *Victorians Institute Journal* 31 (2003): 101–3.
———. "Tale of a Street Walker." *London Evening Standard,* 30 October 2002. http://www.standard.co.uk/home/tale-of-a-street-walker-7384571.html (accessed 7 October 2012).
Ferriss, Lucy. "Uncle Charles Repairs to the A&P: Changes in Voice in the Recent American Short Story." *Narrative* 16.2 (2008): 178–92.
Fielding, Henry. *The History of Tom Jones, A Foundling.* 1749. London: Penguin, 2005.
Finch, Casey, and Peter Bowen "'The Tittle-Tattle of Highbury': Gossip and the Free Indirect Style in *Emma*." *Representations* 31 (1990): 1–18.
Finney, Brian. *English Fiction since 1984: Narrating a Nation.* Houndmills: Palgrave Macmillan, 2006.
Fitzpatrick, Kathleen. *The Anxiety of Obsolescence: The American Novel in the Age of Television.* Nashville: Vanderbilt University Press, 2006.
———. "The Unmaking of History: Baseball, Cold War, and *Underworld*." *Underwords: Perspectives on Don DeLillo's* Underworld. Ed. Joseph Dewey, Steve G. Kellman, and Irving Malin. Newark: University of Delaware Press, 2002. 144–60.
Flaubert, Gustave. "Letter to Louise Colet December 9, 1852." *Madame Bovary.* Ed. Leo Bersani. Trans. Lowell Blair. Toronto: Bantam Books, 1981. 319.
Fludernik, Monika. *The Fictions of Language and the Languages of Fiction: The Linguistic Representation of Speech and Consciousness.* London: Routledge, 1993.
———. "The Linguistic Illusion of Alterity: The Free Indirect as Paradigm of Discourse Representation." *Diacritics* 25.4 (1995): 89–115.
———. "Naturalizing the Unnatural: A View from Blending Theory." *Journal of Literary Semantics* 39.1 (2010): 1–27.
———. "'New Wine in Old Bottles?' Voice, Focalization, and New Writing." *New Literary History* 32 (2001): 619–38.
———. *Towards a "Natural" Narratology.* London: Routledge, 1996.
Foden, Giles. "The Final Gathering." *The Guardian,* 20 October 2007. http://www.guardian.co.uk/books/2007/oct/20/featuresreviews.guardianreview1 (accessed 25 October 2012).
Forster, E. M. *Aspects of the Novel.* 1927. Harmondsworth: Penguin, 1962.
Forster, John. *The Life of Charles Dickens.* Ed. J. W. T. Ley. London: Cecil Palmer, 1928.
Foucault, Michel. "The Functions of Literature." *Politics, Philosophy, Culture: Interviews and Other Writings, 1977–1984.* Ed. Lawrence D. Kritzman. Trans. Alan Sheridan. London: Routledge, 1990. 307–13.

———. "What Is an Author?" *Language, Counter-Memory, Practice: Selected Essays and Interviews.* Ed. Donald F. Bouchard. Trans. Bouchard and Sherry Simon. Ithaca: Cornell University Press, 1977. 113–38.
Fowles, John. *The French Lieutenant's Woman.* 1969. London: Picador, 1992.
———. "Notes on an Unfinished Novel." 1969. *The Novel Today: Contemporary Writers on Modern Fiction.* Ed. Malcolm Bradbury. Rev. ed. London: Fontana Press, 1990. 147–162.
Franzen, Jonathan. *The Corrections.* London: Fourth Estate, 2001.
———. "Perchance to Dream: In the Age of Images, a Reason to Write Novels." *Harper's Magazine* 292.1751 (April 1996): 35–54.
———. "Why Bother? (The *Harper's* Essay)." *How to Be Alone.* London: Fourth Estate, 2002. 55–97.
Friedman, Norman. "Point of View in Fiction: The Development of a Critical Concept." *PMLA* 70.5 (1955): 1160–84.
Fuger, Wilhelm. "Limits of the Narrator's Knowledge in Fielding's *Joseph Andrews*: A Contribution to a Theory of Negated Knowledge in Fiction." 1978. *Style* 38.3 (2004): 278–89.
Gallix, François, Vanessa Guignery, and Sophie Gaberel-Payen. "'From Then to Now and Next': An Interview with David Lodge." *Sources* 18 (2005): 9–28.
Genette, Gerard. *Narrative Discourse: An Essay in Method.* 1972. Trans. Jane E. Lewin. Ithaca: Cornell University Press, 1980.
———. *Narrative Discourse Revisited.* Trans. Jane E. Lewin. Ithaca: Cornell University Press, 1990.
———. *Paratexts: Thresholds of Interpretation.* 1987. Trans. Jane E. Lewin. Cambridge: Cambridge University Press, 1997.
Gibson, Andrew. *Towards a Postmodern Theory of Narrative.* Edinburgh: Edinburgh University Press, 1996.
Gissing, George. *Letters of George Gissing to Members of His Family.* Ed. Algernon and Ellen Gissing. London: Constable & Company, 1927.
Goodheart, Eugene. *Novel Practices: Classic Modern Fiction.* New Brunswick: Transaction Publishers, 2004.
Graham, Robert. *How to Write Fiction (and Think about It).* Houndmills: Palgrave Macmillan, 2007.
Green, Jeremy. *Late Postmodernism: American Fiction at the Millennium.* New York: Palgrave Macmillan, 2005.
Greif, Mark. "'The Death of the Novel' and Its Afterlives: Toward a History of the 'Big, Ambitious Novel.'" *boundary 2* 36.2 (2009): 11–30.
Gunn, Daniel P. "Free Indirect Discourse and Narrative Authority in *Emma*." *Narrative* 12.1 (2004): 35–54.
Gutleben, Christian. *Postmodern Nostalgia: The Victorian Tradition and the Contemporary British Novel.* Amsterdam: Rodopi, 2001.
Hale, Dorothy J. *Social Formalism: The Novel in Theory from Henry James to the Present.* Stanford: Stanford University Press, 1998.
Hamilton, Clayton. *Materials and Methods of Fiction.* New York: The Baker and Taylor Company, 1908.
Hannah, Daniel. "The Private Life, the Public Stage: Henry James in Recent Fiction." *Journal of Modern Literature* 30.3 (2007): 70–94.
Hansen, Per Krogh, Stefan Iversen, Henrik Skov Nielsen, and Rolf Reitan, eds. *Strange Voices in Narrative Fiction.* Berlin: De Gruyter, 2011.
Harrison, James. *Salman Rushdie.* New York: Twayne Publishers, 1992.

Harvey, John. "Lessons of the Master: The Henry James Novel." *Yearbook of English Studies* (2007): 75–88.

Harvey, W. J. "George Eliot and the Omniscient Author Convention." *Nineteenth-Century Fiction* 13.2 (1958): 81–108.

Head, Dominic. "Zadie Smith's *White Teeth*: Multiculturalism for the Millennium." Ed. Richard Lane, Rod Mengham, and Richard Tew. *Contemporary British Fiction.* Cambridge: Polity Press, 2003. 106–19.

Heinze, Ruediger. "Violations of Mimetic Epistemology in First-Person Narrative Fiction." *Narrative* 16.3 (2008): 279–97.

Herman, David. "Hypothetical Focalization." *Narrative* 2.3 (1994): 230–53.

———. "Narrative Theory and the Intentional Stance." *Partial Answers: Journal of Literature and the History of Ideas* 6.2 (2008): 233–60.

———. *Story Logic: Problems and Possibilities of Narrative.* Lincoln: University of Nebraska Press, 2002.

Hickling, Alfred. "Actually, I Don't Like It." Review of *Politics* by Adam Thirlwell. *The Guardian,* 30 August 2003: *Guardian Review,* 22.

Hoberek, Andrew. "Introduction: After Postmodernism." *Twentieth-Century Literature* 53.3 (2007): 233–47.

Hoffmann, Gerhard. *From Modernism to Postmodernism: Concepts and Strategies of Postmodern American Fiction.* Amsterdam: Rodopi, 2005.

Huggan, Graham. "Is the 'Post' in 'Postsecular' the 'Post' in 'Postcolonial'?" *Modern Fiction Studies* 56.4 (2010): 751–68.

Huhn, Peter, Wolf Schmid, and Jorg Schonert, eds. *Point of View, Perspective, and Focalization: Modelling Mediation in Narrative.* Berlin: Walter de Gruyter, 2009.

Humphrey, Robert. *Stream of Consciousness in the Modern Novel.* Berkeley: University of California Press, 1954.

Hutcheon, Linda. *A Poetics of Postmodernism: History, Theory, Fiction.* New York: Routledge, 1988.

Jacoby, Russell. *The Last Intellectuals: American Culture in the Age of Academe.* New York: Basic Books, 1987.

Jaffe, Audrey. *Vanishing Points: Dickens, Narrative and the Subject of Omniscience.* Berkeley: University of California Press, 1991. http://ark.cdlib.org/ark:/13030/ft038n99m1/.

Jahn, Manfred. "Frames, Preferences, and the Reading of Third-Person Narratives: Towards a Cognitive Narratology." *Poetics Today* 18.4 (1997): 441–68.

James, Henry. "The Art of Fiction." 1884. *The Nineteenth-Century Novel: A Critical Reader.* Ed. Stephen Regan. London: Routledge, 2001. 69–78.

———. *The Art of the Novel: Critical Prefaces.* Ed. R. P. Blackmur. New York: Charles Scribner's Sons, 1934.

———. *The Portrait of a Lady.* 1881. New York: Barnes & Noble Classics, 2004.

———. "Review of *Far From the Madding Crowd* by Thomas Hardy." 1874. *The Nineteenth-Century Novel: A Critical Reader.* Ed. Stephen Regan. London: Routledge, 2001. 85–88.

Johnson, Gary. "Consciousness as Content: Neuronarratives and the Redemption of Fiction." *Mosaic* 41.1 (2008): 169–84.

Jones, Edward P. "An Interview with Edward P. Jones." *Book Browse,* n.d. http://www.bookbrowse.com/author_interviews/full/index.cfm/author_number/930/edward-p-jones (accessed 29 June 2010).

———. *The Known World.* 2003. London: HarperPerennial, 2004.

Jones, Gail. "On the Piteous Death of Mary Wollstonecraft." *The House of Breathing*. Fremantle: Fremantle Arts Centre Press, 1992. 105–20.
Joyce, James. *A Portrait of the Artist as a Young Man*. 1916. London: Penguin, 2000.
Kakutani, Michiko. "A Family Portrait as Metaphor for the 90's." Review of *The Corrections* by Jonathan Franzen. *The New York Times*, 4 September 2001. http://www.nytimes.com/2001/09/04/books/books-of-the-times-a-family-portrait-as-metaphor-for-the-90-s.html (accessed 12 November 2010).
Kenner, Hugh. *Joyce's Voices*. Berkeley: University of California Press, 1978.
Knight, James. "Martin Amis." *Vice Magazine* 15.12 (2008). http://www.viceland.com/int/v15n12/htdocs/martin-amis-408.php (accessed 10 August 2010).
Kress, Nancy. "You, the Omniscient." *Writer's Digest* 78.11 (1998): 9–10.
Lanser, Susan. *Fictions of Authority: Women Writers and Narrative Voice*. Ithaca: Cornell University Press, 1992.
———. *The Narrative Act: Point of View in Prose Fiction*. Princeton: Princeton University Press, 1981.
Laurence, Alexander, and Kathleen McGee. "No More Illusions: Martin Amis is Getting Old and Wants to Talk about It." *The Write Stuff [Interviews]*, n.d. http://www.altx.com/int2/martin.amis.html (accessed 6 November 2010).
Lee, Vernon. "On Literary Construction." 1895. *The Handling of Words, and Other Studies in Literary Psychology*. London: John Lane The Bodley Head, 1923. 1–33.
Letissier, Georges. "*The Crimson Petal and the White*: A Neo-Victorian Classic." *Rewriting/Reprising: Plural Intertextualities*. Ed. George Letissier. Newcastle: Cambridge Scholars Publishing, 2009. 113–25.
Levitt, Morton P. *The Rhetoric of Modernist Fiction*. Hanover: University Press of New England, 2006.
Lewis, Barry. "Postmodernism and Literature." *The Routledge Companion to Postmodernism*. Ed. Stuart Sim. London: Routledge, 2001. 95–105.
Lodge, David. *Author, Author*. London: Secker and Warburg, 2004.
———. "Mimesis and Diegesis in Modern Fiction." *After Bakhtin: Essays on Fiction and Criticism*. London: Routledge, 1990. 25–44.
———. "The Novelist at the Crossroads." *Critical Quarterly* 11 (1969): 105–32.
———. *Thinks*. London: Penguin, 2002.
———. "The Uses and Abuses of Omniscience: Method and Meaning in Muriel Spark's *The Prime of Miss Jean Brodie*." *The Novelist at the Crossroads and Other Essays on Fiction and Criticism*. London: Ark Paperbacks, 1986. 119–44.
———. *The Year of Henry James: The Story of a Novel*. 2006. London: Penguin, 2007.
Lubbock, Percy. *The Craft of Fiction*. 1921. London: Jonathan Cape, 1954.
Martin, Wallace. *Recent Theories of Narrative*. Ithaca: Cornell University Press, 1986.
McEwan, Ian. *Atonement*. 2001. London: Vintage, 2007.
McGurl, Mark. *The Program Era: Postwar Fiction and the Rise of Creative Writing*. Harvard: Harvard University Press, 2009.
McHale, Brian. "Free Indirect Discourse: A Survey of Recent Accounts." *PTL: A Journal for Descriptive Poetics and Theory of Literature* 3 (1978): 249–87.
———. *Postmodernist Fiction*. New York: Methuen, 1987.
McLaughlin, Robert L. "Post-Postmodern Discontent: Contemporary Fiction and the Social World." *Symploke* 12.1–2 (2004): 53–68.
Mda, Zakes. *Ways of Dying*. New York: Picador, 1995.
Mezei, Kathy. "Who Is Speaking Here? Free Indirect Discourse, Gender, and Authority in *Emma*, *Howards End* and *Mrs. Dalloway*." *Ambiguous Discourse: Feminist Nar-

ratology and British Women Writers. Ed. Kathy Mezei. Chapel Hill: University of North Carolina Press, 1996. 66–92.

Miall, David S. "Empirical Approaches to Studying Literary Readers: The State of the Discipline." *Book History* 9 (2006): 291–311.

Miller, D. A. *The Novel and the Police*. Berkeley: University of California Press, 1988.

Miller, J. Hillis. *The Form of Victorian Fiction*. Notre Dame: University of Notre Dame Press, 1968.

Miller, Laura. "The War for the Soul of Literature." *Salon.com*, 15 July 2004. http://dir.salon.com/story/books/feature/2004/07/15/peck_wood/index.html (accessed 9 June 2008).

Moody, Rick. *The Ice Storm*. 1994. Boston: Little Brown, 2002.

Morrison, Tony. *Jazz*. 1992. New York: Plume, 1993.

Nabokov, Vladimir. *Lolita*. 1955. London: Penguin, 1980.

National Endowment for the Arts. *Reading at Risk: A Survey of Literary Reading in America*. Research Division Report #46. Washington, DC: NEA, 2004.

Nelles, William. "Getting Focalization into Focus." *Poetics Today* 11 (1990): 365–82.

———. "Omniscience for Atheists: Jane Austen's Infallible Narrator." *Narrative* 14.2 (2006): 118–31.

Neumann, Anne Waldron. "Characterization and Comment in *Pride and Prejudice*: Free Indirect Discourse and 'Double Voiced' Verbs of Speaking, Thinking, and Feeling." *Style* 20.3 (1986): 364–94.

Nielsen, Henrik Skov. "The Impersonal Voice in First-Person Narrative Fiction." *Narrative* 12.2 (2004): 133–50.

———. "Natural Authors, Unnatural Narration." *Postclassical Narratology: Approaches and Analyses*. Ed. Jan Alber and Monika Fludernik. Columbus: The Ohio State University Press, 2010. 275–301.

Nunning, Ansgar F. "Reconceptualizing Unreliable Narration: Synthesizing Cognitive and Rhetorical Approaches." *A Companion to Narrative Theory*. Ed. James Phelan and Peter J. Rabinowitz. Malden and Oxford: Blackwell, 2005. 89–107.

Nunning, Vera. "Beyond Indifference: New Departures in British Fiction at the Turn of the 21st Century." *Beyond Postmodernism: Reassessments in Literature, Theory and Culture*. Ed. Klaus Stierstorfer. Berlin: Walter de Gruyter, 2003. 235–54.

Olson, Barbara K. *Authorial Divinity in the Twentieth Century*. Lewisburg: Bucknell University Press, 1997.

———. "'Who Thinks This Book?' Or Why the Author/God Analogy Merits Our Continued Attention." *Narrative* 14 (2006): 339–46.

Ommundsen, Wenche. *Metafictions? Reflexivity in Contemporary Texts*. Melbourne: Melbourne University Press, 1993.

Palmer, Alan. *Fictional Minds*. Lincoln: University of Nebraska Press, 2004.

Paproth, Matthew. "The Flipping Coin: The Modernist and Postmodernist Zadie Smith." *Zadie Smith: Critical Essays*. Ed. Tracey L. Walters. New York: Peter Lang, 2008. 9–30.

Pascal, Roy. *The Dual Voice: Free Indirect Speech and its Functioning in the Nineteenth-Century European Novel*. Manchester: Manchester University Press, 1977.

Phelan, James. "Estranging Unreliability, Bonding Unreliability, and the Ethics of *Lolita*." *Narrative* 15.2 (2007): 222–238.

———. *Experiencing Fiction: Judgments, Progressions, and the Rhetorical Theory of Narrative*. Columbus: The Ohio State University Press, 2007.

———. *Living to Tell about It: A Rhetoric and Ethics of Character Narration*. Ithaca: Cornell University Press, 2005.

Phillips, Brian. "Character in Contemporary Fiction." *The Hudson Review* 41 (2004): 629–42.
Phillips, Melanie. *Londonistan.* New York: Encounter Books, 2006.
Pike, David L. "*Underworld* and the Architecture of Urban Space." *Don DeLillo:* Mao II, Underworld, Falling Man. Ed. Stacey Olster. London: Continuum, 2011.
Powers, Richard. *Generosity.* 2009. London: Atlantic, 2010.
Pratt, Mary Louise. "Interpretive Strategies/Strategic Interpretations: On Anglo-American Reader Response Criticism." *boundary 2* 11.1/2 (1982–83): 201–31.
Pressly, Thomas J. "*The Known World* of Free Black Slaveholders: A Research Note on the Scholarship of Carter G. Woodson." *The Journal of African American History* 91.1 (2006): 81–87.
Prince, Gerald. *A Dictionary of Narratology.* Lincoln: University of Nebraska Press, 2003.
———. "Introduction to the Study of the Narratee. 1973. *Reader-Response Criticism: From Formalism to Post-Structuralism.* Ed. Jane P. Tompkins. Baltimore: Johns Hopkins University Press, 1980. 7–25.
Prose, Francine. *Reading like a Writer: A Guide for People Who Love Books and for Those Who Want to Write Them.* 2006. New York: HarperPerennial, 2007.
Puckett, Kent. *Bad Form: Social Mistakes and the Nineteenth-Century Novel.* Oxford, New York: Oxford University Press, 2008.
Pullman, Phillip. "'Story' versus 'Literature.'" *The Guardian,* 29 December 2007: *Guardian Review:* 7.
Punday, Daniel. *Writing at the Limit: The Novel in the New Media Ecology.* Lincoln: University of Nebraska Press, 2012.
Rabinowitz, Peter. "'The Absence of Her Voice from that Concord': The Value of the Implied Author." *Style* 45.1 (2011): 99–108.
———. "Truth in Fiction: A Re-examination of Audiences." *Critical Inquiry* 4 (1977): 121–41.
Raleigh, Walter. *The English Novel: Being a Short Sketch of Its History from the Earliest Times to the Appearance of Waverley.* 1894. London: John Murray, 1922.
Rasley, Alicia. *The Power of Point of View: Make Your Story Come to Life.* Cincinnati: Writers Digest Books, 2008.
Reynolds, Susan. "Down from the Mountains." Review of *I Am Charlotte Simmons* by Tom Wolfe. *Los Angeles Times,* 30 October 2004. http://articles.latimes.com/2004/oct/30/entertainment/et-wolfe30 (accessed 12 November 2010).
Richardson, Brian. *Unnatural Voices: Extreme Narration in Modern and Contemporary Fiction.* Columbus: The Ohio State University Press, 2006.
Riffaterre, Michael. *Fictional Truth.* Baltimore: Johns Hopkins University Press, 1990.
Rimmon-Kenan, Shlomith. *Narrative Fiction: Contemporary Poetics.* 1983. 2nd ed. London: Routledge, 2002.
Rody, Caroline. "Impossible Voices: Ethnic Postmodern Narration in Toni Morrison's *Jazz* and Karen Tei Yamashita's *Through the Arc of the Rain Forest.*" *Contemporary Literature* 41.4 (2000): 618–41.
Roth, Philip. "Writing American Fiction." *Commentary* 31 (March 1961): 223–33.
Roychoudhuri, Onnesha. "Books after Amazon: Publishing's Race to the Bottom." *Boston Review* 35.6 (2010): 48–53.
Royle, Nicholas. "The Telepathy Effect: Notes toward a Reconsideration of Narrative Fiction." *The Uncanny.* Manchester: Manchester University Press, 2003. 256–76.
Rushdie, Salman. "Imaginary Homelands." 1982. *Imaginary Homelands: Essays and Criticism 1981–1991.* London: Granta, 1991. 9–21.

———. *Midnight's Children.* 1981. New York: Random House, 2006.

———. "Muslims Unite! A New Reformation Will Bring Your Religion into the Modern Era." *The Times,* 11 August 2005. http://www.timesonline.co.uk/tol/comment/columnists/guest_contributors/article553964.ece (accessed 15 June 2008).

———. *The Satanic Verses.* 1988. London: Vintage, 1998.

Russo, Richard. "In Defense of Omniscience." *Bringing the Devil to His Knees: The Craft of Fiction and the Writing Life.* Ed. Charles Baxter and Peter Turchi. Ann Arbor: University of Michigan Press, 2008. 7–17.

Ryan, David. "Rick Moody: The Art of Fiction No.166." *The Paris Review* 158 (2001). http://www.theparisreview.org/interviews/509/the-art-of-fiction-no-166-rick-moody (accessed 9 October 2012).

Ryan, Tim A. *Calls and Responses: The American Novel of Slavery since* Gone with the Wind. Baton Rouge: Louisiana State University Press, 2008.

Saunders, Max. "Master Narratives." *The Cambridge Quarterly* 37.1 (2008): 121–31.

Scherzinger, Karen. "Staging Henry James: Representing the Author in Colm Tóibín's *The Master* and David Lodge's *Author, Author! A Novel.*" *The Henry James Review* 29 (2008): 181–96.

Schmid, Wolf. "Implied Author." *Handbook of Narratology.* Ed. Peter Hühn, John Pier, Wolf Schmid, and Jörg Schönert. Berlin: Walter de Gruyter, 2009. 161–73.

Scholes, Robert, and Robert Kellogg. *The Nature of Narrative.* London: Oxford University Press, 1968.

Schweickart, Patrocinio P. "Reading Ourselves: Toward a Feminist Theory of Reading." *Gender and Reading: Essays on Readers, Texts, and Contexts.* Ed. Elizabeth A. Flynn and Patrocinio P. Schweickart. Baltimore: Johns Hopkins University Press, 1986. 31–62.

Scott, Walter. *The Fortunes of Nigel.* 1822. Paris: Baudry's Foreign Library, 1832.

Seltzer, Mark. *Henry James and the Art of Power.* Ithaca and London: Cornell University Press, 1984.

Shaw, Harry E. "Why Won't Our Terms Stay Put? The Narrative Communication Diagram Scrutinized and Historicized." *A Companion to Narrative Theory.* Ed. James Phelan and Peter J. Rabinowitz. Malden and Oxford: Blackwell, 2008. 299–311.

Shen, Dan. "What Narratology and Stylistics Can Do for Each Other." *A Companion to Narrative Theory.* Ed. James Phelan and Peter J. Rabinowitz. Malden and Oxford: Blackwell, 2008. 136–49.

Shulevitz, Judith. "Real Thoughts and Fictional Thinking." *New York Times,* 23 February 2003: B31.

Sidney, Philip. "An Apology for Poetry." 1595. *English Critical Essays (Sixteenth, Seventeenth and Eighteenth Centuries).* Ed. Edmund D. Jones. The World's Classics 240. London: Oxford University Press, 1922. 1–54.

Smith, Zadie. *White Teeth.* 2000. London: Penguin, 2002.

Snodgrass, Mary Ellen. "Michel Faber, Feminism, and the Neo-Gothic Novel: *The Crimson Petal and the White.*" *21st-Century Gothic: Great Gothic Novels since 2000.* Ed. Danel Olson. Plymouth: Scarecrow Press, 2011. 111–23.

Stanzel, Franz. *A Theory of Narrative.* Trans. Charlotte Goedsche. Cambridge: Cambridge University Press, 1984.

Sternberg, Meir. *Expositional Modes and Temporal Ordering in Fiction.* Baltimore: Johns Hopkins University Press, 1978.

———. "Omniscience in Narrative Construction: Old Challenges and New." *Poetics Today* 28 (2007): 683–794.

———. "Proteus in Quotation-Land: Mimesis and the Forms of Reported Discourse." *Poetics Today* 3.2 (1982): 107–56.
Stewart, Garrett. *Dear Reader: The Conscripted Audience in Nineteenth-Century British Fiction.* Baltimore: Johns Hopkins University Press, 1996.
Strecker, Trey. "Ecologies of Knowledge: The Encyclopedic Narratives of Richard Powers and His Contemporaries." *Review of Contemporary Fiction* 18.3 (1998): 67–71.
Striphas, Ted. *The Late Age of Print: Everyday Book Culture from Consumerism to Control.* New York: Columbia University Press, 2009.
Süskind, Patrick. *Perfume: The Story of a Murderer.* Trans. John E. Woods. London: Hamish Hamilton, 1986.
Sutton, Henry. "Not as Many Kinks as the Author Thinks." Review of *Politics* by Adam Thirlwell. *The Independent,* 17 August 2003. http://www.independent.co.uk/arts-entertainment/books/reviews/politics-by-adam-thirlwell-536309.html (accessed 12 November 2010).
Swann, Joan, and Daniel Allington. "Reading Groups and the Language of Literary Texts: A Case Study in Social Reading." *Language and Literature* 18.3 (2009): 247–64.
Tanehaus, Sam. "Peace and War." Review of *Freedom* by Jonathan Franzen. *New York Times Book Review,* 29 August 2010: 1, 10–11.
Thackeray, William Makepeace. *Vanity Fair: A Novel without a Hero.* 1848. London: Penguin, 2001.
Thirlwell, Adam. *Politics.* London: Jonathan Cape, 2003.
Thorne, Matt. "Politics, Adam Thirlwell." Review of *Politics* by Adam Thirlwell. *The Independent,* 23 August 2003. http://www.independent.co.uk/arts-entertainment/books/reviews/politics-adam-thirlwell-536731.html (accessed 12 November 2010).
Timmer, Nicoline. *Do You Feel It Too? The Post-Postmodern Syndrome in American Fiction at the Turn of the Millennium.* Amsterdam: Rodopi, 2010.
Van Peer, Willie, and Seymour Chatman. "Introduction." *New Perspectives on Narrative Perspective.* Ed. Willie van Peer and Seymour Chatman. Albany: SUNY Press, 2001. 1–17.
Vernon, John. "People Who Owned People." Review of *The Known World* by Edward P. Jones. *New York Times,* 31 August 2003. http://www.nytimes.com/2003/08/31/books/people-who-owned-people.html (accessed 24 November 2010).
Wallace, David Foster. "E Unibus Pluram: Television and U.S. Fiction." *Review of Contemporary Fiction* 13.2 (1993): 151–94.
———. "Luckily the Account Representative Knew CPR." *Girl with Curious Hair.* 1989. London: Abacus, 1997. 45–52.
———. "Mr. Squishy." *Oblivion.* London: Abacus, 2004. 3–66.
———. "Octet." *Brief Interviews with Hideous Men.* 1999. London: Abacus, 2001. 111–36.
Walsh, Richard. *The Rhetoric of Fictionality: Narrative Theory and the Idea of Fiction.* Columbus: The Ohio State University Press, 2007.
Warhol, Robyn. *Gendered Interventions: Narrative Discourse in the Victorian Novel.* New Brunswick: Rutgers University Press, 1989.
Waugh, Patricia. Metafiction: *The Theory and Practice of Self-Conscious Fiction.* London: Methuen, 1984.
Winterson, Jeanette. *The Powerbook.* London: Vintage, 2001.
Wolfe, Tom. *Hooking Up.* New York: Picador, 2001.
———. *I Am Charlotte Simmons.* London: Jonathan Cape, 2004.

———. "The New Journalism." *The New Journalism.* Ed. Tom Wolfe and E. W. Johnson. 1973. London: Picador, 1996. 15–51.
———. "Stalking the Billion Footed Beast: A Literary Manifesto for the New Social Novel." *Harper's Magazine* 279 (November 1989): 45–56.
———, and E. W. Johnson, eds. *The New Journalism.* 1975. London: Picador, 1996.
Wood, James. *How Fiction Works.* London: Jonathan Cape, 2008.
———. "Human, All Too Human." Review of *White Teeth* by Zadie Smith. *The New Republic,* 24 July 2000: 41–45.
———. *The Irresponsible Self: On Laughter and the Novel.* London: Pimlico, 2005.
———. "The Spoils." Review of *Author, Author* by David Lodge. *The New Republic Online,* 21 October 2004. http://www.powells.com/review/2004_10_21.html (accessed 28 September 2009).
———. "Tell Me How Does It Feel?" *The Guardian,* 6 October 2001. http://www.guardian.co.uk/books/2001/oct/06/fiction (accessed 15 June 2010).
Wutz, Michael. *Enduring Words: Literary Narrative in a Changing Media Ecology.* Tuscaloosa: Alabama University Press, 2009.
Young, Kay. *Imagining Minds.* Columbus: The Ohio State University Press, 2011.
Zunshine, Lisa. *Why We Read Fiction: Theory of Mind and the Novel.* Columbus: The Ohio State Press, 2006.

INDEX

Aczel, Richard: and free indirect discourse, 176; and style, 22, 112–14
Allende, Isabel ("Phantom Palace"), 89
alterity: "aesthetics of," 175–76; as interpretive frame for free indirect discourse, 23, 176–78, 179, 183, 189, 192
Amis, Martin, 2, 22, 62; *The Information*, 25–26, 28–30, 37, 61, 70, 182, 210, 252n2; *The Second Plane*, 16, 251n4
anxiety: about cultural status of literature, 5–9, 21; about cultural authority of novelists, 18, 19; in *The Information*, 26, 28; and narratorial commentary, 70; and postmodernism, 66, 69; in *Generosity*, 161, 210; in *Politics*, 81, 82, 84; in "Octet," 74, 78, 81
anxiety of obsolescence, 8–9, 21, 60–61, 64; and DeLillo, 157
Aubry, Timothy, 2, 174–75
Austen, Jane, 17, 19, 53, 158; and free indirect discourse, 167, 172, 182, 192; *Northanger Abbey*, 14
author: in discursive narratology, 235–39; in narrative communication model, 223, 225, 226–27, 232; neglect of in narrative theory, 22, 233–35; paralepses attributable to (Genette), 198; and unnatural narration (Nielsen), 219–21
authorial intrusion, 219; critique of, 15, 41, 43; in *French Lieutenant's Woman*, 70; and metafiction, 66, 73; in "Octet," 74; omniscience as, 38, 43, 66
authorial narrator: 1, 26, 196, 212–13; comparison with God, 31; compared with other methods of narration, 39; and direct address, 22, 73; as extradiegetic character, 55; Fludernik on, 74, 126; of *Generosity*, 161, 211–12; of *The Known World*, 105; and omniscience, 48, 50, 63, 66, 67; of "Octet," 73, 75, 80; of *Politics*, 82, 83; and pyrotechnic storytellers, 111, 116
authorial presence 1, 13, 19, 36, 40–43, 168, 252n7; effacement of, 40, 42, 180, 229; intrusive, 3, 43, 66–67; and narrative authority, 56; key

feature of omniscience, 91–92; and postmodernism, 68–69; in *Vanity Fair*, 36
authorial voice, 66; in *Author, Author*, 241, 244–45; and commentary, 11, 20–21; and discursive continuum with narrative voice, 15, 24, 61, 150, 153, 163, 236–37, 240, 244–45, 248; and free indirect discourse, 173; in *The Ice Storm*, 203; and narrating instance, 44; nonfictional, 14, 15, 154; and omniscience, 9–10, 23, 36, 58–59, 239
authorship, 33, 36, 39, 52; and author function, 58–59; and gender, 60; omniscient narrator as historically specific figure of, 2, 9, 12, 13–14, 19, 20, 22, 31, 59, 63, 78, 130, 239, 247; in narrative theory, 24–49, 219–21, 222, 233–35; relation to narrative voice, 21, 48, 59
autotelic second person: defined, 77; in "Octet," 77, 79; in *The Crimson Petal and the White*, 96, 193; in *Underworld*, 145

Bakhtin, Mikhail: alterity, 176; authorial agency, 232; monologic novel, 56; double-voiced discourse, 114, 168; social formalism, 175
Bal, Mieke, 46, 205
Banfield, Ann (*Unspeakable Sentences*): "empty deictic center," 47; and free indirect discourse, 173–74; narratorless fiction, 113, 168, 228
Barker, Nicola (*Darkmans*), 2, 22, 60, 111, 135; and free indirect discourse (shared linguistic habitus), 183–85; pyrotechnic storyteller, 116–24
Barth, John, 7; "Literature of Exhaustion," 63, 67, 75; "Lost in the Funhouse," 63, 66; and Wallace, 72–73
Beach, Joseph Warren, 2, 179; on omniscience, 39, 41, 81–82
Bikerts, Sven (*Gutenberg Elegies*), 5–6
Booth, Wayne: dramatized narrator, 55; impersonality, 42; implied author, 42, 222, 223, 233, 234; narrative communication, 222–23; paradox of omniscience, 42–43; on *Tom Jones*, 125
Burn, Stephen J.: on post-postmodernism, 68, 157; on Franzen, 157; on Powers, 157
Byatt, A. S., 2, 59–60, 158, 251n2; the literary historian (*The Children's Book*), 90–91; on omniscience, 95; *Possession*, 94–95, 207

Chambers, Ross (*Story and Situation*), 251n5
characterological cognitive self-awareness, 23, 183, 189–92. *See also* free indirect discourse
Chatman, Seymour: communication model, 223; on focalization, 47, 48; on style, 112
cognitive: facet of focalization (Rimmon-Kenan), 46; frame of alterity for FID, 176–77, 180; frames, 37, 201, 204, 227–28; perspective on free indirect discourse, 176; approaches to narrative, 21, 224, 225, 229; processing, 21, 23, 170, 190, 191, 192, 232; relocation of readers to storyworld (deictic shift theory), 95; theory (and naturalization), 171, 220
cognitive narratology, 224; and paralepsis, 200–201, 204; and readers, 226–27, 229, 231
cognitive science: and neuronarratives, 158–59; and postclassical narratology, 47, 224, 225
Cohn, Dorrit: free indirect discourse (narrated monologue), 170, 171–72, 186, 192; omniscience, 195; psychoanalogy, 191; psychonarration, 34, 50, 186–87; stylistic contagion, 253n1
communication model, 21; Chatman's diagram, 223; critique of by psychonarratology and natural narratology, 226–29; development of in narratology, 222–24; discursive

reformulation of, 24, 231–32, 235–38; and narrative authority, 63, 236, 238; and "Octet," 80; and real authors, 222, 225, 235; and real readers, 225, 235; revised diagram of, 238. *See also* author; extrafictional voice; paratext

contemporary omniscience, 10, 12, 15, 17, 28, 37, 49, 62, 65, 68, 90, 111, 114, 164–65, 182, 231, 239, 248, 251n2; difference from classic omniscience, 14, 62, 63–65, 69, 92, 130, 164; and the direct address, 70; exemplary voice of post-postmodernism, 45, 67–69; and free indirect discourse, 23, 168–69, 182–83, 192, 194; and gender, 59–61; as legacy of postmodernism, 4–5, 10, 64–69, 210, 246; modes of, 22, 23, 61; and neo-Victorian fiction, 93–95; paradox of, 15; *Satanic Verses* as first example of, 15–16; symptomatic of cultural anxiety, 9, 23, 246. *See also* omniscience; postmodernism; post-postmodernism

creativity (authorial), 32, 56: constitutive feature of author/god analogy, 34–35

Culler, Jonathan ("Omniscience"), 17, 49–50, 52–53, 54, 56, 201

cultural authority: authorial anxiety over loss of, 7, 19, 61, 245, 247; crisis of, 9; defined, 18; and Franzen, 153–56; and gender, 57–58; 60–61, 80; and Edward P. Jones, 108–9, 110; and Lodge, 243, 245–46; of novelists, 15–16, 18–19, 21, 56, 130, 237, 243; relation between omniscience and, 9–10, 12–14, 18, 21, 56, 61, 63, 110, 239, 247–48; and paratext, 237, 245; and Rushdie, 219; and Smith, 128, 130; and Thirlwell, 86; and Wallace, 72, 80

DeLillo, Don, 2, 7, 8, 22, 124, 136, 137, 157, 163; on omniscience, 165; "The Power of History," 149–50; and style, 178, 180; *Underworld,* 143–50

Dickens, Charles: Asmodean figure, 37, 96, 252n7; *Bleak House,* 130; omniscience, 19, 31, 36, 39, 51, 97, 130, 138, 213

direct address: apostrophic instantiation of narratee, 20; and autotelic second person, 77, 145, 193; in *The Crimson Petal and the White,* 95–97, 100, 193; and the editorial "we," 27, 128–29; and Franzen, 155; in *French Lieutenant's Woman,* 67; as gendered intervention (Warhol), 79–80, 97; in *Generosity,* 151; and ironic moralist, 22, 62–87; most important device of metafiction, 73, 76, 77, 81, 82; and the narrating instance, 95; as performance of narrative authority, 20, 59, 69, 73, 166; in "Octet," 73–81; feature of omniscient narration, 1, 22, 59, 69, 70, 73, 248; in *Perfume,* 90; in *Politics,* 12, 81–87; in *Satanic Verses,* 70; and self-reflexivity, 69, 73, 161; and "Dear Reader trope" (Garret Stewart), 75–76; in Trollope (Henry James's criticism), 66; in *Underworld,* 143, 144–45; in *Vanity Fair,* 27; in *White Teeth,* 128–29

discourse (and story), 112; breach of in *Vanity Fair,* 27; Chatman on, 47; relation between, 48, 170, 222, 224

discourse: of anxiety, 5, 7, 19; authorial, 175, 229; nonliterary, 14, 16, 24, 232, 247

discursive formation (Foucault): and *Author, Author,* 243, 244; and author function, 58; and communication model, 231, 238; and discursive narratology, 236; as paratext, 24, 65, 237

discursive narratology, 23, 235–38

editorial "we": defined by J. Hillis Miller, 27; in *The Information,* 30; in *Vanity Fair,* 27–28; in *White Teeth,* 128–29

Eliot, George, 79; *Middlemarch,* 14; omniscience, 31, 37–38, 41, 51, 56, 60, 96 epistemological fallacy, 23, 210, 220; defined, 196; and Genette, 199; and Proust, 213, 214

epitext, 254n3; and *Author, Author,* 242, 244–45; and communication model, 238; defined, 236–37; later, 244; public authorial, 237, 245. *See also* paratext

Eugenides, Jeffery, 196; *Middlesex,* 206; *The Virgin Suicides,* 215–16

extradiegetic: character (omniscient narrator as), 55, 81, 83, 137; level, 18, 58, 70; formal status of narrator, 18, 20, 46, 50, 52, 58; narratee, 146; narratorial appeal, 28; public world of reader, 54, 58–59, 83

extrafictional: historical record, 90; level, 20, 235; narrative of Franzen, 156; statements of authors, 19

extrafictional voice, 24, 139; and relation between author and narrator, 239; and communication model, 235, 238; defined by Lanser, 235–36; of David Lodge, 241–46; and discursive narratology, 236; and Foucault's author function, 236; relation to implied author, 235; and narrative authority, 236; relation to paratext, 237, 238, 254n3; of Tom Wolfe; 139

Faber, Michel (*The Crimson Petal and the White*), 22, 37, 109; and free indirect discourse, 183, 193; and hyperomniscience, 95; as literary historian, 88, 90, 95–100; and omniscience, 97–98

feminist narratology, 21, 57–59. *See also,* Lanser; Warhol

fictionality, 89, 92, 98, 100, 197, 208, 219, 239

Fielding, Henry, 31: *Tom Jones,* 34–35, 36, 37, 41, 42, 45, 56–57, 79, 88; and providence, 124–25

first-person narrator: and figure of authorship, 20; John Fowles on, 67; and narrative authority, 20; and unreliability, 3

first-person (homodiegetic) omniscience, 23, 195–221; and *Atonement,* 208–9; and *Generosity,* 210–12; and hypothetical focalization, 205–7, 214–19; and *The Ice Storm,* 202–4, 207; and *Jazz,* 216; and metafiction, 210; and *Middlesex,* 208; and *Midnight's Children,* 216–19; and paralepsis, 196–205; as rhetorical performance, 215–16; typology of different modes, 215; and unnatural narratology, 200–204; and *The Virgin Suicides,* 215–16

Fitzpatrick, Kathleen: *Anxiety of Obsolescence,* 7, 8–9, 60–61, 64, 157; on "Pafko at the Wall," 44

Fludernik, Monika: on authorial narration, 48, 126; on blending theory and first-person omniscience, 253n2; and cognitive science, 47; on free indirect discourse, 170–71, 176, 177–78; critique of narrative communication, 226, 228; on narratorless fiction, 113, 228; on "natural" narratology, 226, 227–29; on omniscience, 48, 74, 126; on relation between voice and focalization, 48

focalization: and cognitive narratology, 226; defined by Genette, 45; external, 52, 93, 132; facets of (Rimmon-Kenan), 46; relation to free indirect discourse, 172–74, 178, 185; internal, 93, 101, 132, 135, 147, 151, 164, 175, 178, 185, 187, 203, 207, 243; multiple, 241; and omniscience, 18, 33, 44, 45, 46–47, 52, 53, 63, 164, 197–98; and paralepsis, 23, 196–200, 202, 204; and point of view, 38, 46; in postclassical narratology, 47; relation to voice, 17, 21, 44, 45–46, 47, 48, 52, 63, 172–73, 198–99, 207, 224; revised by Bal, 46; as rhetorical strategy of narrator, 47–48, 49, 164, 207, 210, 212, 214, 248; and stylistic contagion, 188; variable, 145, 203. *See also* hypothetical focalization; paralepsis; point of view; zero focalization

Foucault, Michel: author function, 58, 236; on literature as discourse, 232; and panopticism, 56
Fowles, John (*French Lieutenant's Woman*), 5, 67, 73, 95, 98
Franzen, Jonathan, 2, 13, 15; and anxiety of obsolescence, 61; *The Corrections*, 15, 136, 150–57, 158, 163; and free indirect discourse, 78–79; 190–91; and Oprah Winfrey, 13, 61; as public intellectual, 14, 137; *Harper's* essay, 15, 76, 153–56, 251n4; social commentator, 22, 136
free indirect discourse (FID), 22–23; in *I am Charlotte Simmons*, 141; in *The Corrections*, 15; in *Darkmans*, 118–19, 120; defined, 169–71; in *The Diviners*, 132; hesitancy of attribution, 169; and history of the novel, 167–69; hypothetical nature of, 167, 170, 172, 174, 181–82, 184, 192–94; and interpretive frame of alterity, 176–81; self-reflexive use of, 182–83; and style, 112; and stylistic contagion, 174–75; in *Underworld*, 146. *See also* alterity; characterological cognitive self-awareness; Cohn; Fludernik; Pascal; shared linguistic habitus; stylistic contagion

gender, 2; and authority and authorship, 57–61; in *I am Charlotte Simmons*, 141; and *The Crimson Petal and the White*, 97; in *The Information*, 30; and "the anxiety of obsolescence," 8, 60–61; and contemporary omniscience, 59–61, 107; engaging and distancing narrators, 79–80; and free indirect discourse, 175; and narrative authority, 58–59; in "Octet," 80
general consciousness: omniscient narrator as voice of, 11, 12, 27; in *Vanity Fair*, 27; absent from *Politics*, 83, 87; in *White Teeth*, 128; in *Underworld*, 144
Genette, Gerard: 17, 44–46, 47, 49, 50, 53, 112, 173, 222, 223; focalization, 45 (defined), 173, 197–98, 199–200, 205; free indirect discourse, 173; function of the narrator, 45, 59, 198; narrating instance, 21, 44, 49, 198–99; narrative level, 58; and omniscience, 44–45, 198–99; paralepsis 23, 196–200 (defined), 202, 204, 205, 219; paralipsis, 207; paratext, 24, 235, 236–38 (defined), 244, 254n3; prolepsis (defined), 90; time of narrating, 89 (defined)

Hale, Dorothy (*Social Formalism*): 'aesthetics of alterity,' 175–76; on Henry James and Percy Lubbock, 252n4
Herman, David: hypothetical focalization, 23, 193 (defined), 205–7; intentionality, 253–54n1; omniscience, 206; possible worlds, 47; *Story Logic*, 225–26
heterodiegetic (third-person) narrator: authoritative knowledge of, 44; and focalization, 199–200, 204; and omniscience, 20, 21, 46, 52–55, 58–60, 63, 114, 196, 212; and voice, 45, 211, 215. *See also* third-person narrator
homodiegetic (first-person) narrator: and focalization, 199–200; and omniscience, 204–6, 213; and voice, 203. *See also* first-person narrator
hypothetical focalization: defined, 205–6; as mode of first-person omniscience, 206–7, 212, 214–15; relation to free indirect discourse, 193–94; and omniscience, 206–7; alternative to paralepsis, 23, 205–7; in *Underworld*, 145
hysterical realism, 4, 124 (defined), 136, 156, 162. *See also* Wood

immersion journalist, 22, 69, 136, 137; Tom Wolfe, 137–43
implied author, 42, 49, 83, 196, 214, 219, 228, 238, 244, 254n2; and authorship, 233–35; and the narrative communication model, 222–23, 225; and paralepsis,199

implied reader: in *I am Charlotte Simmons*, 140; in the narrative communication model, 223, 238; in *White Teeth*, 128
intrusive: commentary, 1, 13, 20, 22, 26, 28, 41, 54, 56, 66, 69–70, 81, 86, 100, 113, 114, 126, 128. 159–61; presence of author/narrator, 3, 5, 12, 22, 43, 53, 60, 63–64, 66, 71, 96, 109, 111–12, 114, 117, 123–24, 125, 151, 157, 168, 180, 193, 239, 248
ironic moralist, 22, 62–87, 157

Jahn, Manfred, 47, 225
James, Henry: in *Author, Author*, 239–44; critique of reflexity, 66; 'house of fiction,' 38; modernism, 44; modernist impersonality, 3; on omniscience, 37, 39; point of view, 40; *Portrait of a Lady*, 158, 253n3; style, 113–14
Jones, Edward P. (*The Known World*), 2, 22, 88; literary historian, 100–110
Jones, Gail ("On the Piteous Death of Mary Wollstonecraft"), 2, 22, 60, 88; literary historian, 91–93

Lanser, Susan: authorial voice, 58–59; on classic realism, 38, 54; cultural authority of authors, 57–58; equation of author and narrator, 60, 61, 107, 238–39; extrafictional voice, 24, 235–36, 237, 254n3; feminist poetics of voice, 57, 60; *Fictions of Authority*, 57–59; *The Narrative Act*, 60, 235–36; on narrative authority, 58, 60, 235; narrative voice, 57, 58, 61; on omniscience, 54, 58–59, 60; public voice, 58
literary historian, 22, 69, 88–110; and authority of historical record, 88; different manifestations of, 89; Faber, 95–100; Gail Jones, 91–93; Edward P. Jones, 100–110; Lodge, 240–46; and omniscience, 104, 106, 107, 110; and prolepsis, 90; and temporal relation between story and discourse, 88–89; and *Underworld*, 144, 150
Lodge, David, 2; *Author, Author*, 89, 91, 239–46; literary historian, 22, 88, 89, 240; on omniscience, 31; "Novelist at the Crossroads," 66; on postmodernism, 65, 69, 138; *Thinks*, 1, 158–59, 190; *The Year of Henry James*, 244–45
Lubbock, Percy (*The Craft of Fiction*): 3, 9, 42, 179, 229, 252n5; on omniscience, 40–41; on point of view, 40–41, 47, 168, 180

maximalism, 5, 179, 249; and omniscience, 161–65
maximalist novel, the, 163–64
McEwan, Ian: *Atonement*, 196, 208, 224; delayed disclosure, 208; metafiction, 208; neuronarrative (*Saturday*), 158; omniscience, 208
McHale, Brian: on postmodernism, 4, 65; on free indirect discourse, 170
metafiction: in *Atonement*, 208; in *Generosity*, 157, 161, 210–12; historiographic, 88, 144; and the ironic moralist, 22, 69, 82; in "Octet," 63, 73–81; and omniscience, 66–67, 100, 210, 249; as privileged mode of postmodernism, 65–67, 68; and post-postmodernism, 68; Wallace on, 72
metaleptic, 96, 145
metaphorical excess: and pyrotechnic storyteller, 112, 115, 116; in Rushdie, 115; as feature of style, 116, 166
minimalism, 10, 162
modernism: 2, 4, 28, 65, 73, 76, 209, 219; figure of authorship, 13; and narratology, 44
modernist: aesthetic, 41, 42, 47, 66, 177, 192, 228, 244; authorial effacement, 13, 168, 228; criticism, 3, 178, 192; difficulty, 28; dramatization, 40, 179–80; exhaustion, 65;

experimentation, 65, 129, 130, 182; free indirect discourse, 173, 177, 180, 192; impersonality, 3, 5, 42, 77, 173, 177, 178, 180, 244; rejection of omniscience, 2, 4, 11, 13, 42, 43, 62, 66, 179–80; poetics, 3; point of view, 44, 179
Moody, Rick, 2, 22, 111, 183, 251n2; *The Diviners*, 130–35; *The Ice Storm*, 196, 202–4, 206, 207
Morrison, Tony (*Jazz*), 216

Nabokov, Vladimir (*Lolita*): style, 114; unreliability, 232, 233
narratee, 45, 49, 214; and authority, 20–21; Chambers on, 251–52n5; in *I am Charlotte Simmons*, 142; and communication model, 223, 238; in *The Crimson Petal and the White*, 96–97, 193; Lanser on, 58–59; Nielsen on, 220–21; in "Octet," 74–75, 78–80; in *Underworld*, 144–47; in *Vanity Fair*, 27; Warhol on, 79–80; in *White Teeth*, 128, 129
narrating instance, 21; and authorial voice, 44; and contemporary historical fiction, 89–90, 93; and *The Crimson Petal and the White*, 95; and the direct address, 90; and figure of the author, 54; and the instance of writing, 81, 44; and narrative authority, 22; and neo-Victorian fiction, 93–94; and *Possession*, 94; and rhetorical narratology, 49.
narrative authority, 9, 14, 24, 25, 49; and the 'anxiety of obsolescence,' 60–61; contingent nature of, 17, 18; defined 18–21; and gender, 57–61; Lanser on (*Fictions of Authority, The Narrative Act*), 57–60; of omniscience, 19–21, 22, 54, 55–56; 58–60, 62–63; and rhetorical narratology, 49; Scholes and Kellog on, 56–57
narrative discourse: and authorial opinion, 21; and extrafictional voice, 235–36; and free indirect discourse, 169, 170, 175, 183; gendered interventions in, 79; Genette's account of, 44–45; and the narrating instance, 113, 198–99; in the public sphere, 24, 232; and story, 198, 205, 222; and style, 112; and stylistic contagion, 172
narrative theory, 165, 249; and authorship, 219, 222; and communication model, 223; different approaches, 21; epistemological fallacy in, 23, 196, 199, 213; focalization and voice, 45–47, 52, 197; and free indirect discourse, 169; key elements of, 21; mimetic bias of, 200; on omniscience, 17, 50, 54, 55, 201; postclassical, 49; on readers, 21, 225, 230; and style, 112
narrative voice: discursive relation to authorial voice, 15–16, 21, 19, 150, 153, 222, 229, 235–38, 247; as element of public discourse, 14, 21, 23–24; and figure of authorship, 20; of first-person omniscience, 195–96; as formalist category, 9, 46–47, 69; and free indirect discourse, 166–94; and hypothetical focalization, 206; and gender, 57–61; and narrative authority, 57–61, 69; of omniscience, 2–3, 4, 9–12, 14, 18, 26, 52, 58–59, 62–64, 164–65, 248; postmodern experimentation with, 66, 247; relation to focalization, 46–48, 164, 199, 207, 212; and maximalism, 162, 163; of modernism, 13–14; neglect of in postclassical narratology, 47–48; as performance of narrative authority, 30, 63; and pyrotechnic storyteller, 111, 114; in *Satanic Verses*, 70; and style, 22, 112–16; and time of narrating, 89
narratology, 22, 55, 205, 225, 228, 233; classical, 44–47, 58, 200, 223; cognitive, 200, 204, 226, 229; 253n2; discursive, 23–34, 235–38; feminist, 57–60; and omniscience, 33, 44–48; postclassical, 47–49, 224; rhetorical, 49, 199; structuralist, 200, 204; unnatural, 199–201, 204, 219–21.

narrator: distancing and engaging (defined by Warhol) in "Octet," 79–81; engaging in *Underworld*, 144; engaging in *The Crimson Petal and the White*, 97. See also first-person narrator; heterodiegetic narrator; homdiegetic narrator; omniscient narrator; third-person narrator

narratorial presence, 43, 45, 48, 60, 63, 64; in *I am Charlotte Simmons*, 142; in *The Corrections*, 151; in *The Crimson Petal and the White*, 96; in *Darkmans*, 117–19, 123; in *The Diviners*, 132, 135; in *Generosity*, 161; in *The Known World*, 109; and metafiction, 66; in *Politics*, 82; in *Satanic Verses*, 70; in *Underworld*, 150; in *White Teeth*, 125; and style, 111–14, 116

narratorial usurpation, 23, 183; defined by Pascal, 177; in Wolfe, 185–89

Nelles, William, 17, 19, 49, 53–54, 252n6

neo-Victorian fiction, 93–95

neuronarratives, 158–59, 190

New Journalism, the, 136, 137–39, 165

Nielsen, Henrik, 200, 219–21

omniscience: as access to consciousness, 43, 45, 48, 62, 63; aesthetic prejudice against, 3–4; anachronicity of, 2; analytic, 37–38, 29, 43, 111; relation between author and narrator, 14, 16, 17, 19, 21, 31, 32, 56; as authorial intrusion, 38–39, 43, 56; classic, 9, 14, 64, 71, 74; contemporary revival of, 4, 7, 9, 10, 12, 162, 246; and creative writing handbooks, 4; and theories of creativity, 34–35; critical neglect of, 2–3; and cultural authority, 5, 9–10, 12–13; fantasy of, 106, 131, 195, 209; and focalization, 45–47, 52–53, 164, 197–98; formal elements of, 1, 5, 18, 26, 31, 35–36, 38, 40–41, 44, 49–50, 53–54, 57; relation between "full" and "limited," 33, 43, 52–53, 55, 59, 63–64, 252n5; genealogy of term, 34–39; and metafiction, 66–67, 69, 210; as method of storytelling, 35–37, 43, 44; modernist rejection of, 2, 11–12, 13, 42; and narrative authority, 9, 14, 18, 25, 28, 54–61, 63, 83, 139, 150, 231, 239, 248; and narrative voice, 45–47; narratological alternatives to, 50; and narratorial commentary, 15, 54, 56, 59; and narratorial knowledge (epistemological problems), 17–18, 19, 21, 26, 29, 33, 62–63, 105; and nineteenth-century fiction, 12–13; paradoxical relation between access to consciousness and authorial presence, 36, 40, 42, 91–92, 168; and paranoia, 164; and point of view, 14, 38, 40–41, 43; as polymathic knowledge, 22, 136–37, 151, 161, 166; and post-postmodernism, 4–5, 67–69, 110; privilege of narrator, 18, 32, 36, 40, 43, 54, 60, 196, 207; as a quality of the narrator, 18, 19, 54, 55, 63, 84, 104, 111, 208; redefined as rhetorical performance of narrative authority, 19, 27, 53, 59, 62–63, 92, 198–99, 252n7; spatio-temporal freedom of, 130, 132, 162; theological associations of (analogy with God), 17, 19, 21, 31–32, 34–35, 42, 53–54, 56, 60; theoretical critiques of, 17, 31–33, 49–54; as unnatural knowledge, 48, 54, 74, 195, 209, 213. See also contemporary omniscience; Culler; Dickens (Asmodean figure); first-person omniscience; Fludernik; Lanser; Levitt; metafiction; Nelles; Rimmon-Kenan; Russo; Royle; Sternberg

omniscient narration, 9; and authority, 21–22, 25, 30–31, 56–57, 60, 222, 232–33, 239; new modes of, 2, 3, 63–65, 245, 247; contemporary turn to, 3, 52; critique of in writing programs, 3–4; difficulty of defining,

16–17, 31; new definition of, 53–55, 63–64, 66, 212–13, 247–48; as exemplary voice of post-postmodern fiction, 4; and focalization, 44–47, 198; and gender, 59–61; and history, 103–110; as historically contingent practice of craft, 17; and narrative theory, 17, 21, 25, 33, 44–45; and nineteenth-century fiction, 10–11, 12, 17, 93–94; and postmodernism, 10, 66–69, 100, 247

omniscient narrator: and authority, 12–13, 18–21, 26, 28, 56–57, 58–59, 162, 166, 168, 248; and competence, 19; as extradiegetic character, 55; and figure of authorship, 2, 12, 14–15, 19, 26, 63, 78; and free indirect discourse, 178, 192; and hypothetical focalization, 206; intrusive presence of, 12, 20, 22; knowledge of, 17–18, 32–33, 44, 53, 55, 91, 136; as outmoded or redundant, 1–4, 40, 44, 64; persistence of term in scholarly community, 50; Russo on, 10; of *Tom Jones,* 34–35, 88; and stylistic presence, 114; as voice of author, 12, 32, 38–39, 41–43

Palmer, Alan, 47; on free indirect discourse, 170, 178; thought report, 183

paralepsis, 23; cognitive parameters, 201–2; defined by Genette, 196–97; and focalization, 196–99; Heinze on, 201–4, 209; and hypothetical focalization, 205–7; and omniscience, 196–99, 201; the mimetic bias, 200–201; and naturalization, 201–4; and unnatural narratology, 199–204; synonym for first-person omniscience, 200; in *The Ice Storm,* 202–4

paralipsis, 207

paraliptic, 218

paratext, 14, 20, 24, 65; and *Author, Author,* 239–46; and communication model, 24, 238; and *The Corrections,* 156; and discursive formation, 24, 65, 237–38; and discursive narratology, 235–38; and extrafictional voice, 237, 254n3; in Genette, 236–37; and *White Teeth,* 129

Pascal, Roy (*The Dual Voice*), 168, 173, 175–77, 187

peritext, defined, 236–38; in *Author, Author,* 241–42; 254n3. See also paratext

Phelan, James: authorial audience, 83; disclosure function, 199; "mask narration," 20; on paralepsis, 199, 219; rhetorical narratology, 49 (defined), 224–25, 227, 232, 234

point of view: references to in *Author, Author,* 240–41; and cognitive narratology, 47, 228–29; and focalization, 33, 38, 44–47, 50, 198; and free indirect discourse, 168, 173, 178; Lodge on, 245; Lubbock on, 40–41; and narrative authority (Scholes and Kellogg), 56–57, 213; and omniscience, 10–11, 14, 33, 36, 40–43; theory of, 38, 39–43, 252n5; Wolfe on, 138, 165; Wood on, 179–80, 242–43. See also focalization

postclassical narratology, 22, 47–49, 224

postmodern fiction: definition and features of, 65–66; and history, 88; and metafiction, 66–67; and the New Journalism, 138, 143; and revival of omniscience, 4–5; Wallace on, 72–73; Wood's critique of, 180

postmodernism, 2, 4; and anxiety over decline of book culture, 7–8, 65, 70; and *Author, Author,* 242, 243, 245; and the problem of character, 165, 166–67; and *The Corrections,* 15, 156–57; and *The Crimson Petal and the White,* 98–100; and death of the novel, 5; defined, 65–66; and DeLillo, 144; and first-person omniscience, 210; and literary historian, 88–89; and maximalism, 162, 163, 179–80; and metafiction, 66–67; and neo-Victorian fiction, 93–94; and the New Journalism,

138; and "Octet," 63, 73, 75, 77, 78–79, 80, 81; influence on contemporary omniscience, 4, 5, 10, 12, 63–67, 69–70, 130, 162, 210, 245, 247, 249; and social commentator, 136; and Smith, 129–30; influence on Wallace, 72–73, 81; and Wolfe, 143

post-postmodern fiction, 7, 22; and character, 23, 81; and contemporary omniscience, 4, 68–69, 100, 247; and *The Corrections,* 15; and *The Crimson Petal and the White,* 100; and first-person omniscience, 210; and *The Known World,* 110; Moody on, 130; and Richard Powers, 157, 210; and Wallace, 72, 80, 81; and Wolfe, 143

post-postmodernism: definition and emergence of, 67–68

Powers, Richard (*Generosity*), 2, 22, 136, 163; first person omniscience, 210–12; free indirect discourse, 192; metafiction, 157, 161, 210–12; social commentator, 157–61

Prince, Gerald, 18, 223

prolepsis: 22; defined, 90; external, 90; extratextual, 90; in *The Known World,* 101–3; in *Underworld,* 143, 148

proleptic (voice of history), 166; in "On the Piteous Death of Mary Wollstonecraft," 92; in *The Crimson Petal and the White,* 95

Proust, Marcel, 44; and paralepsis, 197, 198, 213–14

psychonarration: in *I am Charlotte Simmons,* 185–87; in *The Corrections,* 179, 191; in *Darkmans,* 184; and free indirect discourse, 180, 182; and omniscience, 50, 248; in *Underworld,* 147. *See also* Cohn.

psychonarratology, 226–27

public discourse, 6, 14, 21, 23, 69; authority to speak in, 58, 60; authors in, 65; extraliterary, 12, 161; fiction as mode of, 15, 24, 56, 61, 65, 107, 150, 153, 221, 227, 231–32, 235–36, 238, 239, 245, 247, 249; Franzen on, 15; and gender, 58; narrative voice as, 14

pyrotechnic storyteller, 22, 69, 111–35, 183; *Darkmans,* 116–24; defined, 111; *The Diviners,* 130–35; Rushdie, 114–15; and style, 112, 114, 124; Wallace, 115–16; *White Teeth,* 124–30

Rabinowitz, Peter: authorial audience, 83, 223; communication model, 223; implied author, 234

reader: and authorial audience, 83, 159; cognitive approaches to, 96, 171, 200, 225–29; in communication model, 24, 49, 223–24, 235, 238; empirical approaches to, 229–31; free indirect discourse as interpretive strategy of, 177–78; implied, 128, 140, 223; and implied author, 233–34; as methodological construct, 231; and narratee, 20, 21, 49, 79, 96, 97; and narrative authority, 17, 20, 59, 61; and paratext, 24, 243–44; and postclassical narratology, 47–48, 224; private vs public, 21, 24, 150, 227, 229; public, 231–33; "real," 21, 24, 84, 90, 224–26, 229–31, 242; in rhetorical narratology, 49, 224–25. *See also* Stewart, Wallace ("Octet").

reader response theory, 21, 24, 47, 224–25, 230

rhetorical narratology, 49, 199, 224–25, 232. *See also* Phelan

rhetorical performance: in *Crimson Petal and the White,* 96; of narrative authority, 19–20, 21, 33, 36, 49, 53–55, 60, 63, 66, 116, 166, 212; in *Politics,* 83, 86

rhetorical strategy: of authors, 48, 57, 233, 236, 239; focalization as, 212, 248; free indirect discourse as, 181; hypothetical focalization as, 206–7; of narrator in *Author, Author,* 240, 246; of narrator in *The Known World,* 104–5, 109; of narrator in "On the Piteous Death of Mary

Wollstonecraft," 93; of narrators, 19, 79, 164; of omniscient character narrators, 214–15; paralepsis as, 204, 206

Richardson, Brian (*Unnatural Voices*): autotelic second person (defined), 77; implied author, 254n2; movement away from omniscience, 3; unnatural narratology, 200

Rimmon-Kenan, Shlomith (*Narrative Fiction*): aspects of focalization, 46, 50; narrative authority, 18, 58; narrative communication, 223; omniscience, 18, 46, 58

Royle, Nicholas (*The Uncanny*): critique of omniscience, 17, 25, 31–32, 34, 50–51, 216; on telepathy, 50–51, 216

Rushdie, Salman, 2, 251n4; and contemporary omniscience, 51–52; and first person omniscience, 216–19; hysterical realism, 124; as ironic moralist, 22, 70–71; metaphorical excess, 115; *Midnight's Children*, 51, 195, 196, 216–19; and postmodernism, 64, 71; as public intellectual, 15–16; as pyrotechnic storyteller, 22, 114–15; the Rushdie affair, 16; *Satanic Verses*, 16, 51–52, 70–71, 114–15, 124, 127, 219; and style, 114–15; compared to *White Teeth*, 124, 127

Russo, Richard: "In Defense of Omniscience," 9–10, 64, 251n2; *Empire Falls*, 64

Scholes and Kellogg (*The Nature of Narrative*): on first person omniscience, 213–14; on shift away from omniscience, 11; figures of authority underpinning omniscience, 56–57

second person narration, 76, 149; "autotelic," 77, 79, 96, 145; in "Octet" 74–78

self-reflexivity: in *Charlotte Simmons*, 185, 188; in *The Corrections*, 190; in *Darkmans*, 119; as extranarrative element, 20, 22; in Faber, 96, 99; as feature of omniscience, 50, 66, 248; and first-person omniscience, 210, 214–15; of FID in contemporary omniscience, 23, 73, 167, 182–83, 192–93; in *Generosity*, 161, 211; of ironic moralist, 69; in *Midnight's Children*, 218; in "Octet," 73, 78, 79, 81; in *Politics*, 83; feature of postmodernism, 65, 68, 69–70; in Walter Scott, 167; in Trollope, 66; and metafiction, 66, 67, 68, 73, 100, 210; references to omniscience, 25–26; in *Tom Jones*, 34

shared linguistic habitus, 23 (defined), 183–89. *See also* free indirect discourse

Smith, Zadie (*White Teeth*), 2, 251n4; and character, 178; characterological cognitive self-awareness, 190; direct address, 128–29; editorial "we," 128–29; free indirect discourse, 180–81; gender, 60; hysterical realism, 124; maximalism, 163; omniscience, 64, 130; overt commentary, 111, 128–29; postcolonial, 126, 128–29; postmodernist, 129–30; postsecular fiction, 126–28; satire of providence, 124–26, 127; pyrotechnic storyteller, 22, 111, 124–30; style, 111, 178

social commentator, the, 22, 69, 136–65

social novel, the: and Franzen, 154–56; and hysterical realism, 136; and maximalism, 162; and Wolfe, 136, 138–39

Sternberg, Meir, 17, 32, 33, 52–53, 98, 170

Stewart, Garrett (*Dear Reader*), 75–76

story: distinct from discourse, 18, 27, 47, 49, 93; constructed from discourse, 48

style, 138, 139, 168, 175, 178–81; authorial style, 111–12, 114, 180; and Aczel, 112–14; in *Darkmans*, 116–24; defined, 112; in *The Diviners*, 130–35; and free indirect discourse, 112, 177; expressivity, 111, 113; extranarrative function, 114; and *Lolita*, 114; and narrative theory, 112–14; and omniscient

narration, 111, 114, 116, 123–24; and pyrotechnic storyteller, 111–34; in *Satanic Verses*, 114–15; and voice, 111–14; in Wallace, 115–16; in *White Teeth*, 124–30
stylistic contagion, 23, 174, 175, 177, 253n1; in *Charlotte Simmons*, 186–88; in *The Corrections*, 191; in *Darkmans*, 119–23; defined, 172; and free indirect discourse, 172, 183; in *White Teeth*, 181
Suskind, Patrick (*Perfume*), 89

telepathy: alternative to omniscience, 50–51, 53, 204, 214; in *Midnight's Children*, 216–18
Thackeray, William (*Vanity Fair*), 25–28, 29, 31
Thirlwell, Adam (*Politics*), 2, 12, 22, 70, 183; ironic moralist, 81–87,
third person narration: cognitive approach to, 225; difference between omniscient and limited, 18, 21, 31, 33, 39, 43, 63, 248; and free indirect discourse, 168, 170, 174; limited, 3, 39–40, 179; narratorless, 113; omniscient, 3, 18, 20, 51, 54, 60, 63–64, 95, 195, 201, 208, 212; and paralepsis, 197; and style, 114; and time of narrating, 89; and voice, 44, 57. *See also* heterodiegetic narrator
thought report, 158, 178, 179, 180, 183. *See also* free indirect discourse; psychonarration
time of narrating, 22, 44, 49; in contemporary historical fiction, 89–90; in *The Crimson Petal and the White*, 97

unreliable narration, 3; in *Jazz*, 216; in *Lolita*, 232, 233; in *Midnight's Children*, 217–18; and paralepsis, 201, 202, 220

voice: *See* authorial voice; first-person narrator; heterodiegetic narrator; homodiegetic narrator; narrating instance; narrative voice; third-person narration

Wallace, David Foster, 2, 7, 63, 70; characterological cognitive self awareness, 189–90; "E Unibus Pluram," 72, 74, 155, 251n4; hysterical realism, 124; as ironic moralist, 22, 72–81; maximalism, 161, 162; "Octet," 63, 72–81; as pyrotechnic storyteller, 22, 111, 114, 115–16. *See also* metafiction; postmodernism; post-postmodernism
Walsh, Richard (*The Rhetoric of Fictionality*), 55, 208, 219, 220
Warhol, Robyn (*Gendered Interventions*), 79–80, 97
Wolfe, Tom (*I am Charlotte Simmons*), 2, 22, 136, 137, 165; and Franzen, 154–55; and free indirect discourse, 185–89; as immersion journalist, 136, 137–43; and neuronarrative, 158; and the New Journalism, 137–39, 165; and the social novel, 136–39, 155; "Stalking the Billion-Footed Beast," 137, 138–39
Wood, James: on *Author, Author,* 242–43; on Franzen, 150; on free indirect discourse, 180–81; *How Fiction Works*, 179–80; on hysterical realism, 124, 136, 156, 162; on the social novel, 136–37; on *White Teeth*, 124, 180–81

zero focalization, 50, 60, 63, 64, 111, 198, 252n6; defined, 45; and definition of omniscience, 248; in *The Crimson Petal and the White*, 97; in *The Diviners*, 130–32, 133, 135; and homodiegetic narration (first person omniscience), 199, 206, 207; and hypothetical focalization, 205–6; in *The Known World*, 101; in "On the Piteous Death of Mary Wollstonecraft," 92–93; in *Underworld*, 143, 146; in *White Teeth*, 125

THEORY AND INTERPRETATION OF NARRATIVE

James Phelan, Peter J. Rabinowitz, and Robyn Warhol, Series Editors

Because the series editors believe that the most significant work in narrative studies today contributes both to our knowledge of specific narratives and to our understanding of narrative in general, studies in the series typically offer interpretations of individual narratives and address significant theoretical issues underlying those interpretations. The series does not privilege one critical perspective but is open to work from any strong theoretical position.

A Poetics of Unnatural Narrative
EDITED BY JAN ALBER, HENRIK SKOV NIELSEN, AND BRIAN RICHARDSON

Narrative Discourse: Authors and Narrators in Literature, Film, and Art
PATRICK COLM HOGAN

An Aesthetics of Narrative Performance: Transnational Theater, Literature, and Film in Contemporary Germany
CLAUDIA BREGER

Literary Identification from Charlotte Brontë to Tsitsi Dangarembga
LAURA GREEN

Narrative Theory: Core Concepts and Critical Debates
DAVID HERMAN, JAMES PHELAN AND PETER J. RABINOWITZ, BRIAN RICHARDSON, AND ROBYN WARHOL

After Testimony: The Ethics and Aesthetics of Holocaust Narrative for the Future
EDITED BY JAKOB LOTHE, SUSAN RUBIN SULEIMAN, AND JAMES PHELAN

The Vitality of Allegory: Figural Narrative in Modern and Contemporary Fiction
GARY JOHNSON

Narrative Middles: Navigating the Nineteenth-Century British Novel
EDITED BY CAROLINE LEVINE AND MARIO ORTIZ-ROBLES

Fact, Fiction, and Form: Selected Essays
RALPH W. RADER. EDITED BY JAMES PHELAN AND DAVID H. RICHTER

The Real, the True, and the Told: Postmodern Historical Narrative and the Ethics of Representation
ERIC L. BERLATSKY

Franz Kafka: Narration, Rhetoric, and Reading
EDITED BY JAKOB LOTHE, BEATRICE SANDBERG, AND RONALD SPEIRS

Social Minds in the Novel
ALAN PALMER

Narrative Structures and the Language of the Self
MATTHEW CLARK

Imagining Minds: The Neuro-Aesthetics of Austen, Eliot, and Hardy
KAY YOUNG

Postclassical Narratology: Approaches and Analyses
EDITED BY JAN ALBER AND MONIKA FLUDERNIK

Techniques for Living: Fiction and Theory in the Work of Christine Brooke-Rose
KAREN R. LAWRENCE

Towards the Ethics of Form in Fiction: Narratives of Cultural Remission
LEONA TOKER

Tabloid, Inc.: Crimes, Newspapers, Narratives
V. PENELOPE PELIZZON AND NANCY M. WEST

Narrative Means, Lyric Ends: Temporality in the Nineteenth-Century British Long Poem
MONIQUE R. MORGAN

Joseph Conrad: Voice, Sequence, History, Genre
EDITED BY JAKOB LOTHE, JEREMY HAWTHORN, AND JAMES PHELAN

Understanding Nationalism: On Narrative, Cognitive Science, and Identity
PATRICK COLM HOGAN

The Rhetoric of Fictionality: Narrative Theory and the Idea of Fiction
RICHARD WALSH

Experiencing Fiction: Judgments, Progressions, and the Rhetorical Theory of Narrative
JAMES PHELAN

Unnatural Voices: Extreme Narration in Modern and Contemporary Fiction
BRIAN RICHARDSON

Narrative Causalities
EMMA KAFALENOS

Why We Read Fiction: Theory of Mind and the Novel
LISA ZUNSHINE

I Know That You Know That I Know: Narrating Subjects from Moll Flanders *to* Marnie
GEORGE BUTTE

Bloodscripts: Writing the Violent Subject
ELANA GOMEL

Surprised by Shame: Dostoevsky's Liars and Narrative Exposure
DEBORAH A. MARTINSEN

Having a Good Cry: Effeminate Feelings and Pop-Culture Forms
ROBYN R. WARHOL

Politics, Persuasion, and Pragmatism: A Rhetoric of Feminist Utopian Fiction
ELLEN PEEL

Telling Tales: Gender and Narrative Form in Victorian Literature and Culture
ELIZABETH LANGLAND

Narrative Dynamics: Essays on Time, Plot, Closure, and Frames
EDITED BY BRIAN RICHARDSON

Breaking the Frame: Metalepsis and the Construction of the Subject
DEBRA MALINA

Invisible Author: Last Essays
CHRISTINE BROOKE-ROSE

Ordinary Pleasures: Couples, Conversation, and Comedy
KAY YOUNG

Narratologies: New Perspectives on Narrative Analysis
EDITED BY DAVID HERMAN

Before Reading: Narrative Conventions and the Politics of Interpretation
PETER J. RABINOWITZ

Matters of Fact: Reading Nonfiction over the Edge
DANIEL W. LEHMAN

The Progress of Romance: Literary Historiography and the Gothic Novel
DAVID H. RICHTER

A Glance Beyond Doubt: Narration, Representation, Subjectivity
SHLOMITH RIMMON-KENAN

Narrative as Rhetoric: Technique, Audiences, Ethics, Ideology
JAMES PHELAN

Misreading Jane Eyre: *A Postformalist Paradigm*
JEROME BEATY

Psychological Politics of the American Dream: The Commodification of Subjectivity in Twentieth-Century American Literature
LOIS TYSON

Understanding Narrative
EDITED BY JAMES PHELAN AND PETER J. RABINOWITZ

Framing Anna Karenina: *Tolstoy, the Woman Question, and the Victorian Novel*
AMY MANDELKER

Gendered Interventions: Narrative Discourse in the Victorian Novel
ROBYN R. WARHOL

Reading People, Reading Plots: Character, Progression, and the Interpretation of Narrative
JAMES PHELAN

www.ingramcontent.com/pod-product-compliance
Lightning Source LLC
Chambersburg PA
CBHW030108010526
44116CB00005B/157